MW00949033

Children,
Love One Another

A Daily Devotional Based on Sermons
by Rev. Dr. Norman R. Lawson

KATHLEEN B. POLO, MD

WESTBOW
P R E S S®
A DIVISION OF THOMAS NELSON
& ZONDERVAN

Copyright © 2021 Kathleen B. Polo, MD.

All rights reserved. No part of this book may be used or reproduced by any means, graphic, electronic, or mechanical, including photocopying, recording, taping or by any information storage retrieval system without the written permission of the author except in the case of brief quotations embodied in critical articles and reviews.

WestBow Press books may be ordered through booksellers or by contacting:

WestBow Press
A Division of Thomas Nelson & Zondervan
1663 Liberty Drive
Bloomington, IN 47403
www.westbowpress.com
844-714-3454

Because of the dynamic nature of the Internet, any web addresses or links contained in this book may have changed since publication and may no longer be valid. The views expressed in this work are solely those of the author and do not necessarily reflect the views of the publisher, and the publisher hereby disclaims any responsibility for them.

Any people depicted in stock imagery provided by Getty Images are models, and such images are being used for illustrative purposes only. Certain stock imagery © Getty Images.

Scripture quotations taken from The Holy Bible, New International Version® NIV® Copyright © 1973 1978 1984 2011 by Biblica, Inc. TM. Used by permission. All rights reserved worldwide.

Scripture quotations are] from the Revised Standard Version of the Bible, copyright © 1946, 1952, and 1971 the Division of Christian Education of the National Council of the Churches of Christ in the United States of America. Used by permission. All rights reserved.

ISBN: 978-1-6642-2600-5 (sc)
ISBN: 978-1-6642-2601-2 (hc)
ISBN: 978-1-6642-2599-2 (e)

Library of Congress Control Number: 2021904517

Print information available on the last page.

WestBow Press rev. date: 04/30/2021

PREFACE

A Still More Excellent Way

Over ten years ago, I was helping my parents clear out their storage unit. We came across two dilapidated cardboard file cabinets. The contents took me by surprise. They were filled with files containing all the sermons my dad had preached, reaching back to 1956. His initial response was, "Oh, throw those away; I don't need them anymore." I immediately recognized we had found something to be treasured. We hauled the boxes up to their apartment, and I started to go through the files. The sermons were rich with spiritual insight and paralleled the myriad of current events through the years. The early ones were handwritten, still in the original bulletin covers. We laughed at the photos on the covers and set everything aside. The next morning, I was able to sift through more of the papers, continuously becoming more convinced that the words needed to be shared. I was able to whittle it down to two much smaller boxes and arranged to mail them to myself at home. They sat undisturbed for several years, when I decided to surprise my dad with thirty meditations based on the sermons for his eightieth birthday. The family loved the little booklets, and Dad reveled in reading the excerpts aloud. I felt the nudge from God that more needed to be done—that he wanted me to write out a full year's worth of such meditations. This book is the result.

Many people have encouraged me over the years, especially my sister, daughter, and husband, and later my Bible study friends. Without such encouragement, I may not have been as tenacious. The still, small voice of God continued to nudge me day by day and year by year. I have been deeply moved by poring over these messages, hearing my father speak each word and remembering where we were at the time. I sat in his congregation for almost twenty years but did not fully appreciate the depth of his love for God, Jesus, and his fellow human beings, and his understanding of the Bible. My father continues to feel his words may be unworthy of sharing in this way, but I am fully certain this is a work of the Holy Spirit.

I hope precious moments are ahead for you, as you open your soul to a heartfelt interpretation of God's love. This truth rings out: "Children, love one another."

A Sparkling Word for a New Year

January 1
John 1:1, 4

The first chapter of the Gospel of John is a magnificent passage! The Word, the Word of God—the Word of God became flesh and lived among us. God's Word truly is powerful. We live by words. It has been said that the average person hears somewhere around 192,000 words a day. Each of us has been cut by harsh words and healed by kind words. The Word of God has transforming power, power to move our souls, and the strength to change our lives.

The verses from John's first chapter proclaim that all who receive Christ are born of God. Why do we make New Year's resolutions? Isn't it because, as God's children, we have the hope of a new year as a new possibility, a clean slate, and a fresh start? But how do we keep them? By the force of our own wills? We can't even expect to live up to our own modest expectations!

All who receive Christ are born of God and are new persons because the Word lives with them. Do you want things to be different this year? God is with us wherever we go; Christ is beside us in whatever we confront. God walks with us when things are tough. He uses each of us as his servant. As children born of God, things will be different for us—not of our own wills but with the powerful Spirit of God. Resolutions are different if they are hammered out with God. The new year can become a sparkling one, despite our doubts and worries as we trust the powerful Word of God.

Kick Start Your New Year

January 2
Colossians 3:12–17

Sometimes it is hard to get started as we enter into a new year. Alfred Hitchcock once said, "Drama is life with the boring parts left out." The truth is, a lot of life is boring. It is commonplace, everyday, predictable, and humdrum. How do we put drama into life? How do we keep the faith while battling life's compromises? How do we stay excited with marriage and family and work while dealing with life's endless monotonies? One way is to catch on to "Word Central." We need to place the Word of God as central to our inspiration as the spark of our imaginations.

Every person has a story. Our personal stories are important to us. They chronicle our trials and our hopes. They help to define who we are and where we belong. The Christian faith is also a story. It, too, tells us who we are and where we belong. We find this story in the Holy Bible. To know this story is to know who we are. To be ignorant of this story is to be ill-equipped to deal with the world in which we live! To be unacquainted with this story is to struggle with boredom ad monotony, to find ourselves uninspired and disinterested, and to lack drama and hope in our lives. One saying goes this way:

> *Know* the Word of God in your *head.*
> *Stow* the Word of God in your *heart.*
> *Sow* the Word of God in the *world.*
> *Show* the Word of God in your *life.*

It works! A solid, disciplined study of the holy scripture gives us discernment. As we study and fellowship together in God's Word, we begin to see things we couldn't see before. We begin to acquire the eyes of faith. This allows us to see that God is constantly active and at work in our lives. The Word of God is truly living and active! What would it mean in our lives if we were to truly know, stow, sow, and show the Word of God? I'll tell you one thing: it would give us a good kick start!

A Light Shines
January 3
Isaiah 42:1–9

God is the light that shines through the swirling darkness and mazes of confusion of life. God's first command was, "Let there be light!" (Genesis 1:3). In the psalms, the Lord is described as the light of salvation and the light on the path. The gospels state that Jesus is the light of the world. Light is essential to knowing. If you are trying to fix something, one of the first things you need to do is to shed some light on it.

Some and not others received the light that can enlighten all persons. For those who receive that light, it is life. It is light shining in darkness, and the darkness cannot overcome it. One thing darkness cannot conquer is light. No matter how small the light is, no darkness can penetrate it. It is always the other way around: light can always penetrate the darkest darkness. The light shines, and it cannot be put out.

I will give you as a covenant for the people, a light for the nations" (Isaiah 42:6). There are simply too many people who seem to believe that nothing matters, so they can do whatever they want. They don't see their value in the church, in giving, or in doing. Would you make a difference? Would you be the one who brings light into a dark situation? As the light of the nations, we must believe, with God as our helper, we can and do make a difference. Furthermore, when more are gathered together, the difference is multiplied. Together, we are more than the sum of the individuals. Together, we encourage one another to be bearers of the light. Together, we nurture one another to glow with the joy of Christ—the light.

God Is Light
January 4
1 John 1:5–2:11

Keeping God's light in the center of our vision results in the ability to be guided in our paths and to be filled with light, not darkness; to have joy, not sorrow; to have purpose, not meaninglessness. After the rush of Christmas, it is normal to feel a sense of letdown. Epiphany can bring more thrill than Christmas. We can focus on the implications of the coming of Christ without all the distractions of the holiday season. The season of Epiphany celebrates the revealing of the light of Christ to the gentiles. It harkens to the fact that the source of all light and truth manifested himself to the world.

Humans long for God even when they are not aware of it. Our society bears all the marks of a God-starved community. There is a lack of faith that guides our purpose on earth, which can only be filled by the unique authority of Jesus Christ. God created people to be the highest emissaries in making him known. Therefore, all humans are individually valued over systems; all are individuals, not just a number in humanity; and each individual has worth and dignity in the face of the Almighty. God is light because he lights every soul; he believes in every person. When it is believed that any human has less value than another, evil results. Minority groups and the dispossessed all over the world have experienced what happens when they are less valued than another. God will not let us settle down with the comfortable idea that we need not concern ourselves with *all* people. For God seeks to develop each person's highest potential as a child of his, that he might be made known to all humankind.

We are created to worship. God's light dwells in our spirits. As a nation, we have come to think of diplomacy and world power in terms of armies and navies, guns and air power, missiles and submarines. These things are powerful, perhaps necessary. Yet we forget that it is in the realm of unseen influence that the rule of the world and direction of the future may be found. Even the founding of our nation was accomplished by the power of an idea. Free people stood before a world full of tyranny to announce that because humans are spiritual creatures, their worship of God must be without hindrance or proscription.

As we open the doors of our souls and draw back the curtains of our hearts, God's light casts out darkness and makes us human again. In his light we see purpose and meaning in our universe. We are given the perspective of a view higher and longer than immediate history. God is light, and in him is no darkness at all. He develops persons, he dwells in our spirits, and he frees us to live.

Breathless with New Insight

January 5
Acts 5:29, 39

Sometimes we do things not because we choose to but because circumstances require it. In Acts, the infant church didn't choose to move out into the world. After the first healing in Jerusalem, Peter and John were arrested, and they had to appear and explain. As they were filled with the Holy Spirit, they spoke with such boldness that they became almost breathless with new insight! They knew they were experiencing being under the control of a power quite beyond them.

The disciples discovered they could do more than they thought they could do. God began to move in people's lives, and the apostles became set apart, marked, and honored. They were enjoying the fellowship of one another so much that they wanted to stay there, together, feeding each other. Ultimately, God had to get them in trouble before they began to go out into the world to tell the story. God brought them together so they could learn that they could witness more powerfully in the workplace and with families, beyond their imaginations.

What self-imposed thoughts of inadequacy keep you from moving foward in ministry? Every baptized, born-again Christian can begin to know the joy of being in the ministry. Your baptism in the Holy Spirit is your credential. Your job is to take it from there. You can't stand aside and watch from the sidelines. If you get in there, you'll find you can do more than you thought you could! The Holy Spirit will fill you with more power and insight than you could imagine.

Neon and Candlelight

January 6
John 1:1–13

Epiphany is the season after Christmas that emphasizes that Christ is the light of the world. We live in a world where many lights clamor for our attention. Whereas Jesus is the true light, these worldly lights can be so alluring. Neon calls to distractions such as shopping, eats and drinks, movies, and shows. Far more money is spent on various forms of entertainment than on education or mission.

Candlelight, on the other hand, suggests holiness, awe, reverence, sacredness, and quiet. The scripture states it well: "The light shines in the darkness, and the darkness has not overcome it" (John 1:5). Further, it relates that Jesus is the Word, present from the beginning, God, and life. How is it, then, that we can brush up against Christ and never recognize him? This is the story of the New Testament. Though the Jews had scoured scripture for evidence and knowledge of the Messiah, they missed him when he was right in front of them! How could this be?

Because, whereas neon blares out its message and is difficult to ignore, candlelight whispers and is easily snuffed out. God does not force anyone to believe. He offers salvation and grace to all, but we must accept it for ourselves. The world holds out tangible "goods," Christ offers the invisible—faith and eternal life. Given the choice, it would seem clear which to choose. Yet our natural selves are drawn inexplicably to the world. Only God in us, the Holy Spirit, allows us to see the beauty and comfort of Christ—the light of the world. Will you see it? Will you follow the candlelight and put the neon behind you?

Bread
January 7
John 6:1–71

Bread is the staff of life. It is the simple, the plain, the common. To many, it represents survival, the difference between life and death. Jesus is the bread of life. He is our means to survive, to grow, to stay alive. He is food for the soul, the source of vitality for our faith and our spirits. Jesus, the bread of life, is someone, not something. How often we substitute something for the real One. We spend our lives accumulating things rather than focusing on the source of true, eternal life. Jesus said, "Do not work for food that spoils, but for food that endures to eternal life" (John 6:27). This food is for the spirit. It brings care for one another, building one another up, sharing God's Word, believing in God's power, and living God's way.

Jesus also said, "Unless you eat the flesh of the Son of man and drink his blood, you have no life in you" (John 6:41). In practice, we must receive him into our very lives. This is the significance of Holy Communion. Jesus is the bread from heaven. He is the Way, the Truth, the Life. It is possible to destroy our immortal spirits. It is possible to be separated from God, not because God wants it, but simply because we never put our adult minds to the task, and, by default, choose death even when we are alive. God is in the everyday. He is as close as the simplest of food that keeps us alive: bread.

Don't Rock the Boat—Row It

January 8
Matthew 16:13–20

Do you have a vibrant faith? Do you know what that looks like? When people look at you, are they attracted to who you are (as a Christian) or repelled? Unfortunately, complacency and comfort in faith has become the norm for many of us. "Go into the world and preach the gospel to all creation" (Mark 16:15). The most obvious mark of a vibrant faith is being willing to share the good news. The good news is simple—Jesus Christ is the Son of God; he came to earth, died for our sins, and was risen by God to live forever. Why is that so hard to say? Granted, salesmanship is not required to be a Christian, but what would happen to a salesman if he went to all the meetings, knew his product inside and out, and even made sales calls, but then failed to speak at those calls?

It is said that Christians are, in fact, the fifth gospel: we are the book that the average outsider reads about what it means to be a Christian. People watch us. Why is it that we are so afraid to speak loudly and with a radical voice? Well, we don't want to look ridiculous! We don't want to be outcasts. We don't want to make people feel uncomfortable.

In looking back on the early Christians—indeed, on Christ himself—they had influence because they were not the "norm." They were on the outside, making waves in society. So, how can we get back to that mind-set? First, by opening ourselves to God. "After the Lord Jesus had spoken to them … then the disciples went out and preached everywhere, and the Lord worked with them" (Mark 16:19–20). If you make a fist, you cannot put anything in your hand or take anything out. An open hand receives from the Lord and gives out to others. The same is true of our minds; opening them to God makes us teachable and willing to accept his guidance. Through his strength and wisdom, the words will come, as will the vibrancy.

Enthusiasts, Situated to Serve
January 9
1 Thessalonians 1:2–10

Who are you? What do you want out of life? Where is it that you are willing to put your life on the line, freely, without law or accident? Our lives can be spokesmen for the gospel; we can be co-operators, not tearing at the word of truth, but mending it; we can be students, endeavoring to know God's will. We can also be enthusiasts: filled with the grace of God and delighted to be an instrument of his love. The source of our enthusiasm is God himself. Zest for life comes from a quality of relationships. "We continually remember your work produced by faith, your labor prompted by love, and your endurance inspired by hope in our Lord Jesus Christ" (1Thessalonians 1:3). The truth is that when we are out of harmony, we are miserable, and when we are in harmony, we are happy.

We are his, chosen for a special purpose. We have a work of faith to do, which energizes our own souls and the souls of those we touch. This is a labor of love by which we care for one another. Further, it requires a steadfastness of hope. Hope is like an anchor for the soul, firm and secure. We have an exciting and important work to do. A work that grows out of being possessed by God, inspired by him, vigorous and bold in him. Enthusiasm for Christ is like a laser beam. Let God represent the light; Christ reflects and unifies the light, so that our thrust into the world is intense with passion and specific with purpose.

God Is the Lion
January 10
John 1:1, 14

In Kenya, a Masai elder observed that the Swahili word most missionaries used to convey the word *faith* was not a very good word in their language. The word they were using for "faith" meant literally, "to agree to." It was a rather passive word, as in operating from a distance. For one to really believe, said the Masai elder, is more like a lion going after its prey. A lion's nose and ears sense the prey. He sniffs the air and locates it. Then he crouches and slithers along the ground virtually invisible. The lion gets into position, then pounces. As the animal goes down, the lion envelops it in his arms, pulls it to himself, and makes it a part of himself. This, said the elder, is the way one believes—making faith a part of oneself!

The analogy continues, as one considers that although we believe we are seeking God, it is really him seeking us. As John writes, "This is love, not that we loved God, but that he loved us, and sent his son to die for our sins" (1 John 4:10). So often in this life, we think we have to search out God, stalk God, pounce on God, and make God take us in. In fact, it is God who has made us, and it is we who have wandered. We may have thought we were the lion, while in fact, God is the lion, seeking us. Faith is to embrace that reunion like a lion embraces the catch. God is the lion; our part is the embracing.

How's Your Vision?
January 11
Matthew 6:22–23, 7:7–14

Farmers and foresters have vision for the things about them because of an eye trained through study and practice. A walk through the field or forest with one of them opens one's eyes to subtle details that are vital to the professional but remain invisible to the untrained, without their enlightenment. The peeks we get into ways and workings, wonders and developments around us serve as an illustration of how important our ability to see and discern is to our lives.

In awareness of God, "How's your soul-vision?" In sensitivity to others, "How's your heart-vision?" In faithfulness to religious truths, "How's your mind vision?" God, revealed in Jesus Christ, is our light, who, when we open our eyes, will help us to share that light with others. This is a concept that needs to be repeated again and again until we may never forget who is the source of our lives. Who is our God, and what he expects of us. It is surprising how much the New Testament scriptures speak of light and darkness. The eye, in Hebrew thought, was the spirit of humankind—their moral and religious faculty. If the spiritual light is turned off, selfishness takes over. The problems in too many relationships are due to self-centeredness. True love is not based on self-concern but rather on other-concern. On a larger level, darkness will prevail if we ever stop hurting with concern over those who are in pain.

On the other hand, how great is the light when the eye is trained, when the vision of others is good. The light is great when we catch a vision of God and a vision of the holiness of all of life—every individual. Holiness reaches into every aspect of life—work and play, home and away, near and far. How's your vision? Is it open to the light of our Lord who is the way, the truth, and the light, that our whole body may be full of light?

I Promise
January 12
Deuteronomy 31:8

It is a brand-new year. Naturally, our thoughts turn to resolutions on this day. The break of the old year with the new perpetually provokes reflection on the last year and inspires promises for this year. On New Year's Day, promises have many different meanings. Most of the time, resolutions are taken lightly, but there are other times where the words "I Promise" are deeply hallowed and sacred. A promise is a pledge, which anticipates and hopes for the expected performance.

In faith, Christ promises eternal life. God has made a promise to us: "The Lord himself goes before you and will be with you" (Deuteronomy 31:8). Today, we can make a promise to God. It is with him that we begin, continue, and end. We promise to uphold his name with all our hearts, minds, and strength. Further, we promise to love our neighbor as ourselves.

How can we keep these promises? These promises of faith lead us to a prayer. We pray for the ability to freely yield all things to God and to further his will on earth. We pray that our faith will find expression in action. We pray that our hearts might be softened in deeds of love and mercy. We pray that in helping, even in the least of our actions, we are helping our holy heavenly Father. At this time of beginning the New Year, we must also remember that Jesus is present with us. God has promised to never leave us or forsake us. He is helping us become the people he envisioned us to be. God is a promise keeper. With him, we can look forward to new life, redemption, forgiveness, and hope. He will never let us down.

Jesus Is Lord

January 13
Mark 1:21–28

Jesus chose to open his ministry in a way that had never been seen or heard before. He was preaching in the synagogue, when a man with an impure spirit cried out, "Jesus of Nazareth, what do you want with us?" Jesus spoke sternly to the spirit, and told it to come out of the man. It did so with a shaking of the man and a shriek. "What is this? A new teaching and with authority" (Mark 1:27). The people were so amazed, they spread the news about this man through the whole region. Jesus was something incredibly different, in fact, he is LORD. Jesus is the Lord of life and all that happens in it.

What is the lord of your life? We all have them. They are the things to which we give our allegiance, that demand our attention, require our obedience and devotion. It could be drugs or alcohol; ambition; money. Self is the most common of all false gods. The specific demon is not as important as how easily we come under the sway of a false god.

How does one come free of such a thing? The only way is to focus on the Holy One, the true Lord, Jesus. Nothing is outside his sphere, he is involved in the everyday-ness of life for all of us. He transforms our everyday-ness from a treadmill of dread to a pilgrimage of adventure! This is not old news. He is present now, with us. He lives with us every day in a partnership, helping and guiding us. We must choose to give him control, and truly let him be Lord of our lives.

Let There Be Light!
January 14
John 8:12–20

Light has a particularly eye-catching facility, and we are all familiar with its many uses—in advertising, in our homes, in all forms of work. Most all of us have experienced that moment when we are busily going about our lives and suddenly the power goes out, plunging us into darkness. What a difference that makes! Yet even a tiny match repels the darkness to be able to reorient one's self. The light that Jesus provides is far beyond the mundane, everyday illumination. He provides light to live by, light for the heart, light for the soul. Sadly, there is still much darkness in the world.

Christ's claim as the light of the world is supported by his revelation of God's true nature. The disciples who walked and lived with Jesus experienced this in his every action. Jesus himself said that those who had seen him had seen the Father. Their time with Jesus changed their lives forever, and through them, the entire history of the world has changed. No other person has had the influence of Jesus. Through the teaching of Christ and those who follow him have come reforms such as the abolishment of slavery, equal rights for all, prison reform, and the very constitution of the United States.

Even now, millions of men and women all over the world can testify to the light and power of Christ in their own lives. Those who walk in the way of Christ are those that bring food to the hungry, hope to the hopeless, a hand up to those in need. We who walk in the way of Christ are the light of the world through him. It is our actions that others see as different—special. It is the power of Christ that sustains us and brightens our lives. May we each walk in the light as he is in the light.

Mission Is Possible
January 15
Matthew 28:19–20

The secret of life is dignity and worth. The "how" of that is to give of oneself. Mission means "sent." It means a task of function assigned or undertaken. As God sent Christ to us because he loves us, so we too are sent. We are sent with the message of reconciliation, giving, adventure. In the face of war, mission is possible. In the face of crime in the streets and rioting, mission is possible. In the face of drugs, unwed mothers, and broken homes, mission is possible.

Mission is possible for individuals. We need to change our mind-set from analyzing the problem to doing something about it; from showing how or why something won't work to making it work; from complaining about how poor the teacher is to showing how good the student is; from griping about what a sick society we have to making it a healthy society.

The real challenge is to get out there! It starts with the understanding that sometimes faith isn't about being safe and cozy at home. Sometimes it is about risk. That doesn't mean we risk our lives, but it might mean risking our dignity for a little bit to come alongside someone struggling where they are, even if it isn't a place where we are comfortable. Distant travel doesn't even need to be involved. A mission is possible right in your own city—needy to be fed, lonely to be comforted, helpless to be helped. All that is needed is a desire to reach those that are left out of today's society.

Jesus's last words to his disciples were: "Go and make disciples of all nations, baptizing them in the name of the Father, and of the Son, and of the Holy Spirit, and teaching them to obey everything I have commanded you" (Matthew 28:19–20). What more motivation could anyone need? Where will you start?

Let's Go Fishing!
January 16
Luke 5:1–11

Jesus is the greatest fisherman in the world! He is the one to learn from, to keep your eye on, to follow after, to give your heart to. Jesus is the master of all time and eternity—the master of the past, present, and future. When Jesus called the disciples, he entered into their world first. He borrowed Simon Peter's boat, and after preaching from there, told them to go out to deep water to fish. They had been luckless that night, but they followed through and caught more fish than they could handle! Then Jesus said, "Follow me; now you will fish for people." Jesus continues to call to us to join him.

Then and now, Jesus comes to where the people are. He preached on the shore, in the marketplace, and on the mountainside. He comes to us and gives us words to live by. Jesus taught by example. He looked out for people who were in need and came alongside them. There are innumerable such stories: the blind, the beggars, the widows, the prostitutes. When we seek to follow Jesus, we, too, need to go to those in need. It is a little scary to reach out to people we don't know, who are not like us. But the reality of faith is that we have to die to ourselves a little bit. We have to let go of self-consciousness, fill ourselves with the love of God, and let it spill out to those around us. Jesus takes ordinary, common folk like us, like the disciples, and speaks to our hearts, shows us the way, and makes us winners of souls.

On to Perfection
January 17
Matthew 5:38–48

"Be perfect, therefore, as your heavenly father is perfect" (Matthew 5:48)

This is a heavy verse. How can we imperfect humans ever hope to attain such perfection? Christ himself is calling us to reach for the perfection he attained on earth. The key word is *calling.* We know that on our own, we would surely fail. We're only too likely to think, *Ah, I'm nearly perfect now,* and then think, *Why look how much better I am than that poor sinner!* And we have thereby denied even a closeness to the kingdom of God. So, we have to ask, what did Jesus mean when he said, "Be perfect?"

We know that if God asked us to be perfect, then he would give us the means. The answer is so simple: God sees us as sinless because of the sacrifice of forgiveness Jesus made on the cross. Forgiveness means sinless. This freedom from sin allows us to be in the presence of God. It allows us to press on to the prize of our high calling. The crux of the matter is that we should not be dismayed by the enormity and complexity of living Christian lives in this world but that we expect great things of God—and we shall receive them.

Were we ever meant to attain anything like perfection on our own strength? When we try it alone, maybe our failure is trying to tell us that life is an affair, not of humankind alone, nor of human with human, but of humankind with God and God with humankind. Jesus could say, "Be perfect," because he believed staunchly in the seed in us which, given into God's care and power, can grow into eternal life. With that, we can truly press on toward perfection.

Son of Thunder

January 18
Matthew 20:20–28; Mark 10:35–45

The disciples were men very much like ourselves. Peter was hot and cold and denied his Lord at a crucial moment. They all deserted Jesus in the Garden. They sometimes misunderstood his message. They argued among themselves. Judas betrayed him. They were great men, and it is essential to see their humanity. There must have been some contact, some touch, some experience that made these men into godly men. What made these men disciples? What transformed them?

James was one of the inner circle of Jesus. The circle consisted of Peter, James, and John. There is little written specifically of James, as he is mostly mentioned with his brother, John. We do know that he was known as a Son of Thunder due to his hot temper. He once wanted to rain fire on a Samaritan village for denying them a place to sleep. James got angry at the wrong things, fussing about people instead of causes. Spending his energy on the argumentative rather than the eternal. Jesus appreciated people of passion. To confuse the Christian spirit with one who never becomes angry is to relegate the faith to the inanely meek and the innocuously mild.

As James walked and talked with Jesus, the fire of the Holy Spirit transformed him into an effective man of passion for Christ. Those of us who would serve Christ must let our Lord work in our lives that even our damning faults are turned into forces of fruitfulness.

James was also famous for his attempt, with his brother John, to gain the top seat, next to Jesus. Ambition is another human trait that is both good and bad. We need to have ambition to do the right thing—to help build the kingdom of God. We need to do away with the ambition for personal gain. God always knows the heart. Ultimately, James was most ambitious for the kingdom. He was beheaded by Herod for witnessing for Christ. Like James, we, too, can be molded by the Holy Spirit into righteous anger and righteous ambition, furthering the kingdom of God.

Special People
January 19
Isaiah 62:1–5; 1 Corinthians 12:1–11

Once God through Jesus announces that his wonderful kingdom is no longer distant but at hand, in our very midst, and wide open to us, God says to us that we are beautiful. He says there is a special relationship between God and the people of God, like that between a bride and a groom. God is shouting out that he chose Christ as his means of coming to be among us. Abundant life lies in the direction of being in harmony with God and with God's Word. Sadly, in the world, the tenderness of love for God must be hidden behind a faceless mask. No weakness must show. No vulnerability. We must survive by being so strong none would dare to approach. Fortunately, for the world, there are those who break and ignore the world's code of coldness. They are God's special people who understand that in Christ the joy inside is like the joy of first love, like weddings.

God's special people know that God's love is so abundant it simply cannot run out. That's what the story of water into wine is about. It is not just to save the reputation of the groom; it is to proclaim that God's love is *big*. It is so humungous it cannot run out. Abundance means there is plenty for everyone, no need to shove, no lines, no need to panic, there is plenty— more than enough—a lot left over. His love is big enough to fill the huge empty hole—anger and misunderstanding inside all of us. Enough to heal and repair and fulfill and enable us to give away endlessly without being emptied and instead to come away fuller still! His love is not magic; it cannot be bought. God's love is a for-real item. To gain its joy takes our real response, understanding, giving, and sacrifices. It is like raising a loving family. There are times of disappointment, anger, uncertainty, discipline, tears. But if there is abundant transforming love undergirding, grounded in God's love, and rooted in the scriptures, the end result will be like a wedding party. Deep, abiding, Christ-guided love is at once difficult and attainable, demanding and worth it.

The Courage to Be Christian
January 20
Philippians 1:12–21

It takes courage to be a Christian these days. It is somewhat encouraging to know that it has always been so. A quick look at the life of Paul shows that he endured far more than anything we will do in our time, but the need is there. Jesus warned the disciples that following him could lead to hardship; in fact, hardship is a sign that we are truly following. The ways of the world are so contrary to the ways of Christ.

One of the chief stumbling blocks to courageous Christian living is confusion over that which is really significant—the confusion over heaven and earth. As humans, we are very much a part of this world. We cannot live without many of the things it supplies. No matter how high or humble our station, we have to have food, water, air, and so on to live. Unfortunately, the necessities of obtaining a living take over our total attention. The earth is so visible; often spiritual things appear imaginary. The real question comes when we consider humankind's place on the earth and its relation to it. Our relation to the earthly should be only tentative, our relation to wealth only as stewards. We are here for a short time only, at best. As surely as we count on the things of the earth, we will be bound by them. The Christian faith is that God is love and wants harmony with us. When we live in harmony with him and our fellow humans, we live in accord with the intention of God and the structure of the universe. If we realize this and live with it, we will find that it gives us a courage we have never had before. We will know we're on the side of the right and the true and the good, and that regardless of what may appear to be the earthly outcome, we have the victory. Take courage in the knowledge of the eternal and the truth that is behind you, and, let yourself be wholly given to him who has the final victory.

The Dearly Beloved

January 21
Mark 14:32–42

More men are named John than any other single name. It is a good name. In Hebrew, it means, "God is Gracious." The apostle John is central to our faith. He authored the beautiful passage, "For God so loved the world that he gave his one and only son, that whoever believes in him shall not perish but have eternal life" (John 3:16). John was given to anger and ambition, like his brother James. He was intolerant and overprotective of Jesus's very name. As he walked with Jesus, he changed as well. While it is true that we cannot change the fact that as human creatures, we love and hate, fear and forgive, but with God, we can change our attitude and perspective.

John left to follow Jesus seemingly on the spur of the moment. He didn't pack; he followed Jesus just as he was. He took with him all his prejudices, angers, and ambition. He also carried a longing for spiritual renewal, and a hunger for God in terms he could understand. He may have thought he was going along just for the day, but it became his for life. This is the way it happens; when we follow Jesus, we find it becomes a life of joy.

John had some growing to do as well. He walked, lived, and talked with Jesus, and witnessed his sermons and miracles as well as his crucifixion. He was one of the first to see the risen Christ and receive the gift of the Holy Spirit. His change was gradual, learning that there were things that were of this world and there were things that were of eternity. He lived long enough to see the church become more than a gathering of believers. He was able to draw truths from experiences, ultimately realizing that if we can love one another, all else will fall into place. The apostle John is an example of how Jesus can take a man as he is and use his natural gifts and powers and temperament for greatness.

The Fullness of Faithfulness

January 22
Colossians 3:16

What in this world really pays off? What gives the maximum returns in the long run? What is worth giving yourself to? Faithfulness. That may not have been the first thing to come into your mind, but it really does. The world has a different message, of course. It's a matter of attitude.

The world says use threat to get action. Look around you; there are plenty of illustrations. War. Parenting. Even the legal system. Now contrast that with Christ's example of cherishing persons, investing in them, giving them value. In fact, that was his life's work. He came to earth to experience the pain of being human so that he could be the ultimate sacrificial priest. So that he could guide us to a true and good path. The world says threaten. Christ says cherish.

The world says wealth is power. Again, it stares you in your face. Bigger houses, faster cars, more, more, more. Yet what does that bring you? More work to pay for those things and less time to enjoy them. What is truly valuable? Persons, memories, relationships of lasting worth. Consider a funeral. There are no gut-wrenching stories about material things. The stories are about lives touched and paths changed. The world says "Mine." Christ says, "You are worth my time."

Finally, the world says take care of yourself. After all, who else will? Christ would add, take care of yourself, and give yourself away. It's a little bit scary. Maybe God will want you to do something you don't want to do or can't do. Thankfully, that's not the way it is. God gives you everything you need to serve him and yourself. It is an ongoing work in progress, but the payoff is far greater than anything the world has to offer.

The Joys of Fishing
January 23
Mark 1:14–20

This passage, where Jesus calls the fishermen from their work, is always a bit puzzling. How is it that he could just walk up to these men and say, "Follow me," and they would drop their nets and do it? It may have been that they were already acquainted and that there was a prearrangement. Even so, people can come up with so many excuses about why they can't do something when the time comes, that this seems unusual. Somehow, the disciples were convinced that what they had heard Jesus say earlier was true. "The kingdom of God is at hand" (Mark 1:15). What was ahead was part of God's plan; in fact, it is still going on even now. The opportunity to participate in the salvation of others is a privilege for all believers.

There are always things to be taken care of—everyday life requirements. Yet if these are tended to to the exclusion of God's matters, God will not force the point. Only those who choose to join God get the opportunity to be a part of his works. Further, If we choose to place God in our lives, we need to have the courage to live that priority. This priority means to say yes to all that upbuilds love; and to say no to all that does not upbuild love. This is not the way of the world we live in.

To be a fisher of men, it is vital to choose to build one another up, to come alongside with praise and kindness. To be a fisher of men, we must reach out to those with whom we swim in the stream of life, letting them, too, catch the joy of flowing with our God.

The Persecuter Preaches

January 24
Acts 9:1–20

The greatest journey in the world is the journey from a question mark to an exclamation point. The apostle Paul made such a journey. When he was struck down on the road to Damascus, he asked "Who are you, Lord?" He spent the rest of his life answering the question. He went from declaring sentences of death to writing words of life because of the forgiving love of God, which is available to all humankind.

In the language of faith, Paul experienced conversion. The drama of this conversion has puzzled many people seeking Christ. Too many have expected Christ to knock them down before they would accept his saving power. However, there are important steps in Paul's conversion that may guide those who await a vital experience of God.

The first step for Paul was a question—a growing awareness that he could not save himself. He could not meet all the requirements of the law of Moses. Despite devoting his life to learning and understanding the law, he developed a dissatisfaction. He then was a personal witness to the stoning of Stephen, and his height of dignity through Christ. After such preparation, he experienced Jesus face-to-face.

No one comes into true faith without such an experience. There must be a firsthand knowledge of God and a firsthand decision to follow him. This knowledge that God's hand is upon you is a gift that only God can give. We can point to the steps, witness its effects, and share it with others, but only God can give it.

Upon This Rock
January 25
Matthew 16:13–26

Jesus saw potential in Simon that no one around him had seen, even himself. Jesus saw through the eyes of God, and gave him the name Peter—the rock. To this time, he had been rather unsteady in his life, going from one thing to another. His association with Jesus changed him forever, from drifter to great rock of the church.

Peter was rather quick to speak, often blurting out things that others were likely thinking, and thereby giving Jesus the opportunity to teach them. While Peter was the first to recognize Jesus as the Christ, Son of God, he also tried to protect him from his destiny of pain in Jerusalem. Jesus saw this statement as a temptation from Satan, when he declared, "Get behind me, Satan!" Jesus was well aware of what lay ahead and reminded Peter, and therefore us, that much sacrifice is expected of those who follow him.

Peter followed Jesus so closely that he was in the courtyard when Jesus was arrested. It is here that he made his infamous denial, which Jesus had predicted. It is Peter's humanness that reaches out to console us when we, too, make mistakes. Which of us have not missed an opportunity to witness to our Lord, or withheld service to him when asked? These lapses are not defining, if we are able to rise above them as Peter did. Jesus redeemed him by asking him to feed his sheep—three times—the same number of times he had denied Jesus.

William Barker said, in *Twelve Were Chosen*, "There is an angel in every block of marble, but no matter how rough-hewn, a master sculptor can bring it out. There is a disciple, a man or woman of God, standing in every human life. No matter how chipped or rough-hewn, the Master-carpenter can carve it out." Peter, in his lovable, bumbling manner, reminds us that God will use us as we are, as long as we will give our lives to him.

We've Got a Way to Go

January 26
Ephesians 3:1–21

The turning of a new year is like a road sign that marks a point on the way. As we pass the road sign, we pause to think about where we have come from and where we are going. We are reminded that we are on a journey. We are travelers; we are pilgrims. We each have a way to go in our personal lives of faith. We may have caught a good glimpse of the Light, but at best we have only done a little. We know of the beautiful fruits of the spirit: love, joy, peace, patience, kindness, goodness, gentleness, faithfulness, and self-control. And we want these fruits. Many of us display them often, but none of us hold true to that fruitfulness all of the time. Until we know our journey is an ongoing one, and respect others for where they are along the pathway and journey with them, we have a way to go yet!

Another part of the journey is in the name of faith. It is easy to care for and about those closest to us, including ourselves. Only the most mature capture the universal nature of God's love. We need to continue to expand our vision of what we can give to the world around us. Wherever we are currently, the goal is still ahead. There is always more that can be done. Until we give ourselves here and now with greater joy and less reserve, we have a way to go yet. We are pilgrims of Christ on our life journey. We see the light and head for it. And we have a way to go yet.

What Comes First?

January 27
John 1:1–18

What comes first? What are your basic assumptions? What are you trying to accomplish? What is your life about? Life can be like a treadmill—a constant round of the same thing to achieve a static and boring result. Even with the boat and trailer, the camper and cook kit, the motel and seashore, our existence can be a treadmill! No mass of people have ever had the leisure time we Americans have or the finances to exploit it, but it can still be a treadmill. What changes life from a treadmill into a pilgrimage are the goals of life.

Generally, I suppose, we would say we are striving for happiness. But, as a goal, we discover happiness to be like a mirage; like a pot of gold at the end of the rainbow; always moving, fleeting, elusive. The New Testament asserts that the end is holiness. We seek godliness, work at loving the unlovely, and to make ourselves to stand with what is worthy. Too often, all we can say is that we are running around, doing, flitting from place to place; with nothing having much meaning or thought or purpose behind it at all. The purpose of our days needs to be seen in the light of what comes first. John wrote, "To all who received him, who believed in his name, he gave power" (John 1:12). So, when our activities are toward God, there is power with them. The nonessentials sap our strength and make us weary with well-doing.

Where does all this lead? What is it all worth? The great end is holiness; the great beginning is God. Any worthwhile goings and comings must be on the road between the two. It doesn't seem to matter which comes first, as much as *what* comes first.

What Do You Say?

January 28
Matthew 28:16–20

Has the church become outdated? How often do you hear, "I don't want to go to church, it's boring." How has this happened? Jesus was certainly not a boring man. In fact, he was quite controversial. He did not follow the common path or worry about what others would think. His story is not boring either—he is the most influential man ever to live! He is God among us—not far away, but here, in partnership with us. When did this qualify as boring?

Perhaps the problem is the members of the church—us. We have watered down the message so that it is "acceptable" to everyone. We need to contemporize Jesus. When you think of Jesus, do you think of a man dressed in a sharp suit and tie, driving a modern car? Or are you stuck with the Sunday school version of a kindly man with a beard and long hair wearing a robe and sandals? When we say Jesus lives, we mean he lives in our living. So when we speak of Jesus, we need to know that he is here, now, every minute of every day.

This gospel—our faith—is genuine and real. It is neither a bad joke nor an ancient, boring relic. So, what do we say? When Jesus rose from the dead, the Roman soldiers were actually *paid* to keep it quiet! Let us not make the same mistake. Faith is power. It is the power for the alcoholic to walk past that "first drink," for the person to walk away from a risky relationship, for the couple to stay strong through the tough parts of marriage. Faith is here and now; let's shout it out.

Where Is He?

January 29
Matthew 2:2

One of the problems we consistently face in this hectic world is that it is hard for us to work our way back into the origins of the faith. The stories of the birth of Christ and all that surrounded that event are so long ago, yet the event was so important and means so much to this day. It is important for us to work our way back into the original because we need it for reality's sake and for the sake of truth and understanding.

Picture the wise men. We don't know much about them, really, but we do know that they were wealthy enough to travel, to study, and to bring gifts. From the question, "Where is he who has been born king of the Jews?", we can safely assume they were expecting royal surroundings for this infant. But, as is often the case, God amazes us with his own plans. Things were not as the wise men expected, nor as the prophets expected, nor as the shepherds expected. In fact, the common thing we can rely on is that God chooses to operate in unexpected ways. Imagine their surprise, then, when they found him. Not in a palace, not in an inn, but in a stable. They must have been shocked! In the window of our minds, we clean things up a bit, probably quite a bit. The reality must have been shocking.

Now fast forward. Where do we find Jesus? Some say, "in the church." Others say, "absolutely not in the church!" The reality is somewhere in between. Jesus cannot be contained in a church. He is, however, in its people. He is in the darkest alleyway as much as in the beautiful home. He is in the prison, the hospital, the shelter, as much as in the office building, the mall, and the cathedral. Christ today is doing just what he did long ago. He chooses to be whom he will be: servant, spirit, redeemer, friend. He is in the persons we deal with every day. We do not need to look farther, but rather, in front of us. This is the great gift of God: that he offers us to engage in mission every day with the persons with whom we get angry, with whom we fight, with those who are the nearest. The most tragic mistake we can make is to look elsewhere. He has come. He is here.

Who Do You Think You're Kidding?
January 30
Matthew 7:7–24

Our human tendency is to want to do it ourselves. An early phrase in a child's vocabulary is, "I can do it myself!" As adults, we learn more sophisticated ways of asserting our independence, but the desire to hold the reins in our own hands is still there. Independence and self-reliance are important virtues. Taken to excess, they can also become vices, because it is not a far step from self-reliance to self-centeredness. So we become lord instead of God as Lord, and all kind of havoc results. Who do we think we are fooling? God knows our frame. We're not kidding him. We're probably not kidding those with whom we work and live. Alas, we are our own worst enemies.

God is vibrantly alive, yet we are so preoccupied with ourselves that it doesn't seem that way sometimes. God won't make us listen. There are no laws that compel you to ask what it is God wants for your life. There is nothing that requires you to praise him for all things. There is no compulsory believing. He certainly plays beautiful music, and his words certainly make sense. We do need guidance—we cannot go it alone. God is very real, and he knows us by name and longs for us to be one with him. So we are called upon to do what is better, to persuade, to win, to beseech, to live what we believe is Truth.

Who Would Betray Him?
January 31
Matthew 22: 14–16

Do you know anyone named Judas? Yet how many guys named John do you know? Interesting. They were both disciples of the Lord. The difference is that Judas betrayed Jesus and delivered him up to the hands of the authorities who crucified him. So, no one calls their child Judas. The name Judas is synonymous with betrayal. How could a man betray the Lord? It is easy to say that we would never do such a thing, but would we?

After all, we're nice in his presence. We wear nice clothes, say nice things, smile nicely, and are courteous and kind. Well, at least we do those things on Sunday! We may not betray him in such a way as Judas, but what about the little things? What about not speaking up when someone is being beaten down; what about not fulfilling our true potential; what about missed opportunities to share our faith? When we miss these "little" things, we betray the Lord … and just as much, we betray ourselves.

The reason Jesus came to this earth was that we might have life and have it more fully. When we miss the mark of our own capacity, we have betrayed our reason for being created. The saddest part of the work of a pastor is not the conduct of funerals. It is seeing people go through life missing the mark, losing their lives for their own sakes, missing out on the joy of faithfulness, denying themselves the joy of fellowship.

Who would betray Jesus? Why, none of us, surely! Yet we know we do. With God's help, we can do better. That is the secret: with God's help, we can do better. Jesus came to earth to help keep us from betraying ourselves; and he came with the power to follow through. Now that's good news!

A Call, a Gospel, a Task
February 1
Romans 1:1–7

There is a deep need to sharpen our awareness of the truth of the good news of God and to discover new power in that faith through fresh commitment, discipline, and dedication. The day for lackadaisical Christianity is past. The time of the complacent must be left behind. A new and vigorous breed, who know their scripture, who know the Lord, and who are willing to do something about it, are taking their place. The faith of Jesus Christ is too vital, too important, too filled with meaning and significance to be viewed haphazardly, lazily, or witlessly. We are called to total commitment to Christ to spread the gospel.

What is the gospel? It is the good news that there is a way for us to be at one with God in spite of the fact that we have broken with Him. That way is Jesus Christ, who says to us, by the fact that he rose from the dead, "I really am who I say I am, and I offer you forgiveness and a new start." A life of total commitment is a good life, full of meaning and significant work and an eternal hope. Each confessing Christian is called to be separated to God's service—a servant of Christ. There is almost infinite variety to what we may do in being in God's service. The common tasks to all who are called in this way include worshiping together, being constant in prayer, knowing our Bibles, and supporting our gathering of believers. Through these tasks, we will each be blessed with a specific means of serving God as loving, nurturing persons and have a truly abundant life.

Agony and Ecstasy
February 2
Mark 8:27–38

The Agony and Ecstasy is the title of an excellent book by Irving Stone about the life of Michelangelo. The agony of Michelangelo was his attempt to create. The ecstasy came when the creation was wrought. Is it offensive to think of Jesus as one who agonized and who also had some periods of ecstasy? It is not hard to see Jesus in agony. We know he wept at the loss of Lazarus, pined for the renewal of Jerusalem, and agonized in the garden of Gesthemane. But what of ecstasy? To be ecstatic is to be nearly beside oneself with a powerful emotion. Jesus clearly felt these emotions as well. He rejoiced when Thomas came to believe, and with the blind and paralyzed whom he healed. He enjoyed watching Peter become alive and the best self he could be. Jesus had strong emotions. He laughed, he cried, he shared, he carried, he lifted. How often we cloister the Lord in the walls of the church and leave him out of the everyday. It is good to know that he is with us in everything.

It requires agony to live life. To live life well requires discipline and sacrifice. It is important to place our relationship with Christ front and center. We need time to read and study the word, to pray and to listen to the answers. Without such disciplines, it would be like a basketball team that never had a practice; it takes practice to win the game.

Renewal is equally important. There are so many tasks that need to be done to just get through the day. In fact, it can become a giant treadmill. Yet with Christ as our guide, it is a journey, a pilgrimage. What God has done in Christ is the difference. With him, life is no drudge; it is an adventure. Knowing Christ puts a new spring in the step, teaches us beauty and hope so that we see life with new eyes that find ways to care. The great story of humankind is that God came to us in the form of a man to call us to fullness of life. To follow him costs quite a bit, at times. But it's worth it!

Chances
February 3
John 4:5–42

The biblical story of the woman at the well is a wonderful story. The season of Lent is set aside by the church to encourage us to examine our lives spiritually. It is an opportunity to ask ourselves how things are with our souls. For the woman at the well, life had been a series of broken and painful relationships. Her initial response to Jesus reflects a kind of flirtation. No man should be seen in the daytime talking with a woman, particularly a Jewish man and a Samaritan woman. Yet Jesus is somehow able to help her see that he is the Christ! He knows things about her yet is still interacting. He sees an opportunity to change her life and those around her and gently guides her to the truth. This event has been used as an encouragement to discipled Christians to think positively about sharing the good news with their network of friends and acquaintances. It has been used to promote evangelism. Clearly it is an invitation to every baptized, believing Christian to witness to what we know wherever and whenever we can. Never mind the outward appearance or even the reputation of the person involved. Each is a child of God, and none are outside the reach of God.

Jesus offers real hope. Now. Today. Jesus was able to see beyond the outer woman and reach in for her soul. Things were never the same for her; she became a different person. That is what happens when Christ catches hold of your soul. We become different persons; our horizons change. We begin to see new possibilities; hopelessness is replaced by vision. To be captured by the all-encompassing love of Christ is to have a new chance.

Choose Life
February 4
Deuteronomy 30:15–20; Matthew 5:20–37

The scene is Jesus talking to the disciples. They have been steeped in the law all their lives, and know them down to the letter. However, Jesus is saying something new. It is about going beyond the law. God said, "I have set before you life and death; blessing and curse; therefore choose life" (Deuteronomy 30:19). Don't be caught in the negative restrictions of the law. Be caught up in the reason for the law: that we might be free! That we might have real life!

Take murder. Obviously we shouldn't kill another, but what about the attitudes surrounding murder—the hostility of the heart, self-centeredness, greed, anger? Consider marriage and divorce: marriage is holy; love and loyalty alone avail as the foundation of a happy home. Divorce hurts everyone, despite being within the law.

This was truly instruction in the nature of discipleship. We are called upon to be the same blessing that has blessed us—to be salt, light, and leaven. The whole perspective is to concentrate upon the choosing of life.

We wonder what Jesus would say today about human sexuality, marriage, pollution, population, poverty, energy, tension between the rich and the less rich. Likely, he would say that the source of bloodshed is in the attitudes that forget to care deeply about the whole creation. Yes. In our humanness we experience brokenness. Jesus says to us, "Do not wallow there. Be reconciled; give and receive forgiveness and through that, grace. Stand again and choose life. Choose not what takes away but what puts together." We have been given life and death, curse and blessing. Which is best is not at issue. What we will choose is at issue.

God's Ways/Our Ways

February 5
Mark 8:32–33

In this passage, the disciples saw the ministry of Jesus taking a turn that they did not like and that they did not understand. Amazing events were taking place. Jesus was standing up to the self-righteous leaders. Peter even blurts out, "You are the Christ; you're the Messiah; you're the *one*." Then Jesus gives them a glimpse of what is to come. He would suffer and be rejected. He would be killed and rise again after three days. They were shocked! When Peter expressed their resistance, Jesus actually says, "Get behind me, Satan." It was unthinkable. God's ways are different than our ways. We are in God's ways whenever we understand that love is better than hate and that building is better than destroying. If we think, as Paul states in Philippians, on things that are honorable, just, pure, lovely, gracious, excellent, and praiseworthy, and do these things, the God of peace will be with us. (Philippians 4:8–9)

To follow Jesus, we must get beyond ourselves. In Jesus's words, "deny self … follow me" (Mark 8:31). He even expressed that we need to lose our lives to save them. It's perplexing but true. What it takes is partnership with our Lord. It requires that we align God's ways and our ways. The world has some nice things, but that's all they are. They turn to dust, and they can't love back. Peter was a blustery guy, but ultimately, he got the message: "I'm poor but rich; I've lost but won; I've denied self and my self has somehow come into real being." There are God's ways, and there are the ways of the world. Take God's ways.

Hard-Headed Christianity

February 6
Ephesians 6:10–20

It is easy to become discouraged in your faith. Even to have doubts sometimes. It feels like the world is descending into sin anyway ... is there any hope? It can feel like the cards are stacked against those who try to do the right thing, like teachers, parents, pastors, law enforcement officers, and so on. People seem to hesitate to take responsibility for their actions. You may even feel others are making fun of you for believing in something that cannot be seen or touched.

How do we overcome such discouragement? First, we must believe strongly in God and his work here on earth; next, we must have a solid concern for others; finally, be convinced that the Christian view of life is a real, valid perspective. The first point makes sense; otherwise, we wouldn't be concerned about doing the right thing in the first place. This leads to the second point—a solid concern for others. Now that goes against the grain of society, doesn't it? Society has fallen into the mantra of me, me, me. Jesus said to love our neighbor as ourselves. So, is the Christian view valid? Jesus said he would care for us, not that things would be easy. In fact, one might say that if your faith walk is easy, you are missing something. This is where our passage comes in.

The armor of God tells us that there will be battles and that we will be enabled to stand firm. With the belt of truth, the breastplate of righteousness, the shield of faith, the helmet of salvation, and the sword of the spirit, you are ready to combat anything that tries to get in your way. So, be a hardheaded Christian, withstanding the blows of others, in the knowledge that yours is the better way—God's way.

Holy Smoke!
February 7
Leviticus 19:1–2, 15–18

The passage for this message is known in scholarly circles as "the holiness code." Some of the concerns listed are obeying father and mother, observing the sabbath, avoiding idols—the basic lines of the Ten Commandments. Other scriptures concern wages and cattle breeding, weights and measures, incest and witchcraft, haircuts and tattoos. The interesting question that emerges from the words is, "Why should these particular things be observed?" The first answer is written in the passage numerous times: "I am the Lord your God." These instructions were given directly to Moses by God after he began leading the Israelites. He was initially called by God through the burning bush. God calls us by dramatic means to reflect on who we are. When Moses saw the burning bush, what he saw was not as important as whom he met.

The holiness code is the first instance of social welfare work in that it called to leave the edges of the field or orchard for the poor and travelers, rather than stripping it completely bare. It also calls for fairness to the stranger and right dealings with the unwary. But the real source of goodness is our identity as children of God, and our responsibility before him. Our lives are lived not according to "holy smoke," but by "Holy Spirit." We know in the depth of our souls who we are and whose we are.

Who we are deals with all thoughts of life. Our religious experience can never be compartmentalized. When we accept that we are the sons and daughters of God and that he is our Lord, everything is his and nothing is excluded. This allows us to begin to minister to others. The grace of God leads us to care about social issues that are not within our immediate family but within the family of God. Issues such as drug addiction, war, and homelessness are brought home when we experience the grace of God in our own hearts. It would be more comfortable if we could ignore it all and go about our business—and that is our natural bent. But we must resist that nature and reach out to the challenges of society at large. Knowing who we are allows us to meet the challenge because there is a Holy Fire within us.

Hope Beyond Our Wilderness

February 8
Matthew 4:1–11

Each one of us has our own experience with and in the wilderness. We each have our own stories. Personal wilderness comes when you simply don't know what to do. Not knowing where to turn, not being able to decide, confusion, indecision, anguishing uncertainty, and doubt and depression. The temptation of Jesus in the wilderness was actually a trinity of temptations—bread, sensationalism, and kingdom. Jesus gave three answers, all from scripture. In this setting, the temptations were more of a test, to see how he would respond. The concept of testing is a good insight into our own experiences in the wilderness. Rather than a reaction of anger, we could see what occurs in life as an opportunity to see what we can learn. In living, there are trials, and God seeks to bring us through them with applications of living truth. The Word of God is a wealth of resources from which to draw, which is why it is so important to be familiar with it.

The reality of life is that we will each experience our wilderness. We will know what we believe is betrayal. We will experience brokenness and hurt and pain. But God, through the scripture and the worshiping community of faith, has resources that surround us with understanding and love; with hope and joy. These lead us beyond our wilderness.

How an Easy Choice Gets Slippery
February 9
Deuteronomy 30:15–20

We would all choose life and good and blessings. No one wants death and evil and curse. No one purposely tries to ruin their future. So, what happens? There is a crisis. Everywhere there are choices that seem good but aren't the best. We fall into "community standards," complacency, selfishness, rebellion, rationalizing, deceit, dishonesty. We know better, but the deceiver is after us. He loves to make wrong sound so right. He cloaks our destruction in words of goodness, hides the truth with deception. We have all heard this—a lie is a "misstatement," and foul language is an "expletive." Slippery ways include convincing us that the bad is good ... try it, you'll love it.

With all this slipperyness, it's important to grab onto something solid. You have to keep your eyes on your destination. Statistically, 95 percent of the people in this nation believe in God. But only 60 percent of those belong to any church, and half of those only rarely attend. It seems that these people don't think that it is important to be active in their faith. Believing in God isn't enough. True saving faith requires action. In fact, if one has true faith, the action is a natural result. The destination is life and good and blessings. Keeping ahold of God with true faith will bring you to that destination.

How to Be on the Winning Side
February 10
Genesis 2:15–17

The greatest stories of our faith, found throughout the Bible, strengthen us in our own daily efforts to be faithful. The Genesis story is a marvelous one. It is the story of what we could call the "first sin." Adam and Eve had been given everything they could possibly want. Yet Satan, the great deceiver, points out the one thing they were to stay away from. He twists the words of God, so that Eve questions the reality, and, in a moment, their innocence was gone. There were some pretty hefty consequences. In fact, this moment set the pattern for humankind even to this day.

Thankfully, God already had a plan. After the consequences come words of Grace. He teaches us to come to him so that we might experience forgiveness. Oh, the joy of forgiveness! Forgiveness brings a fresh start; forgiveness brings hope. This concept is outlined clearly in Romans 5:17: "If, because of one man's trespass, death exercised dominion through that one, much more surely with those who receive the abundance of grace and the free gift of righteousness exercise dominion in life through the one man, Jesus Christ." Sin comes by way of Adam; reconciliation comes by way of Jesus Christ. Christ breaks Adam's disobedience; Christ gives us the opportunity of a fresh start. Christ becomes the Lord of a justified, redeemed, triumphant community! We are on the side of victory!

If You Knew; If You Only Knew

February 11
Exodus 17:1–7

It is easy to imagine that the Israelites wandering in the wilderness might be a bit cranky. They were impatient and demanding. Moses was leading them, and he surely felt a bit cranky himself. After all, he had spoken with God, broken them out of slavery, led them across the Red Sea—on dry land. Moses does exactly the right thing. He cries out to the Lord. God, being infinitely patient, answers with water rushing out of a rock!

Fast-forward to your own life. You may have come to the end of your rope. You have been a good person but now find yourself in an impossible situation. What do you do? We tend to call on others, our earthly support system. They don't have the answers either. It is humiliating. That is when we cry out to the Lord! It feels like giving up; it *is* giving up—to the only One who can actually fix the problem. The trouble is that it is hard to give up. We think we can do everything on our own. It is hard to admit that we need anything—that we need a savior.

This is the deceiver, hard at work. The deceiver convinces us that we are good enough. We become annoyed that we are not. It feels like God is asking for too much. That is exactly where he wants us. In need of him. Humbled enough to kneel at his throne and ask the Lord of the universe for help.

Knock, Knock, Knock
February 12
Revelation 3:1–22

Who can resist a knock? Even if you're putting on your coat to leave, you look out to see who is knocking and what they want. It was part of the technique of the writer of Revelation to use figures of speech and colorful words daubing their way into pictures in order to reach his hearers with a relevant message for their condition and experience. The book of Revelation is a provocative one. Many approach it with caution, if not fear. Numerous notable passages get lost in the swirling imagery and veiled numerical references. One of the most notable is our text for today: "Here I am! I stand at the door and knock; if any one hears my voice and opens the door, I will come in to him and eat with him and he with me" (Revelation 3:20).

At the time of Jesus and his disciples, sheep were a large part of daily life. In the ancient sheepfold, there was no gate or door. There was a single opening, the shepherd himself would lay down across the opening, so that none could get in or out except over him. In the above reference, we are the door. We control the door to our own hearts, as well as to the sheepfold, which is our home. By our answering or ignoring the knock of Christ, we give our homes the abundance of Christian life or the lack of such abundance.

It is interesting that there is a prevalent idea that Jesus has no right to stand at the door of one's heart. It is almost as if people have staked out "stay away" signs. Don't talk to me of my responsibilities; just leave me alone. In point of fact, if we accept that Jesus is the Alpha and the Omega, the beginning and the end, the first, last, and always; then he has a right to stand there. In one sense, he stands in judgment. If the door is opened, he is welcomed with wide arms. Often, he simply stands at the door. He stands mercifully, patiently, but sorrowfully. Our response to his knock is life altering. When the door opens, he doesn't stay in the doorway. He comes in and stays for a while. Jesus comes to our door with a desire to have a relationship with us. We must decide whether to answer.

Listen
February 13
Matthew 3:1–17

One of the most wonderful of the senses is our ability to listen. Listening is different than hearing, in fact, we hear what we listen for. The chief problem speakers have is that the listener won't listen or that the audience hears only what it wants to hear. One of the softest sounds from heaven came at the beginning of the ministry of Jesus … his heavenly ordination at baptism. Lent is a time for listening to and for a voice from heaven … a spirit breaking out from the traditional forms, a breath of eternity whispering words of restoration to tired souls. The first act of Jesus after his baptism was to go into the wilderness to fast and pray for forty days and forty nights. He went to listen to the still, small voice. There he struggled with Satan, but because he had selective listening, God's purpose for him won out. Now, none of us are Jesus, but we are from common stock with him. And we, too, can listen if we will. It is a gift God gives to all if they will take it. If we take the gift, we, too, can take footsteps along eternity.

Having made us, God seeks nothing more or less than our fulfillment. We must listen carefully for the voice of God. The critical step to hear the voice of God is to be quiet. If we believe that our real nature is spiritual, we must take time to listen. Another aspect of finding the voice of God is to listen to others around us, seeking together the words of God. This includes husbands and wives, children and parents, students and teachers. If there is any general area in a relationship that has trouble, it virtually always stems from trouble with communication. All too often, we talk at one another, but not with one another. Listening to one another and listening to God must go hand in hand, or we hear nothing from either. Let us relearn the art of listening, not just of hearing sounds blaring through day and night, but of selective hearing and most especially for that still, small voice. Let us tune in an eternal transistor in the depth of our souls, so that, centered on eternity, we may walk confidently through noisy days.

Modeling
February 14
1 Corinthians 11:1

To be a model who is admired and appreciated is a tremendously natural aspiration. In fact, most of us become something of a model for someone, whether in action, dress, or behavior. Jesus was such a man that he made an impact on his world and is still making that impact. He is a worthy image to model after. Yet how do we go about imitating him? What do we really know?

Jesus was tough. He was a protector who used strength for the benefit of those without strength. He laughed and cried and had callouses on his hands. He enjoyed doing things with his hands. He wasn't naïve about the world, in fact, he was indignant over situations where the rude and the crooked and the dishonest cheated the weak and the poor. He was also gentle. He would toss children in the air and make them feel secure. He recognized that he was accountable to God. He was in touch with the world. He analyzed it and picked out what was lasting. He was whole, not partial. He knew himself. He was always able to take persons who would respond and help them to want to do what they knew would make them whole people. To be like him is to grow toward completion, to be strong for others less strong, to be gentle with others, drawing out their best. Wow! Who wouldn't want to be like him, to seek to embody his characteristics? It is worth giving your life to seeking to grow toward his likeness.

This is not easy. Christ in the flesh was rejected. Many don't want to be like him; many don't even want to know what it would be like, or fear asking about it. If we model our lives after him, we will also model those lives for someone else. We will not be everything to everyone. But we can be something to someone. We may even be a lot to many. The thing is, we are being copied. What will the template produce?

46

Mountaintops and Marketplaces

February 15
Mark 9:2–9

Consider the differences between the values of the "world" and Christian values. Several comparisons come to mind. Me first versus other first; get ahead versus care for one another; get even versus be forgiving; success means material things versus success comes from the spirit. What is your mountaintop? When Jesus, John, James, and Peter were on the mountain, and God said, "This is my beloved Son, listen to Him" (Mark 9:7), Peter wanted to build booths so that they could stay there. That is what we want sometimes, isn't it? It would be amazing if we could stay in the "mountaintop" experience, yet, just like Jesus and the disciples, the real work is in the marketplace. Down in the marketplace, among each other, day after day, and when we're out of sorts and crabby, is where it works or fails to work. This is where the good news of Christ must be shared. Such is the work of God.

We need the inspiration of mountaintops, when we *know God* deeply and richly, because then we can be what God is calling us to be where we live every day. Inspiration is what gives us the impetus and motivation to work diligently on behalf of our Lord and Savior. Inspiration changes our hearts and souls from partnership with the world and its values to partnership with Christ and our Lord's values. It is a constant battle. The winsomeness and hype of the world snag us repeatedly. But be of good cheer. Christ is in our heads and our hearts and our attitudes. We are not alone.

Narrow Passages
February 16
Luke 13:22–35

One of the challenges of life is knowing the limits. The question of the crowd in this story was, "Lord, will those who are saved be few?" His answer was startling. "Strive to enter by the narrow door." The first reaction most of us would have is, "OK, so how narrow is the door? What are the rules?" The nature of most of us is to try to determine the minimum requirements. One of the most natural of human reactions is to test the limits. Children test their parents. Drivers drive four miles over the speed limit. Kids face peer pressure to be like "everyone else." The first story of humanity was Adam and Eve, who had everything, just one limit, the tree of good and evil. What did they do? They had to eat from that tree!

Of course, some are content to stay within the limits. They are sure goodness will get them through the gate. And then, they puff up on how good they are, how much better they are, until the gate is too narrow again! The most common human stumbling is to understand all things literally rather than spiritually. The Lord does not speak literally. He spoke of the quality of relationship, process, direction, striving, acceptance, trust. Most of us are solid, sound believers. We love Christ, and we love his church. But eventually, if we are not careful, our faithfulness becomes habit; it becomes routine. We must see how delightful it is that God gave us each and every day to be fresh, like no other, and never to be again. Invest in quality; search for that first, tingling love. Once the door is open, we are not alone. The door must be kept open so we can come and go and remain full.

New Religion
February 17
Mark 1:22

The people surrounding Jesus were astonished at his teaching and power. It seems like nothing is astonishing anymore. The true source of all joy and astonishment is that God himself has come into our world! Jesus spoke with authority. The people of that time noticed that there was a significant difference between the way Jesus spoke with them and how the scribes and Pharisees spoke. When they spoke, they quoted other sources and persons of authority. But the authority of Jesus was not from tradition. The authority of Jesus was directly from God.

We are able to speak with authority and authenticity as well, if we truly share a personal experience with Jesus. This allows us to speak from deep within our own hearts and souls. Having intimate knowledge of the scriptures is also important. Jesus possessed such knowledge. It is vital to do more than simply study scripture. We need to truly internalize it. This means spending time in God's Word. Another element of authenticity is humility. Having a deep conviction of the truth that God is our creator is the final aspect that gives our speech true authority.

The context of the people's astonishment was that Jesus had just cast out a demon from a troubled man. Consider the demons of our day—fear, worry, anxiety, insecurity. These are the things that make people "crazy" today. What Jesus did was to restore the soul of the man. His Word still speaks with the power of God to those who are burdened, distressed, or sick. For those of us that already rely on God, we have received forgiveness and direction for our lives to overcome envy, jealousy, and hatred—with the love of God. The crowds asked, "What is this? A new teaching?" Yes! This is a new and wonderful teaching. This teaching has the authority of God in it. What could the teachings of Jesus do for your life? When you have been set free by Christ, you have been set free to serve. That results in astonishment from the crowds of our day as well.

New Testament, Not "New Age"
February 18
Deuteronomy 4:35–40

Either God is God, or there is no God. Either Jesus is Lord, or there is no Lord. This is not believed by all, and the struggle has been with us for a long time. We call it the New Age movement. The New Age movement would have us believe that *we* can be *God*! That is certainly not what the Bible says, though, is it? Today's text states, "The Lord is God; besides him there is no other" (Deuteronomy 4:35). To believe otherwise is purely and simply rebellious.

Some of the New Age beliefs are worth examining. First, they believe that everything is relative. There is no absolute truth, there is nothing ultimate, or solid, or sure. From this standpoint, some will even go so far as to say that they shouldn't impose their beliefs onto their children. In other words, there is no heritage, no legacy, no values; there is nothing that is for sure. Really? Is that what we want our children to hear? Or do we want to give them something to really believe, to have an assurance, to have an advocate pulling for them? Unfortunately, you can't have it both ways. It's either the New Testament or the New Age; it simply can't be both.

Another belief is that God is impersonal. In this belief, one is to empty one's mind. It's like in *Star Wars*. Luke Skywalker is in the swamp with Yoda: "Empty your mind of all thoughts, let the force flow through you." You are god! Whatever god there is, you are it! But, with a personal, transcendental God who knows your name, who has you listed in the book of life, who knows what goes on with you every moment of every day, who loves you and cares for you … there you have something you can stand on, something solid, something you can teach your kids.

A final belief to examine is that of reincarnation. It comes under the doctrine of karma. It is one of the filthiest jokes Satan has ever played. "Listen folks," Satan says, "you don't get it right this time … there's another time." How many times around do you want? Besides, if there is no ultimate truth, if everything is relative, and if you are god, and that's it, how are you ever going to get it right?

Think of it as a bee in the car. The family is driving around happy and singing. One of the children is allergic to bees, and it comes right for her. She screams, and just as it comes toward her, the father swishes his hand and catches the bee in his fist. The bee zaps Dad. Daddy says, "It's all right now, honey, look at my hand, there's the stinger." That's the way it is with God. The Bible says Jesus took it all for us! Now that's something to stand on—that's the New Testament.

Ordinary Men
February 19
Isaiah 56:1–9

The first disciples were simple, ordinary men. Matthew was a tax collector, Peter, Andrew, James, and John were all fishermen; Judas was a rebel. They all had their families, their habits, and their personal hopes. Give one of them a jacket and tie, and you wouldn't know he was any different than a multitude of businessmen. There is a tendency to think of them as special, almost holy. Yet Peter, James, and John fell asleep praying for Jesus, Thomas blatantly doubted who Jesus was, and Judas stole from the group and ultimately sold Jesus out. All of this to say that when we put an ordinary group of people together and allow God to work among them, great things can come about. The difference is the presence of God.

Jesus has changed more people, changed more history, and influenced more lives than anything or anyone before or since. Ordinary people are changed by an extraordinary Christ. God often, almost preferentially, uses the local and commonplace for the biggest things on earth. He can transform any person. If you have given yourself to Christ, you have become extraordinary. Such are the people that God has chosen to build his kingdom. The strength of the instrument does not come from within, but from God. Even as an ordinary carpenter's hand enfolds a rough fisherman's hand and leads him into a rich fellowship with God that calls forth his most unusual discipleship—even so that extraordinary hand can enfold yours, regardless of how ordinary—and make you a doer of good and godly things.

The Art of Hating
February 20
Proverbs 8:1–13; Romans 12:9

An old song written by Spike Jones in the '40s used the line, "You always hate the one you love." If we were to be candidly honest with ourselves, we could recognize more hostility, more anger, animosity, and old-fashioned hate mixed into our relationships with others—including loved ones—than would be, to say the least, respectable. Hate is a dilemma in our world. It is here. It is a fact. It is something we have to face. Christianity is a divine goodness held in tension by a divine fierceness. It is loving the good and true, hating the bad and evil. It is a tension. Some say that all wars are fought on the basis of religion; others point out that too much peace softens people.

The risk of modern Christianity is that we have emphasized the softer side of faith to the point that we risk becoming indifferent. We are called to hate evil. We must be sensitive to injustice, detest unthinking prejudice, and loathe arrogance and haughtiness.

The art of hating comes in a balance between gentleness and fierceness. There is a tension between seeing red at wrong and being kind toward the wrongdoer. The art of hating comes with hating the evil and loving the evildoer. Many people have gone wrong hating a person for what he has done wrong and not being able to separate the person from his wrongdoing. Love without backbone and discipline is mush. On the other hand, discipline without gentleness and love is brittle and hard and defeats itself. Gentleness and discipline, love and hate must come together. The same God who made the tiger made the lamb. Christianity separates the sin from the sinner. Toward the sinner, it is more forgiving and gentle than any other philosophy has dared to be. Toward the sin, there is an undying hatred. We must learn the art of balancing these things. It is as true in the love and discipline of our children as it is in the world, seeking to love and understand those who would be our enemies.

The Ship
February 21
Hebrews 9:1–5

In order to successfully navigate the voyage of life, we not only need God's plan for our lives, we also need the ship of faith—the church. Participation in the local church is as essential for our successful voyage through life as having a vessel is essential to cross the ocean. Throughout history, people have crossed the ocean in ridiculously small vessels. From the first solo circumnavigation in the 53-foot Gipsy Moth to a twenty-four-foot sloop, to crossing the Atlantic in a six-foot sailboat, and even rowing across the Atlantic—3,075 miles in fifty-six days! But no one has ever made it across an ocean swimming. Yet spiritually, folk plunge into the ocean of life and try to make a crossing without so much as a life vest! The vessel God gave us for the voyage is the church. This is not a new idea. It dates all the way back to Noah and the ark. Eventually the Israelites were led to form the ark of the covenant.

The deceiver isn't happy about the church. He tries to destroy it with the put-downs of many sources. He uses our human nature to break down the unity of the church and to encourage us to argue among ourselves. But the church belongs to our living God; it is the SS Jesus. Our captain, Jesus, calms the storms both outside and within our hearts and souls. Thank you, Jesus. Let the Lord take the helm of our faith.

The Story of Salvation
February 22
Genesis 2:4–3:15; John 14:1–11

This story begins with understanding that God created the earth and everything in it—Including man and woman. Adam and Eve lived initially in perfect harmony with God and the earth. They fell out of that harmony through a very simple act of disobedience. The serpent twists the words of God to imply that the restriction of one specific tree was unreasonable, not in their best interest. This type of persuasion comes to every one of us, presenting the idea that we can know better than God. One man's rebellion against God is far-reaching, and the effect of his sin has lasted for generations. The reaction of Adam to his sin can be seen in our own selves today. We hide. Like Adam, we know how naked our sins appear in the eyes of God. God created us with freedom of choice, and one of the choices we could make is to go to hell, if we wanted to. Many times we forget that that path is open wide and clear.

The Old Testament is filled with actions and prophecies that make humankind's rebellious nature unquestionable. The New Testament is the fulfillment of these prophecies. The new covenant supercedes the old covenant and gives it real meaning and significance. Christ is the core of God's work of salvation. God seeks to draw humankind back into real and true harmony throughout the scriptures.

In the fullness of time, God sent Jesus Christ, who could show us God in the flesh. Who could reveal God in terms we could understand: fatherhood, brotherhood, love, kindness, integrity. This was fulfillment, because it meant salvation. Christ's death and resurrection was witnessed by the men he had developed throughout his ministry, and they were the first to see the truth. Christ is God, and his sacrifice was for every one of us. He has covered our sin with his righteousness. He is humankind's hope, because he opened a way of escape from meaninglessness. Life becomes rich and full, centered around upbuilding one another in love. Furthermore, he puts eternity into living. He is our salvation.

The Way

February 23
Acts 9:2

The first instance of the Christian faith being referred to as "The Way," was Paul's persecution of those belonging to The Way. It is an interesting touch that he became one of the chief evangelists of The Way. We are followers of The Way. It is the way that leads to life. It is the way of our Lord. It is a way that has proven its trustworthiness over the years. A way that will serve a lifetime well is something everyone longs to discover. I don't know anyone who wants to fail. Everyone wants to do well, to be thought well of, to have counted for something.

The Way is a way of discipline. In the dictionary, the definition of discipline includes: to act in accordance with, to train in the conduct of, and third, punishment by way of correction. Yet societally, we often think first of the negative connotation of punishment. The Christian use of discipline is to act in accordance with one's profession of faith and to train one's spirit to be like that of Jesus Christ. It comes down to a frame of mind. The nature of humanity is a mixture of wanting what is right and good yet procrastinating and rationalizing and excusing. To stay steadfast in The Way means to discipline one's tendency to put things off, to care more about the good of others over one's self. We worry about our world's ills, but if we were all truly followers of The Way, many of those ills would cease to exist.

We can have a steadfast conviction that The Way is the right way. The truth was told by Jesus: "I am the way, the truth and the life" (John 14:6). To really follow Him is to move toward the truth and the fullness of life. That doesn't mean Christians don't have low moments or that they never have doubts. It just means a confidence that they are moving with the way God made the world. Hold steadfast in The Way that leads to life eternal.

Throwaway Living
February 24
Romans 12:1–21; Philippians 4:8–9

It seems we have passed from stone age to iron age to science age to paper age! We used to eat out of a can or a jar if it was a prepared food. Now we eat out of a box and throw it away. Not only do we live in an age of disposables, it is also a time of rapid obsolescence. We are urged to drop the old product and get the new one. Perhaps the ease of disposables has given us a tendency to throw away some values too. Paul's injunction is to "cling to what is good" (Romans 12:9). One such thing is the sabbath. The sabbath was made for humans, not humans for the sabbath. It was made for humans to renew their spirits, give reverent worship to God, and experience the sanctifying quiet of holiness. Too many people are about to explode from the sheer noise of it all—no quiet time, no time for renewal, no higher value than the next thing we must have.

Consider national freedom. It often seems that the processes of freedom impede what is a desirable end. The justice system gets bogged down in protecting the rights of the accused criminal—and it is easy to think it would be better to just assume guilt. Our system is designed to protect any who may be falsely accused.

Even our freedom to pursue our own religion seems to be at risk. God gives each of us the light to see our way. No religious group may be allowed to impose its will upon others with the use of unscrupulous means. The point is that if we call ourselves Christians, we must love our fellow humans. We must be informed and willing to act in Christian love and concern. Otherwise, we will be in the clutches of throwaway living and be dangerously close to casting away permanent values and cherished ideas for fleeting pleasure or popularity. "Finally, whatever is true, whatever is honorable, whatever is just, whatever is pure, whatever is lovely, whatever is gracious, if there is any excellence, if there is anything worthy of praise, think about these things" (Philippians 4:8).

Traveling Incognito
February 25
Hebrews 13:16

Travel is so impersonal. The people around us have no knowledge of who we are or what we do. As human-beings, we have a tendency to write off certain people. We tend to treat important persons with great courtesy and consideration and tend to be short with those of lesser station. We need to remind ourselves that every person deserves consideration and courtesy. Every stranger, every contact, every act, can call us to ask of ourselves: "Is this how I would treat Jesus himself?" The process is that of holding common things, unpretentious people, and ordinary events in reverence. How often have you met a person and changed your behavior based on what you learn about them?

The Lord is in our midst in a form not immediately recognizable. There are many stories that tell of persons receiving great rewards for having befriended someone of great importance unbeknownst. Our Lord gave us the guideline in the words, "Whatever you did for one of the least of these, you did for me" (Matthew 25:40).

When we accept Jesus Christ as our personal savior and Lord, it changes our whole lifestyle. He becomes our helper, leading us to care less about what others will think of us and more willing to give. God travels incognito. He comes in the person of the mailman and the telephone repairman and the worker in the next cubicle. With the Spirit within us, we can recognize the Spirit in others and approach each interaction with reverence.

What's This?
February 26
Matthew 5:1–20

The most famous teachings of Jesus came from the Sermon on the Mount. It was there that the people became intrigued by his teachings and there that the scribes and Pharisees realized they were heading for trouble. Jesus spoke with an authority that the people had never heard before—even from their teachers. That makes sense, since the authority of Jesus was God himself. Jesus is the exact representation of God, who came to earth so that we might know God. Through Jesus we know God is love, we know God longs for our fellowship as his children, we know that by repentance and reconciliation we can be forgiven and return to wholeness and fellowship with God. We know God's presence is here, that our lives can be guided by him; we know he lives in our very hearts.

Jesus viewed behavior differently than we can. He looks on the heart. He is concerned with the beginning, the motive and thought, the attitude and intent. We will never achieve purity of thought, but with Jesus, we can at least be going in the right direction. In following the right direction, we are blessed. Confession of mistakes leads to freedom and joy, a clean heart, and a righted spirit.

As humans, we are free to do as we please. But this freedom can enslave us if we are not responsible. Service of others flows from the full heart of love of Christ. Through service, we put into action the authority and the righteousness and the responsibility shown to us by Jesus himself.

Why He Came
February 27
1 Corinthians 9:16–23

Would you like to be wise? It is a common wish for all of us. Wisdom is the ability to separate out of the swirling mix of life what is true and what is false, what is fleeting and what is eternal, what is glitter and what is substantial. Wisdom is separating what has value from what is of less value. It is like pulling weeds in a garden and then tending the plants. Unfortunately, what is evil is always parading around in the costume of a better and an easier way. There is nothing more difficult than separating good from evil—nor more important.

Having analyzed the parts and chosen what we understand is true, creative growth can happen. We live in the midst of the swirl of the world. It is in the mix of good and bad, greater and lesser, that we practice our faith. Within that constant interplay lies the possibilities of growth, redemption, and hope. The key is to have the will to live by the truth while in the midst of that mix. Jesus moved in the midst of health and disease, wholeness and brokenness, hope and despair. In that midst, he spoke the truth and cast out disease, brokenness, and despair. Jesus also knew that he had to seek quiet and solitude to recharge. Our power in the faith is connected to our "who-ness." If we would have faith power in the mix of life, we have to know to whom we belong! We have to have his image of living etched in our minds and on our hearts. Jesus is light in the mix of life.

Winter Green Shoots
February 28
1 Corinthians 3:6

In the midst of winter, when the grass is brown and the trees are bare, it is good to think of winter green shoots. Nothing warms the heart of a gardener than these first testaments that spring is coming. The crocus sticks out a first tentative shoot skyward; the daffodil pokes through the dark, crusted earth. There are deep concerns for the churches in today's economy. Many can be described as "stable and declining." We are in great need of some green shoots. The green shoots of faith don't have to wait for spring. Each day is a warm spring day for the faith. God's beautiful plan for our lives is silently urging the spirit within us, which was planted in our very fibers from the beginning.

It is a spiritual green shoot to seek for harmony. Plants are a tremendous illustration of being in harmony with God's creation. Flourishing plants are evidence of God's plan for planet earth. Plants are a lesson for humans. Spiritual green shoots indicate growth. Plants simply fulfill their design. They strive to become what they were intended to be. The spiritual stirrings were also built into us. We are relentlessly spiritual. Each of us is on a spiritual journey. We can deny those stirrings, we can bury them, but they are still there. We are not fulfilled until we release those stirrings and let them climb to the sky. God made us that way. God put green shoots in us that can sprout even in the middle of winter!

Charting the Voyage 1, The Chart
March 1
Ephesians 1:1–10

In Ephesians, we find a key instruction for the Christian faith. "God made known to us the mystery of his will according to his good pleasure, … to bring unity to all things in heaven and on earth under Christ" (Ephesians 1:9–10). These words tell us that the most important goal of the Christian life is to unify—to find out how to bring things together.

God has a plan for us to be holy and blameless before him. This does not mean that we act like tin soldiers under the command of God, more that we become sons and daughters of God. We are to come together as a family. Jesus came to bring redemption from sin. We are able to correct our paths and try again because of the forgiveness and reconciliation that redemption brings in our lives. The words given in Ephesians are like a chart that is used to map a voyage on the ocean. Without a chart, a ship may get into dangerous waters, shallow waters, shipping lanes. With the correct chart, it is easy to see where you are headed and arrive safely.

The path to redemption for our sins was mapped out by God from the beginning of time. He gave us the ability to make our own choices, knowing that we would not choose wisely. If love for God was not a choice, however, it would not be love. He gave us prophecy and landmarks to Jesus throughout the Old Testament, finally bringing Jesus into the world in the fullness of time. Having the correct chart doesn't guarantee arrival at the right port, nor does it provide complete safety, but without the correct chart, neither destination nor safety are possible. The Word of God is our chart; we need to read it, study it, *know* it to negotiate the voyage of faith.

Charting the Voyage 2, The Rudder
March 2
Hebrews 10:19–25

On the voyage of Christian faith, the scriptures are vital to steer the path that God has laid out for us. The Bible is such a unique book in that it is truly a living Word. Somehow, as one reads, different passages have varying perspective, in keeping with the stage at which they are read. If you have written in your Bible, you know this to be true! The Hebrews passage has specific guidance that goes along with the analogy of faith as a voyage.

"Let us draw near to God" (Hebrews 10:19). There is no separation from God, apart from our own sin, which causes us to move away. Baptism in the Spirit has washed and purified us to stand in his presence. Draw near each day by daily inviting the Holy Spirit to open our hearts and minds. "Let us hold unswervingly to the hope we profess" (Hebrews 10:23). Remember the most important laws as given by Jesus—to love the Lord your God with all your heart and all your mind, and with all your soul; and to love your neighbor as yourself. If our lives are guided by these principles, we will never be off course!

A rudder is useless unless the vessel is moving. So it is with faith. We must be active in the body of Christ and working toward the good of others to continue to move toward the goal of becoming more and more like Christ. In this way, we come together as Christians to help each other as well. The input of like-minded brothers and sisters in Christ will ensure unswerving progress.

Charting the Voyage 3, The Ship
March 3
Hebrews 9:1–5

God made us with strong wills. By the nature of God's creation, we had to be free. We had to be free because love cannot be coerced, commanded, or forced. It can only be freely given and freely received. It was risky, doing it this way, so God laid out a plan—a chart for the voyage. He knew, however, that we would not make it without a vessel. No one has ever made it across the ocean swimming. Yet spiritually, folk plunge into the ocean of life without so much as even a life vest! The vessel God gave us is the church. The idea of the church as a ship roots all the way back to Noah.

Christian believers get very mixed messages from the world we live in. There is admiration and appreciation for the church sometimes. There are also plenty of put-downs. People can be derisive, dismissive, and even despicable. These put-downs come from ignorance and guilt. Satan is not happy about the church, so he throws storms at our lives and rocks the boat.

Thankfully, the church truly belongs to the Lord. You might say it is the SS Jesus. It is built by the angels of God for our salvation. The captain of our ship is Jesus, who calms the storms both inside and outside, within our hearts and our souls. As we go along on the voyage of life, our ship is guided and protected by the King of the universe. It may be rocky sometimes, but the destination is well worth the challenges.

Charting the Voyage 4, The Crew
March 4
Colossians 3:1–4

Once we have the chart, God's plan for our lives; the rudder of the Holy Bible; and the ship of the church, the next thing needed is the crew. The crew is the body of Christ—the people of faith. The crew must work together for the good of the whole, or no one gets anywhere. Every member of the crew is important, with similar but varying responsibilities, and overall, personal wants are set aside in order to accomplish the goal. In the letter to the Corinthians, Paul uses the illustration of one body with many parts. The foot cannot say to the hand, the eye to the ear, the head to the feet … I have no need of you. It is all together or nothing.

Together, we can run the race, fixing our eyes upon Jesus. It is critical to set markers along the way of the voyage. Of course, it is vital that the markers are the right ones. We will never go wrong with Jesus as the focal point. There will be troubles, but working together and reminding one another of the goal, they are surmountable. Colossians gives us this guidance: "Set your hearts on things above … bear with each other, forgive … let the peace of Christ rule … be thankful … and let the word of Christ dwell in you richly" (Colossians 3:1–2). It works for the ship of faith and the crew of the Lord. It works in everyday personal things too. God wants us to make a safe and successful voyage. Be sure you rejoice in the gifts of all. Keep your eyes on the marker of Jesus. Together, we will arrive safe in home port.

Charting the Voyage 5, The Storm
March 5
Ephesians 2:1–10, 3:7–10, 6:10–13

When you start out on a voyage, you cannot expect all fair weather. There will be storms. It can be terrifying, but the God of Grace is invincible. We can't make it safely to home port because we're smart enough, because we're nice, because we're sincere … we make it because we've decided. Decided to sail the good ship of faith by the plan of God with the rudder of the Bible, and the captain of the crew, Jesus. It is a choice—a deliberate choice.

In Ephesians, Paul talks about the principalities and powers. We are not contending against flesh and blood but against the world rulers of this present darkness, against the spiritual hosts of wickedness. It is not possible to never have negative thoughts cross your mind. But to entertain, to encourage those thoughts, that's when a demonic power has entry and can begin to build up a storm around you, meant to destroy you. We need to be aware of these principalities and powers, because if we think we can fight the storm alone, we are mistaken. When we are in the bite of the storm, we are not a helpless people. There is a beautiful song by Luke Garrett called "I Choose Jesus." Here are a few of the lines:

> All my life I sailed the sea of reason.
> I was captain of my soul;
> There was no need for a Savior
> I could live life on my own.

> Then I heard Him speak the language of compassion,
> Words of healing for broken lives.

> I choose Jesus! I choose Jesus!
> Without a solitary doubt, I choose Jesus!
> —Luke Garrett

Charting the Voyage 6, Bouyancy
March 6
Luke 12:22–32

The joy of Easter comes from knowing God's incredible power as I live my everyday life. As I struggle to cope with the everyday defeats of living, Easter gives me strength to know that Jesus walks with me. Because I believe that Jesus gave himself for me and then was raised from death by the Easter act of God, I know God has also made provision for me in all things. As Jesus was lifted from the grave, so the ship of faith is lifted on the sea of life. As Jesus was lifted to the right hand of God, so individual Christians are lifted and buoyed in everyday living.

The largest ships on the sea weigh up to 477,000 tons, and yet they remain afloat. Water actually buoys an object of lesser density. It is truly a leap of faith to trust in this property of ships and water. God gave us natural principles to harness on this earth, like iron ships that float. And God gave us faith principles to harness as we walk this earth like Easter, which gives us buoyancy for the voyage of life. God wants to give us the kingdom; it gives the Father great happiness.

God's design is so good. It is an absolute assurance. God is the designer of the vessel of faith; Jesus is the engine powering it, and the Holy Spirit is the fuel. God wants us afloat; he wants to enjoy eternity with us. Believing is reasonable, but is it beyond reason? Believing is a leap of faith. Believing is tossing caution and doubt aside and saying, "Lord Jesus, take me. I give myself to you without reservation. Do with me what you will." The day you do that, nothing can stop you. Praise be to God.

Crisis Days
March 7
Matthew 12:9–28

Jesus faced many crises during his life on earth. In fact, every time he connected with an individual, it was a crisis. When Jesus stood face-to-face with a person, and they had the courage to look straight into his eyes, there was a point of decision from which one could not turn without a yes or a no. Christ offers his yoke—he doesn't say the way will be easy, but he does agree to walk and work alongside as a perfect partner.

The claims that Jesus is God, that he is alive, having resurrected from the dead—are tough for educated minds to understand and accept. The reality is that Jesus was simple and also profound. He was compassionate and also strong. He was mentally sharp as a tack and at the same time able to listen and to hear the voice of God. When Jesus looked at a person, he was able to see how to touch them in a way that kindled their faith and returned them to health and to God's love. God in him allowed him to reach into that person and bring forth a response that made them a whole person, sensitive to others and open to God.

Jesus is reaching out to you. He is saying something like, "I know that your days find many problems to be solved. Many temptations to overcome, many frustrations to meet. I am concerned. I can help you if you will let me. I can give you the joy and happiness of a full and healthy life. Sometimes my medicine will be tough, as you struggle with your fears and reservations. But I can give you the strength to stand fast and be healed. You need do only one thing: meet the challenge. Then you will have begun on the road to recovery and eternal life with God." Will you meet the challenge?

Excuse Me!
March 8
Isaiah 55:1–2b, 6–11

Pardon is to the soul what ballast is to a ship. Our human tendency is so pronounced when it comes to overlooking our own faults and overcondemning the faults of our neighbors that we desperately need to practice forgiveness and even more desperately need to be forgiven. Pardon is the way to bring balance in a situation, and put things right again. In fact, pardon and forgiveness are crucial to wholeness of life. The word *pardon* can mean three things in Hebrew: to cover, to lift up, and to let go.

It must be remembered that sin is expensive. It is costly. Forgiveness is not cheap. There are really three steps to forgiveness in our faith relationship. First, one must actively seek the Lord as he seeks you. One must change the way of life that led to the sin in the first place. Then, God will abundantly pardon. Forgiveness and pardon are essential in our broken world.

As much as we must recognize and accept that we are forgiven, we must also be quick to forgive others. Forgiving changes attitudes; it frees the soul. Know the beauty and the fulfillment of the grace of God in your heart.

God and You, Inc.

March 9
Luke 15:11–32; 2 Corinthians 5:16–21

Mostly, we don't take God too seriously. God is there, of course, like sun and rain, like air and water, like food and shelter. Most Americans believe in God, or some higher power. Belief in God is not the issue. We are too taken up with our own stuff to get mixed up with God or Jesus. Yet God calls us to be partners with him. In the words of Paul, "We are ambassadors for Christ, God making his appeal through us" (2 Corinthians 5:20). God doesn't need our help; he has all the resources to reach out on his own. Consider advertising; the most powerful appeal is through personal witness. God wants our partnership simply because it is through us that God has chosen to make his principal appeal.

Truly, there is more in this deal for us than for God. He draws us beyond ourselves to carry his message. The partnership, in turn, gives us joy. Most importantly, this partnership makes a serious connection with God. It takes God seriously, and we find ourselves absolutely amazed with what God can do even with common folk like us. Once we take God seriously, we find he is doing wondrous works among us daily. God and You, Incorporated. What a team. There is no limit to what can happen in his glory.

God's Plan for Action
March 10
Acts 17:22–31

The book of Acts has never actually been finished because it is still being written. We are today's apostles being urged out into the world by the Holy Spirit. God has a plan, and he will make us alive for it. Without the power and presence of God, humans are truly dead. In Athens, the people had altars for many gods, even one to "the unknown god." Paul recognizes that each of us has a place that hungers for meaning and spirituality. When we follow the course of this world, the spirit at work in us is the spirit of disobedience, and we have become so accustomed to it that we don't even notice the hollowness of it.

When we follow Jesus Christ, we become open to meaning, connection, harmony, and friendship. These desires that come from the Holy Spirit draw us together in support of each other. In groups of like-minded people, we can pray, study together, and support one another in Christ. Together, these groups can help those who are still spiritually dead. It cannot be done in our own power. It is the work of God, the giver of every needed gift through Jesus Christ, by the empowering of the Holy Spirit within. We are Christ fed and Spirit led.

Hostility
March 11
Isaiah 53:1–11

Jesus was received in various manners. Sometimes receptively, sometimes in rejection. We often think of Jesus as gentle and meek, but his message was so dramatic and revolutionary that he almost immediately was met with harsh, severe, dangerous hostility. As present-day Christians, we cannot view the life of Jesus as his contemporaries. They had no way of knowing that this attractive and compelling Jesus was really the Son of God. Occasionally they would catch glimpses of his true identity. But mostly, Jesus was a puzzle to them. Many questioned him and made evil plans against him. He was rejected by his townspeople. He was thought crazy by his family; he was misunderstood by his own disciples. In short, the world did not receive him. We have a tendency to think that Jesus was really quite successful, and it is true. Jesus was ultimately successful by the grace of God and his own obedience. Jesus was impressive, and many were impressed. Some with adoration and faith and others with hostility and hatred because they had been exposed, and their lives judged them. Hostility to Jesus was encountered from the day of his birth and mounted from the moment he entered his active ministry.

The world would not believe him because they did not want to. They held that the world is to be gained by force and that many things would be righted only by direct intervention by God. In fact, the world was being righted by the intervention of God, in his Son Jesus, the Messiah. Jesus met the hostility that faced him by never deviating from his task of revealing what God really is. Jesus lived the message he was sent to reveal. Justice in love. God, not as unreachable and unconcerned but as a father and personal. Jesus was not surprised by rejection. He knew that the love of God could not be rammed down people's throats. He revealed to us that hostility is not overcome by greater and louder shouting but by greater loving and forgiveness.

How Jesus Can Feed You
March 12
John 6:1–14

Spiritual food and physical food … we need both. The spiritual food of faith in Jesus is amazingly abundant. We begin with a growing relationship with the Lord until we ourselves become mature. It is in giving that we receive; it is in feeding that we are fed. The story of the feeding of the five thousand is the only miracle of Jesus that is found in all four of the gospels. The people wanted to make Jesus a political king, interpreting the feeding as something that would be economically beneficial to them. But Jesus escapes and later speaks to them of how he is the bread of life.

A common image of being fed is that of baby birds in a nest. They peep and open their mouths wide, waiting for the food. They are passive recipients. Clearly, they are immature—babies. The parent birds are mature. They bring the food; further, they had to go through so much to get there! They spent time keeping those eggs at just the right temperature, trading off, in order to keep themselves fed. Then, it takes both parents flying back and forth to feed the growing chicks. Finally, they make their way out of the nest.

Hebrews 5 speaks of immature Christians needing the basics—spiritual milk—whereas the mature are ready for solid food. They have trained by practice to distinguish good from evil. Mature Christians are fed by being in ministry, not by sitting with their mouths open. Mature Christians are nurturers rather than asking to be nurtured. How does Jesus feed us? First, one has to be in relationship with him. Then comes commitment—to prayer, study, and ministry. Finally, one finds others and teaches them how to fly. Involve yourself in that and you will have twelve baskets full and running over.

How Jesus Can Unbind You
March 13
Luke 11:14–23

The people surrounding Jesus were worried. The word was going around that he was going crazy, possessed by the devil. His family came to take him home. The common folk were trying to protect Jesus by not saying anything—whispering their concern. So, Jesus called them all together and told them that he knew they were talking, saying he was casting out demons by the power of Satan. This is great news, not bad news. How can Satan cast out Satan? Clearly that isn't the case. Only God could beat Satan, meaning that Jesus was truly God! Satan had been bound up by God.

Satan would bind us up. He tries to insert fear and doubt into our minds, binding us with apprehension and misgivings. There are so many kinds of bindings—things that we want to do, but never get to do. Things we are told we cannot do because we are not old enough, or not smart enough, or not strong enough. Whenever we are bound, we lose hope, faith, joy, confidence, aspiration. We lose our joy in the Lord. We often let ourselves be bound by our doubts and fears; moreover, we bind ourselves up by worshipping at the altars of false gods. Thankfully, Jesus is persistent; he loves us when we are unlovely. He continues to show us the truth that builds hope and sets us free. Jesus is in control.

I'm Sorry
March 14
Psalm 51:1–17

While it is true that our ideas of God are very individual, there is common agreement that God is *love*. The approach has changed, over time, from "hellfire and damnation," to an emphasis on the dos rather than the don'ts. We do respond well to positive stimulus, and the living of the faith is a glad and joyous thing. Nevertheless, the doctrine of repentance remains a truth of life. Repentance means to be sorry and to turn to amend one's life. There's nothing quite so healing as saying, "I'm sorry."

There is a clear trend with increase of crime, addiction, divorce and violence; a good number of persons in our population are confused about what is right and what is wrong. The commandments stand, not because they have the authority of centuries and the Word of God, but because they are true principles of life. To violate these principles of life results in hurt as surely as to place your bare hand on a hot stove results in hurt! Jesus commended the Great Commandment to us not because it was his authoritarian right to command our obedience but because living by it, our lives could be filled with joy and our homes abide in peace. Sadly, to relax moral effort and "let nature take its course" is to drift into indolence, sensuous indulgence, cowardice, and selfishness. We simply do not drift into industry, purity, courage, and loyal generosity!

The words "I'm sorry" are healthy words, redemptive words. They are words that signify a new start. The words of the Psalm say it well, "The sacrifice acceptable to God is a broken spirit; a broken and contrite heart you, God, will not despise" (Psalm 51:17). When we realize an error and do not repent of it, there remains a contradiction in our lives, and we cannot be at peace until it has been confessed, and we have acted upon it.

Jesus's Victory, My Victory
March 15
John 20:1–18

At the time of the resurrection, the first person Jesus appeared to was Mary Magdalene. She was a prostitute. She was the woman Jesus saved from being stoned by telling the accusers that the only ones worthy of stoning her were those that had never sinned. He told her to go and sin no more. His appearance to her was completely unexpected, yet it tells us that we are never too far away from the love of God to be able to return. Mary had a special kind of integrity. She realized what she had been, and that she was totally, awesomely different.

That's what Christian faith is all about. It is about the fact that Jesus can make you totally, awesomely different. We will never truly know why Jesus came to Mary first, but I believe it is because God wants us to know that he knows us by name. No matter what you have experienced in the road of life, God wants your victory. The resurrection is the sign and the seal of the promise that Jesus's victory, God's victory, is *our* victory. What God wants for us is to win in life. He wants us to experience joy. Joy is not surface happiness. It is more than entertainment, more than diversion. Joy is about having a deep and lasting relationship with those around us; holding and cherishing high values that are permanent. It is about making a connection with our maker in a significant way.

Jesus wants you to be filled with joy. We celebrate the victory of Jesus over death because it is also our victory.

Mending Brokenness
March 16
Exodus 20:1–17; Matthew 5:21–26

We all know the Ten Commandments. At least, we know the gist of them. We also know that Jesus came to change all of that. And he did, giving us the beautiful truth that we are truly saved by grace, justified by faith, and that it is God's love and mercy that make us whole. We simply cannot be good enough or smart enough to demand that God take us in on our terms. Consequently, many Christians fail to understand the Ten Commandments on Jesus's terms. Somehow, many of us fail to see that the commandments were given to bless! God doesn't want to punish us … he wants to give it *all* to us. Prior to giving the Ten Commandments, God, through Moses, reminds the Israelites of what he has done for them— released them from slavery, fed and clothed them through the journey, to bring them to himself. He tells them that the earth is his, and he wants to give it all to them! The commandments were intended as a covenant gift.

Jesus compresses and expands the commandments throughout the Sermon on the Mount. He brings out anger, abuse, integrity, revenge, and love. He starts with anger. Anger is rooted in caring for "me" first. When we come to God in anger, he seems distant. To get back into harmony, we must "first be reconciled" (Matthew 5:24). It's a simple, round, healthy truth. Anger cuts us off from the source of joy. The commandments were given, not to judge, but to bless. God bears us on eagles' wings, as a father, that we may run and not be weary, that we may walk and not faint. God wants to give it all to us, because he loves us that much.

Preparation
March 17
Luke 9:51–52; Mark 10:42–45

Jesus's face was resolute as he and the disciples made their way to Jerusalem. Although they did not yet understand, Jesus was preparing them along the way for the events that were ahead.

Jesus told the disciples at least six times what was to come. They needed to know, for they were to go on from the point of his death to proclaim God's action in history. They did not understand until it was all over, then they began to realize what it was he had been saying. Jesus was the Christ, the Messiah, but not in the way they had always thought. Jesus chose the cross to reveal that love transforms hearts and changes needs. Jesus chose sincerity and honesty in relationships in such a way that holy divine love could flow through human vessels.

Despite living on this side of the cross, we need to learn what serving and dedication mean so that in times of doubt and immaturity, we may recall what has been said that will lead us back to God.

Jesus was also preparing himself. He was as courageous a man as ever lived. He had a clear-eyed knowledge of the nature and power of the forces set against him. This awareness did not reduce the cost of obedience to God, but it was an armor for conflict, a preparedness so that when the attack came, the shoulder was braced. When we try to be obedient in this way, it seems to not work out so well. Why? We forget one drastically necessary ingredient: communion with the strength of God. This is why Jesus was what he was, because God was part of him. Obedience to God is not gained except through learning total giving, total laying of one's heart and mind, soul and strength in the hands of God. He returns our gifts with strength that endures, power that transforms, wholesomeness that makes life here victorious and happy in the best sense because it is lived in harmony with God.

Reaching Out
March 18
Philippians 3:12–14

It is in the nature of life to be reaching out. It is in our nature to explore, discover, experiment, and expand our frontiers, no matter what our age is. The context for this passage was that the Jewish Christians were still enamored with tradition. They insisted that every new believer had to pass through the old portals, such as circumcision. Paul responded that he was living proof of one who had done everything right, followed all the rules, but it still wasn't enough.

He called the new Christians to "forget what lies behind, and strain forward to what lies ahead, press on toward the goal for the prize of the upward call of God in Jesus Christ" (Philippians 3:13–14). There is a constant battle between clinging to the past and bracing against the future on one side and dropping what is no longer useful of the past and embracing the future. God is calling us to reach out! Our past is behind us; the future is where God is calling us. We look not only ahead but up. This is what happens when we center our lives on helping others win. The upward call of Christ is a call to a relationship, a quality, a context, a trust that is eternal. The upward call of Christ finds its joy not so much in our own achievements but in enabling others to achieve. Reaching out is not so much for our achievement as it is to minister and to thank God. Get your God-focus right, and the rest falls into place.

The Commitment of Hope
March 19
Luke 23:13–43

The final words of Jesus on the cross have traveled through history intact due to their significance. He really didn't speak much, just a few phrases, but each has specific meaning to those of us in the family of God. The words Jesus uttered to the thief hanging next to him were a response to his words of belief. "Today you will be with me in paradise" (Luke 23:43). These words underscore the fact that no one earns salvation. It is a gift given by God through Jesus Christ. While it cannot be earned, there are some necessary elements. First is openness. Jesus was placed between two thieves. One scoffed at him along with the soldiers and onlookers. He had no ability to see what was occurring right next to him. The other saw the truth that God is the final judge and that without belief, death was truly final. Repentance and belief led him to paradise through Jesus.

Openness to the meaning of salvation and repentance of sin results in hope on this side of eternity. One of the consequences of disbelief and a hard heart is that one lives without hope. Once we can see the gift of eternity, the entire picture changes. Hope leads to a desire for obedience that truly gives meaning to life. We could wait to repent until the last minute, like the thief, but we would miss the chance to glimpse paradise here on earth through hope.

The Heart's Song
March 20
John 12:24

Comparing ourselves to one another seems to be an inevitable way of life. Children compare one another endlessly; youths seek independence and individuality, yet find themselves conforming to the most popular peer image. And with adults, it seems like everything involves a comparison. In some ways it is useful to compare. By comparing, we can improve ourselves; we can improve our product. We can learn how to do things better and analyze and instruct ourselves. These are compelling comparisons. They lead us to model ourselves after some positive role model. It is wanting to be like someone else because that person does it well, and we want to do it well also. On the other hand, there are crippling comparisons. These result in running ourselves down and losing confidence. Crippling comparisons come from feeling ourselves unloved and not knowing what to do with the anger of that. Crippling comparisons need to die within us. Our faith is a faith of victory over sin and death. In all of us, some things need to die. Not for death's sake, but to bear much fruit.

There are five important qualities in a community of faith: community, caring, responsibility, commitment, and challenge. So often we become motivated by challenge and commitment, when what is really needed is caring and community. God's work is to be written on our hearts, and we need to desire to have clean hearts. What ties it all together is the heart song, or universal truths. The heart's song is what moves us so powerfully. It is uniting all the forces for good that reside within us. We are won to Christ primarily because Christ touches our heats and thereby awakens our souls. We are called to live such that we sing the heart's song by living after the examples of Christ. We are called to live life for life—for fruitfulness, for service, for one another.

The Incredible Lesson
March 21
John 13:1–17

Foot washing is an amazing experience. It is quite humbling, both to wash the feet of another and to have your feet washed by another. When Jesus washed the feet of his disciples, he told them that he was giving them an example. Though he was their Teacher and Lord, he was willing to wash their feet. They also should be willing to wash each other's feet.

What was going on behind this scene was that the disciples were feuding. They were fighting about who was going to get what position in the lingdom that Jesus was going to establish. Judas was already contemplating his betrayal of Jesus. They were so embroiled in their own desires that they weren't even paying attention to the Lord. What a tender way to reveal to them their haughty arrogance! He quietly prepared, then knelt at each one's feet. He demonstrated that their (and our) relationship with Christ, though he is the incarnation of God, is that of equals. He reaches out his hand to us. He invites us to be a part of his incredible kingdom of humble service. The disciples were brought into such a depth of understanding that they transformed the world in the name of Christ. We, the present-day disciples, continue to do the same.

The kingdom of Jesus Christ is very much alive—teaching us, lovingly revealing our mistakes, reaching out to draw out the best in us. That's a kingdom in which I am proud to claim citizenship and can strive, with all my energy, to serve in!

The Power of a Name
March 22
Mark 1:16–17

The most beautiful word to most people is their name. Calling a person by name immediately brings a spark to their eyes. Try it sometime; learn the name of a normally anonymous person in your life—a housekeeper, server, grocery clerk—then use their name when you see that person. It will bring a smile. After the resurrection of Jesus, Mary recognized him as soon as he spoke her name. That's pretty powerful! When Jesus called his first disciples, they were anonymous fishermen. They were rough, tough, uneducated men who, when called by Jesus to become fishers of men, left their life's work immediately. They became some of the most important names of the Bible: Simon (Peter), Andrew, James, and John. Where would we Christians be without the testimony of these simple fishermen?

Later in the gospel of Mark, Jesus asks the disciples, "Who do people say I am?" (Mark 8:27). They answer with what they have heard: John the Baptist (who had been beheaded by then), Elijah, Jeremiah, a prophet. Jesus then asks, "But who do *you* say that I am?" (Mark 8:29). This brings a revelation. Peter says, in awe, "You are the Christ, the Son of the Living God." Jesus goes on to say that this has been revealed to him by God himself, and further names Peter the rock upon which his church would be built. At this, Peter began to allow God to mold him into what he was to become. The name Jesus gave him had the power to transform him from the rough fisherman into the leader of the early church.

The name Jesus means "Save." Jesus saves. Of course, when you commit your life to the name of Jesus, you also receive a new name: Christian. As we claim this name and seek to live up to it, we are transformed as dramatically as Simon transformed into Peter the rock.

Transactions
March 23
John 3:14–21

John 3:16 is likely the most quoted verse of the New Testament. What parent cannot identify with the sacrifice involved in willfully giving one's only son to bring about the salvation of others? This is the ultimate transaction: an exchange of one thing for another. In this case a life for all others to be at one with God. Quite bluntly, we will either be at one with God's way, or we will reject that oneness, whether knowingly or unknowingly.

We are all hopelessly broken. Even the best humans fall short of the glory of God. God gave humanity countless chances to bring us back—Abraham, Moses, the prophets, and finally Jesus. There is always sacrifice involved; early on it was precious animals, then the sacrificial lamb at Passover, finally the Lamb of God. Each was a transaction to atone for the sins of the people to become right with God. Each was also a gift—to God and to us in the gift of his Son. God lovingly calls us back to him to enjoy life the way it was meant to be, without fear into eternity. Ultimately, it is a life or death question—a life or death transaction.

Wait for Me!
March 24
Matthew 4:12–25

We've all seen a little youngster stumbling, half-mad, half-crying: "Wait! Wait for me!" None of us want to be excluded. We may exclude ourselves, at times, but that is different, that is by choice. To be excluded against our wishes is a cruel experience. As Jesus went about his earthly ministry, more and more people followed him. He spoke to them. He loved them. He fed them. Clearly, Jesus was something special. Slowly, these people began to recognize that he might be The One they were waiting for. When asked, he quoted prophecy, saying in effect, "Decide for yourselves." The blind see, lame walk, deaf hear, lepers are cleansed, dead raised, good news preached to the poor. Finally, Peter is the first to say, "You are the Christ, the Son of the Living God!"

When Jesus walked along the shore of the sea of Galilee and said to the men, "Follow me, and I will make you fishers of men" (Matthew 4:19), what is amazing is that they *did* it! Whatever could be enough to make a man leave his job and follow a wanderer? But what Jesus touched when he appealed to the disciples was the key that makes life worth living: meaning and purpose. No one wants to be pointless. The disciples were rescued from dullness and dreariness. Jesus inspired them with the nobleness of life and brought them the enthusiasm of his spirit. What a privilege to tread that footstep of eternity.

Wouldn't it have been great to have followed along with Jesus in his ministry … to have known the Master personally, intimately? The power of the Christian message is exactly this—that we worship no dead master. Jesus lives! He said, "Repent, the Kingdom of God is at hand" (Matthew 4:17). The kingdom that is at hand is silent and has unseen influences. The kingdom is in the hearts of humankind. The kingdom is in your heart, if you believe.

Want a Master Card?
March 25
Romans 5:2

Don't we all just love our plastic credit cards? They certainly have a convenience appeal. They give us access to things in a way that is unprecedented. The passage for today, "Through him we have obtained access to this grace in which we stand, and we rejoice in our hope of sharing the glory of God" (Romans 5:25), brought the connection to mind that it is like a Master's Master Card! All the dazzling splendors of all the ads for credit cards are nothing compared to accessing the amazing, wonderful glory of God.

Truly, access is a good thing. Why, not one of us can achieve access to the president of a corporation without good connections, or good reason. Yet access to God is ours for the asking. God can process all of our prayers at one time, and know every name and every intimate detail about every single one ... even the numbers of hairs on our heads. And we take this access for granted. God is always in. The door is always open. There is no waiting, no line, no time limit on our stay. The price of the visit—gratitude, love, a smile, a hug.

Think now of the benefits of access to God. His grace is more than we can even comprehend. Grace cannot be earned, unlike what most of us were taught in the rules of life. In life, hard work, study, time, and sacrifice lead to success. In God's economy, with the Master's Card, there are no monthly billings. Instead, access is given through humility and acceptance. We become members of the body of Christ. Out of our gratitude comes the privilege of grace. We get the privilege of serving, of giving of ourselves and our money, of teaching others about this amazing grace. God actually wants us to come alongside of *him*. Now that's better than any rewards card I know of! You make a difference when you have the Master's Card.

What Next?

March 26
Hebrews 13:8; John 11:17–44

When the bottom of our world has dropped out, these two words express our yearning for a faith to cling to; they indicate our struggle to find an answer to: "What next?" It has been said that all thinking must start with some assumption—be guided by some polestar. One of the most secure polestars in history is Jesus Christ. It is genuinely grounding to remember the truth that Jesus is the same yesterday, today, and tomorrow.

In considering the question, "What next?" it is truly faith that guides us to that next step. True faith allows deep trust in God. We may not know what will be next, but knowing that God is in control and has the power to carry us through whatever is ahead results in the ability to continue to move ahead. In the Christian view of life, our preparation is for each day as it comes. God promises that his grace is sufficient for us at each moment.

Our own faith, however is insufficient for any crisis without the dimension of eternity. Each element of everyday life is spiced with the touch of eternity. Each moment brings the opportunity for creativity, each activity must be done to the glory of God, each day we are a part of eternal life. Because eternal life isn't a place. It isn't a system. It is a quality of life. A life lived—by God's grace—in the footsteps of our Master. If we know this, then we have no qualm when crisis stuns and causes us to stammer, "What next?" Our answer is: Jesus Christ. The same yesterday and today and forever.

What's Impressive

March 27
Mark 11:17

Jesus was angry. He was not impressed by the Roman Empire, the temple's grandeur, the priestly apparel, the priestly rituals. He was especially not impressed with the money making capacities of the temple and the money changers. The temple people were completely caught up in the busyness of the temple ... as if it were only business! The moment we make the place the holy of holies and not the soul the holy of holies, we have missed the mark. Jesus wanted people to build the temple of their soul, not some substitute. If you were to build a cathedral of your soul, what would impress you as important things with which to build it? What would impassion you as vital? Of course, it is important to be impressed by those who help you build it—parents, pastors, teachers, peers. Thousands of people make up the foundation and walls, the ceilings and windows of the cathedral of your soul. Who are the persons who helped you discover and thereby are part of the cathedral of your soul?

Some of these people help us to love; others inspire faith. Within the household of faith, we are loved members of the family of God. Not everyone. Some are on the learning and growing side; some do not yet have much to give. Let those who have much to give become building blocks and sparkling windows in the cathedral of your soul. Be impressed by the nurturers. All of us have gone through challenges, loss, and sorrow. These experiences help us grow in the faith. We need to be grateful that Jesus considered us worth enough to get tough with us. That day when Jesus drove out the money changers from the temple in Jerusalem was long ago. But the spirit of Christ, which is impassioned for our soul's sake, is as fresh as your next breath. Jesus was saying that the temple of the future would be wherever Christ was. Not the building, the body. In our souls, in our hearts, in our spirits is the temple, the dwelling place of our God. It is a place of holiness, sacredness, a place of grace that reaches right on into eternal life. That's impressive.

Where There Is Life
March 28
Ephesians 2:1–10

Did you ever stop to think of how much different types of communication can excite our attention? Such as a knock on the door, a ring on the phone, a letter in the box? Each of these things cause a different response. A knock on the door must be responded to now. The ring on the phone is maddeningly persistent, and hard to endure if we don't want to answer it. And the letter in the box depends on who it is from, but we still always like to "check the mail." Saint Paul wrote amazing letters, letters that still speak to us today. This passage deals with the gift of God in Jesus to give us life in spite of our bent to kill ourselves in the darkness of sin. Where there's life, we mortals still have a chance to receive the beauty and peace of God in place of the lack of direction that finally overwhelms the ungodly.

Life without Christ has no purpose. We start out bad, being born with evil natures, and without Christ are subject to God's anger. Rightness with God is life, and separation from God is like death. Brokenness is death; wholeness is life. The definition of the Greek word *sin* in this instance is, "to miss the mark." Sin kills innocence. Once we've done it, we can never return to a state of having not done it. A cut can heal, but the scar remains. Sin kills ideals. Once we let down, it is easier the next time. Sin kills the will. Initially people engage in some forbidden pleasure because they want to; in the end they engage in it because they cannot help doing so. It is slow, almost imperceptible. Until we find, to our sadness, that we haven't broken any of God's laws; we have been broken on them. Our disobedience grieves God. Sin is not so much stumbling against the law as it is breaking God's heart.

Grace is the answer to sin. Grace invites us to return. It reawakens ideas in the hearts of persons. Jesus revives and re-creates the will. To be one of Christ's disciples is to live, to be free, to find a life of joy, deep peace, and godliness. We cannot earn grace; it is a gift given freely to all who will accept it.

Yeah, But How?
March 29
Hebrews 11:1–12

Once one has decided to become a Christian, the critical question becomes, "How do I live the Christian life?" The beautiful passage of Hebrews 11 has been called the Hall of Faith. It recites the virtues of the ancient fathers of the faith. The author of Hebrews drew the people with whom he spoke into a sure and steadfast understanding of their need to be faithful to the end.

How? First, receive the word. "By faith we understand that the world was created by the word of God … For whoever would draw near to God must believe that he exists and that he rewards those who seek him" (Hebrews 11:3). He made us; he wants us. Our creation was for a reason. It is filled with meaning, and it has a direction to it. When I receive the word that God created me, I know I am a part of his plan. If I can be in harmony with it, things will go well, because what he created he called "good." It means I belong, and I have a meaningful purpose.

The second element of "how" is to accept forgiveness. It is a beautiful thing to see someone discover that God has set a path back for us. Despite the nature of humans to pull things apart and to struggle in relationships, God draws us near. He sent his only Son, Jesus, to guide us back. The entire Bible is the blueprint for that path. It is filled with stories of people just like us, who made mistakes, and God called them back into relationship.

Finally, put your faith into action out of gratitude. The work of a Christian should never come from duty or from guilt, but from gratitude. Any other attitude will dry it up. Our good works come from the awareness that our cup overflows. We must constantly remind ourselves to give out of gladness and not grudging. Our faith is that what God has done for us in Jesus is incredibly beautiful. It is so precious and so marvelous that it has no choice but to be shared with all we can, winning them to the friendship we have in Christ. Receive the word. Accept forgiveness. Act from gratitude. That faith will bring gracious peace, amazing happiness, and joyful fulfillment throughout the arduous pilgrimage.

20/20: The Vision of Jesus

March 30
Colossians 1:15–23

God has a plan for us. His vision is clear. He said it to Adam, he said it to Abraham and Sarah, he said it to Moses, and he says it to us: "I will be your God, and you will be my people" (Leviticus 26:12). The Old Testament is full of examples of people who tried to live up to the standard set by God, and it was impossible. No one could possibly keep all the laws. God taught them to worship him and use sacrifices to help cover their sin. Ultimately, God cleared the path for us to truly be his people through the perfect life and death of Jesus Christ. He paid the ultimate price, and he showed us an exact image of God.

How do we get in on this vision? First, we must accept Jesus as savior, who brings us back to God as God's friend. It is vital to take this step and to share it with others so that it becomes a true commitment. The next step is to be so enthusiastic about what you have learned and the joy that it gives you that you cannot help but tell others about it. Joining up with Jesus is life changing, it is challenging, and God gives us the power to make this change through the Holy Spirit. The Holy Spirit does not overpower us; he is gentle and patient. He teaches us, guides us, and helps us bounce back when things don't go as planned. The Holy Spirit's empowering is an inflowing of enthusiasm. Jesus's vision for us is that we partner with him to bring the kingdom of God to this world and fill our lives with joy. Thanks be to God.

Come On, Let's Go See
March 31
Luke 19:28–42

One of the most interesting characteristics of human life is our insatiable curiosity. We always want to respond when told, "Let's go see!" This is likely what prompted the multitude to go see the entry of this prophet of Galilee into Jerusalem, and to shout, "Hosanna," after him as he came along. They had heard of his doings, his miracles, some things he had said, how he infuriated the people of pious position and important respectability. But they missed the point. They didn't know what was going on. The most important things of life cannot be seen. The most important things of life occur in the soul, at a moment of insight, at one white instant of vision. It seems that God travels incognito in this world. He is not seen on a white charger but on the back of a donkey. He is not found in royal robes but in a manger for a cradle. He is hidden from the proud, the powerful, and the too respectable.

This life without the eternal is hopeless. Without it, history is little more than a madhouse, and faith itself has neither root or substance. We try to encompass the world by doing more things, by being busy. Yet the eternal is not found merely by adding things together. It is found in observing the little miracles in every day—like roses and sunsets, and birds singing in the trees. It is found as we catch the mystery of life and as we commit our lives in sharing the depth of our being. We must prepare ourselves for the miracle of Jesus by recapturing a sense of wonder and awe, opening our eyes to see, and our lives to do, and our souls to be.

Behold the Man!
April 1
Matthew 27:22

Palm Sunday is pictured as a celebration, a triumphal entry. But the man on the donkey was weeping as he went along. He was weeping because he knew what was ahead. He knew that he would be rejected, denied, betrayed, and finally killed by the very crowd swarming around him on that day. We, too, know what is ahead. Palm Sunday is somewhat clouded by our knowledge of the events that would come hurtling along in the coming week.

One way to approach this day is to look at it through the question posed by Pontius Pilate: "Then what shall I do with Jesus?" He was torn by the desire to exert justice while maintaining an uneasy truce of military occupation. He offered to release Jesus, but the crowd shouted for Barabbas. We, too, understand this dilemma. Will we stay with him or drag him through our everyday crosses; will we serve him or betray him; will we learn to hear his voice above the noise of society, or will we deny him?

What shall *we* do with Jesus? Many ignore him completely. Some offer lip service. We could commit our waywardness to his cross and our faith to his resurrection. We need new conviction, new direction, refreshment of soul and spirit. We need to have help in throwing down the barriers we put up between ourselves and others. We desperately need to pull off the masks of public politeness from our shell of emptiness. The joy and sadness of Palm Sunday combine in truth when we answer the question "What shall we do with Jesus?" by "Behold the Man." By beholding him in faith. By beholding him in truth and glory. Jesus wept that day because he saw with unusual clarity how we deny his triumphal entry. May it be that we can behold the Man with new vision and clarity, to then move forward in his majesty.

Take This Cup Away
April 2
Mark 14:32–38

The victory God gained in Christ was gained for us. The confidence we have is thereby eternal. The hope we have is thereby inextinguishable. How do we best live our days? How do we translate the truths of God into victories for our own lives? We must balance our will with God's will for us. This is beautifully played out in the garden of Gesthemane the night Jesus was arrested. His struggle comes down to a useful thought for most of us: "Not what I will, but your will be done" (Mark 14:36). We so want to be in control of ourselves! We struggle with simple decisions such as whether it is important to go to church. Viewed through the lens of the Ten Commandments, the answer would be yes, but there are so many things that get in the way. The critical action is to foster friendships in Christ and to support one another in godly relationships. All of us are in ministry in the name of Christ, ministry to one another, and ministry to the world as best we can.

A challenge is to filter each activity through these two lenses: God's will over our own, and the Ten Commandments. Motivation drives the first lens. Is this activity or behavior for my own good, or is it helpful in building the kingdom of God? Who benefits? The first four commandments have to do with keeping right in the worship of God. The last six have to do with keeping things holy between ourselves and others. Doing the right thing for both godly and human relationships is the goal. This is not a thing we can learn to do by our own sheer judgment. We must allow for God's will to prevail over our own.

The Meaning of Holy Week
April 3
Mark 14–16

Holy week is really a chapter of the greater events stretching before and after this time. The entire Bible truly could be called the story of salvation. Not because it is a fictional story, but because it gives an account of God's great plan for the salvation of humankind. The story begins with God and creation, the fall of Adam and Eve, and the evidence of ongoing sin in humankind's separation from God. Humankind needed help to return to harmony with God. God chose Abraham to start the nation that would be fathered by God himself. They, too, experienced the pain of sin and separation of God. Moses brought the Ten Commandments, but no human could ever fulfill all of them. "All have sinned and fall short of the glory of God" (Romans 3:23).

Then God paid the ultimate price: he came down from heaven as his Son, Jesus, who was wholly God and wholly man. Jesus is undoubtedly the one single person who has made the greatest impact upon the history of this world. Starting with his birth at Christmas through his life, death, and resurrection, Jesus fulfilled the prophecies of the Messiah—Immanuel. He showed the world the nature of God; he told them he was the only way back to God the Father. Holy week contains the details of his grizzly death, further solidifying the fulfillment of prophecy from the Old Testament. His death appeared to be the end; it was all over in failure. But Easter day came, and they found that he had arisen from death to life and is indeed with every one of us even now. Resurrection day says by faith in Christ you can become the best that is in you. By believing in your heart God acted for *you*, God can grant you entrance into a genuine and right life here and now. So it is. Amen.

Three Crosses
April 4
Luke 23:32–47

Good Friday is the day Christ died. It can be difficult to conjure up a feeling of sadness and mourning, for the event is far away and seems unreal to us. What would we have felt if we had been there? Would it have come home to us that God will even go to this extent in order to open my blinded eyes and to unstop my closed ears? Or would we have mocked as the soldiers did? It is hard to say. It is crucial to reenter this scene, to be reminded of what it cost to redeem souls.

There were three crosses on Golgotha. Only one has eternal significance. In God's great provision, the other two crosses serve as reminders. They remind us that unrepentant blindness existed even at that moment and that anyone who will abandon himself to Jesus can gain paradise, regardless of who or what he is. These two factors are not often separated, but are usually present to some degree in all of us. Each of us somehow resists God's saving grace while at the same time we are accepting it and finding power from it. We can become so blinded to things close to us that we cannot allow God's will to work in us. The one criminal scoffed at Jesus in unbelief, unable to see the difference in the countenance of the one beside him.

The other perceived a difference. Had he heard about the betrayal, the unlawful trial, and the setup of the crowd to call for Jesus's death? Or did he catch an open glimpse into the eyes of Jesus and feel the flame of faith flicker? The man cast aside all mental reservations and appealed to Jesus, leaving his fate in the hands of God. At that instant, he received assurance: "I tell you the truth, today you will be with me in paradise" (Luke 23:43).

The three crosses on Calvary have significance because they teach us. One cross brings us to confession of our lack of faith in God; the other criminal's cross tells us to cast ourselves upon Jesus in absolute trust. None of the crosses would have had significance except for the actions of God on our behalf. That central cross became divinely proven on Easter day, when newness is offered for all life. Beginning now. The cross proclaims the urgent majesty of God's plan for our redemption through the darkness of death to triumphant life.

It Is Finished
April 5
John 19:30

It is a great feeling when we complete a tough task and say to ourselves, "Ah, that's finished."

What did Jesus mean when he uttered from the cross those words: "It is finished?" Was it a sadness, relief, sorrow? Clearly, we cannot truly know what they meant to Jesus, but we can comment on some of the possibilities. They may have been a prayer to God. In this sense, Jesus had finished the *work* God had set out for him to do—the work of salvation. The word used in this passage translated directly from the Greek means to complete, execute, perform, or fulfill. This would indicate that it was a triumphant statement, not one of loss.

Jesus came to seek and save the lost. He came to give us life in its fullest. He came to establish a kingdom that would build men into a brotherhood. And he came to reveal God ... to make him known. All these things were completed as Jesus breathed his last breath on the cross. Finally, he said those words for us. What he accomplished then is what he is still accomplishing now. Christ willingly gave his life for us, but it was also an act of obedience. Jesus knew that his death would bring everlasting life to us—forever. Now that is something to shout about.

Business as Usual?

April 6
Acts 9:1–20

Easter is not just a day in the year. It is a celebration of transformation. Right after the crucifixion, the disciples didn't know what to do. Some of them went to Emmaus; most returned to their previous lives ... business as usual. Yet truly, everything was different; they just didn't know it!

Jesus was a revolutionist. That was the political reason for his crucifixion. We, as followers of Jesus, are called to continue his work. That means that we should stand out as different from ordinary society. It is our obligation to work for systems of fairness, to condemn exploitation, to proclaim the power of love, and to come alongside the hungry, the broken, and the poor. We generally don't think of the church as revolutionary. Perhaps we should. Perhaps that would change the way we approach our faith.

After the resurrection, nothing was ever the same. Jesus had said it very clearly to Pilate: "My kingdom is not of this world" (John 18:36). In fact, the kingdom of God is in our midst—in our very beings. We need to live every day as "Easter people." Just as the disciples had to learn to go about their lives proclaiming the truth of the news of the resurrection, so we must proclaim the difference that Easter makes. Business as usual simply isn't good enough. Each day is alive in the face of death, transformed by the power of our Risen Christ. In light of this, nothing should ever so fill us with sorrow as to make us forget the joy of Christ risen.

God Is at Work
April 7
John 20:22

It is easy to let the celebration of Easter become ho-hum. We know the story, and it has become so familiar that it can lose its relevance. The fact is that the celebration of the resurrection is both old and new. It is the best of the old. One of the longest held emotions of humans has been awe. Our highest capacity is to worship. Our greatest need is to be understood. What the world longs for is someone who understands, who accepts us as we are, and gently leads us into what we can become at our best. What the Easter truth means is that Christ himself lives and moves among us and walks beside us and cares about us.

The Easter truth is also the best of the new. New insight is always a joy; new awareness of beauty and goodness is a delight. To have the truth of Easter come flooding in upon us with a freshness that gives us new life … that is the best of the new. When Jesus came to the disciples in the room after he had risen, he breathed on them, and gave them new life. Death cannot contain Jesus. He comes to each generation and to those of us that have grown tired to make us agents of God. He sought them out to bring them this new life breath. Our risen Lord seeks every one of us to bring us the breath of life. Hallelujah!

He Is Risen
April 8
John 20:19–31

Though the Easter event celebrates something that took place in the past, the real significance of Easter is in the present tense: He *is* risen. He *is* here. He *is* present. He is always becoming new. It is a matter of catching a fresh glimpse of Christ for our own lives; he is unmistakably real and alive. He is available every day to nourish our souls. The realness of God is that he is not a far-off idea, but a real Spirit, close at hand, caring, drawing us to newness of life, opening new possibilities for wholeness right now. God has no grandchildren. The one thing a believer cannot give a nonbeliever is his believing. For one who has not received Christ into his life and made him the rule and guide for living, Easter is just a history that is told. It is not until what God has done in Christ is what God is doing for me, personally, right now, that Easter makes any sense. Christ is alive and well in the life of a believer.

To maintain this newness, we must continually be growing in the faith. It is not some status symbol, bowing at the shrine of a tomb, but a vibrant, living, growing thing. No archeologist will ever unearth the bones of Jesus, because *he is risen*! Every day some new insight can push its way up through the crustiness of our understandings and give us the gift of fresh and restored vibrancy. As we experience the major changes of the living of our days, we change our viewpoints on life. We can take those changes and become angry and bitter or give them over to God and thank him for teaching us to know the pain that others experience so we can better share their pain. Christ is with us. He is bringing about his will and way with his people for our wholeness and for bringing the world into a new oneness and unity with God.

What a Deal!
April 9
Acts 1:3–5

It is all too easy for us to coast along on the spiritual high of Easter. Then, Easter is over, and we believers are coasting, taking little or no responsibility ourselves for spreading the good news. Jesus returned repeatedly after the resurrection. The purpose of Jesus returning was to be sure the apostles and disciples knew what was expected next. He returned and appeared to the eleven apostles and told them to "do and teach" and said that the Holy Spirit would be coming to them soon. He then appeared to the apostle Paul three separate times, to delineate his mission among the gentiles. Then, five hundred brethren met the risen Lord at one time. He came personally to Thomas, to verify his presence. He returned to provide physical proof of a spiritual truth.

The resurrection guarantees that Christ is truly the Son of God, that the Father accepted the atoning work of Jesus, that the believer has an advocate with the heavenly Father, that the believer may enjoy the assurance of eternal life, that believers will also be raised, and that we shall be like our risen Lord. Wow! What a deal!

The consequence of Easter for the believer is that we must bear fruit. God the Father and Jesus Christ the Son have provided the pathway for our daily ministries. Spreading the good news is now our job. Those who do so enthusiastically shall receive a reward. The reward is that we shall also be raised and shall be like our risen Lord and will spend eternity with him and our loved ones.

A Still More Excellent Way

April 10
1 Corinthians 12:1–13:13

Paul's illustration about the body of Christ being the church and being like the human body is so obvious that any of us could have thought of it! Nothing is actually closer to us than our physical bodies. We hear our own heartbeat, know about our own thoughts, feelings, hopes, fears, aches, and pains in a way no one else can. It is indisputable that our physical bodies are important to us and that we spend a tremendous amount of time and money tending to them. So, Paul takes our obvious central interest and draws fascinating parallels for our lives together in the church. If we were as interested in the finest functioning of the body of Christ, what could happen? What a challenge: put as much into tending Christ's body as you put into your own body. Not only tending the body of Christ like our own but also recognizing the significance of each single person, each and every one who make this body of Christ what it is.

Incredibly, God has chosen to work this way. God has chosen to be limited, to work through us. It is wonderful, and it is frightening. Because, if we do not rise to the hope, the hope falters. If the hope of the world falters, illness deepens instead of health thriving. Some things we know about healthy bodies: Healthy bodies have healthy attitudes—like faith, love, joy, peace, patience, kindness, goodness, faithfulness, gentleness, and self-control (Galatians 5:22). Healthy bodies look outward. They are not inward-looking but find their glory in bringing about good results. Healthy bodies know God is sufficient. God hasn't gone home for the day. Quite the contrary, God has given us the gifts, powers, capacity, and the ability to be healthy, productive bodies of Christ. If we have hearts to receive the Christ of life, if we have minds to grab hold of the wisdom of Christ, if we have the energy to interact interdependently, if we will be the hands and feet of Christ, and the voice and Word of God, we will embody the more excellent way.

Pruning
April 11
John 15:1–8

The images of the vine, the branches, and the fruit were all very familiar in the time and places of Jesus. We know little about the art of vine-dressing, but most of us are aware of the need to care for, prune, water, and fertilize plants. Jesus starts by saying he is the Vine. He is not a branch or a shoot, he is the trunk, the main source of power to the plant. Pruning can seem downright brutal. You must cut off every branch that will take away from the strength of the others that will ultimately bear fruit. The rest is cut off and tossed away.

The only way to approach pruning is with hope. Hope that the result will be fruitfulness. Pruning has a finality to it. There is no way to go back and put things back together. Why is that so important? Because all branches that will not produce fruit are wasting energy and resources. We spend our days constantly in a rush of doing. It is critical to assess all of these activities for what is coming from them: fruit or waste, joy or sorrow. When the wasteful branches are pruned, the remaining twig sends out hidden buds. The Lord Jesus has hidden talents within you that you don't know you have, plans that you are unaware of. By cutting out those things that distract you from God's plan, your life becomes more fruitful. Prayerful focus on God's plan for you leads to boundless fruit for his kingdom.

Blessed Are ...
April 12
Matthew 5:2–3

In the Sermon on the Mount is found God's answers to some of life's most challenging questions. Of course, the answers are not what we would expect; many of them being almost polar opposites of how the world would answer them. The beatitudes are familiar to most people. Even if we cannot remember them in order, most people have heard them and can use them when needed. The Sermon on the Mount contains the most important words of Jesus for us, and they are intended to make a difference now! None of us are immune to the wooing of the world. It is a constant struggle, a constant conflict.

Jesus says, "Blessed are the poor in spirit"; the world says, "Be elite, climb above the crowd." Jesus says, "Blessed are those that mourn, that are caring." The world says, "Look out for number one." Jesus says, "Be pure in heart." The world says, "Take what you can get without getting caught!" These sayings draw out the contrasts—the realities. Following the way of the world is easy—go with the flow. Jesus's way takes courage and sacrifice. Yet it is only in Jesus's way that we are blessed, happy, fulfilled. The Beatitudes truly are the best way to be.

By What Power?

April 13
Acts 4:8–12

Power is a word that may have different meanings to any given individual. Some think of political power, financial influence, popularity. Others will imagine brute force such as military strength. Perhaps the power of nature comes to mind. Power. Power to build. Power to destroy. We live by power of conviction and ideals. We are moved and motivated by visions of right and good, fairness and justice, love and peace. There is a distinct contradiction in the powerful positive images of God and the motivation of personal gain.

The story in Acts is one of healing by the apostles Peter and John. The establishment is disturbed. "By what power did you do this?" "The power of Jesus Christ of Nazareth." In him is found the power that transcends all others. By what power will you choose to live your life? We must live by something; by some need or some dream, by some greed or by some hope. Those who live by such images of power as are found in Christ Jesus become shepherds. True shepherds, those who stay with their flock, those who will lay down their lives; in them, God vests an amazing power. The power of God's love for one another is the ultimate power by which to live. With it, we can change the world.

Christian Commitment
April 14
Ephesians 3:17–18

How can we make our Christian commitment more *real*? Christian commitment is belief and trust in something beyond oneself, to something that gives ultimate meaning, coherence, and a goal to life. To have these benefits, however, our commitment must be real and purely our own. St. Paul said it this way: "I pray that you … may have power, together with all the saints, to grasp how wide and long and high and deep is the love of Christ" (Ephesians 3:17–18). To grasp this is to realize that commitment to Christ is the ultimate act of all. Everything else in life will eventually let you down. We must reach out to God, who offers his power freely.

Next, we must make it complete. There can be no halfway. Commitment to Christ requires that it be without conditions, modifications, or reservations. This kind of commitment allows Jesus to come down and live in us. We stop being at war with ourselves.

Finally, we must make it live. To make our commitment live is to give of ourselves. Jesus said the greatest commandments are: "Love God with all your heart, and with all your soul, and your neighbor as yourself" (Luke 22:27). In order to truly absorb any concept, the best way is to teach it to others. Such it is with God's love. To make it real, we must reach up to God, selling out to him completely, and reach out to others.

Christic the Door
April 15
John 10:1–16

Have you ever considered the properties of a door? It can be made in an amazing variety of sizes, shapes, and materials. Some doors are made to keep things out, others are designed to hold things in. Yet what is the major function? A door is something to go through to get somewhere else. Jesus is the door through whom we come to God. Christ brought an understanding of God to us that we could grasp. What would we know of God if it were not for Christ? We would know his wrath, anger, the vastness of his creation. But Christ allows us to see the intimacy with which God knows, understands, and cares about us. Christ allows us to have harmony and right relationship with God.

Christ truly brings the abundant life to us. The world is always searching for some secret formula or miracle to answer the question of how to get the fullness of life. People have sought fullness through opium, alcohol, materialism, and power, but these things are hollow. Life in its fullest can only come with a right relationship to God through the self-sacrifice of Christ. With Christ as the door, we may step into the splendor of life spent following the exciting possibilities he puts within the reach of anyone who would take them.

Dwelling Places
April 16
Ephesians 3:7–21

Just about everyone likes to take pride in their home. We redecorate, remodel, and relandscape. A home is a lot more than just a place to live. It is where we come together with family and friends. It is where we grow relationships. Given our attention to our physical homes, how much energy do we spend developing a spiritual dwelling place for God?

A home must have a firm foundation. It must be level, and it must be true. Without such, the home will settle and even become weak or unsafe. Accordingly, Christ may dwell in our hearts if we are rooted and growing in love. In fact, we must be rooted and growing in the Spirit and love of Christ. Truly, Christ is the one foundation.

Next, there must be the physical structure: floors, walls, ceilings, roof. In the words of Paul to the Ephesians, the house is defined by its breadth, length, height, and depth. These are also the elements of faith. We need to acknowledge and understand the all-encompassing claim that Jesus has made upon the world. We must build firm floors of repeated experience with our Lord—in prayer, in fellowship, in study. We need walls of scripture—reading, making our interpretation and comparing it with the interpretation of others. Finally, a strong roof of commitment and loyalty. Commitment that won't leak and loyalty that won't blow away in the wind.

Ultimately, a house is just a structure until it is occupied, really lived in. An empty home will soon be in disrepair. Spiritually, this corresponds with Paul's prayer: "to know the love of Christ which surpasses knowledge, that you may be filled with all the fullness of God" (Ephesians 3:19). We deepen our lives in the Christian faith by sharing sorrows and joys, by carrying one another's burdens, and learning from one another. In such a manner, we can fill our spiritual home, which has been rooted and grounded in love, enlarged by breadth, length, height, and depth, and filled with the fullness of God, furnished with the riches of his glory, and indwelt by Christ.

Experiential Religion
April 17
Acts 9:1–31

The Christian faith is the most exciting, wonderful, creative, and dramatic experience that can befall a person. It is more adventurous than Huck Finn; it is more exciting than first love, it is more dramatic than skydiving. That is, if it is real. Full acceptance and participation in the Christian faith is more wonderful even than a fruitful marriage. It can change the whole direction of life: it can redeem the damned; it can save the lost; it can direct the drifting; it can give meaning to wealth, significance to success, and purpose to promise ... if it is real. How can we make our faith vibrant and alive, enthusiastic and joyous? How can it be more real? There are hundreds of ways, of course. The ways differ with the persons involved. Each way has something in common: a genuine experience of God.

The conversion of Saul to Paul is one of the most famous and dramatic conversion experiences known. Saul was truly seeking after righteousness. He followed every law, learned every text. He was so zealous that he began persecuting Christians. This zeal carried him through the conversion into even further zeal for following Christ. He had not felt fulfilled in his quest for perfection in the practice of Judaism. Once he met Jesus face-to-face, everything was new; it all fell into place. The conversion of Paul was astounding to those around him. It demonstrated that some impossible things are possible with God. Most important for the average person is the fact that the call of God requires a clear response.

Once the experience has occurred, it is necessary to proclaim its effect to others. We must give testimony to our faith, for it is our eyewitness account of our experience. No two people will have the same experience, but true faith cannot exist without changing the person. It is by these changes that the fruit of faith is proclaimed.

Get the Book
April 18
Deuteronomy 10:12–13

The Bible is God's Holy Word. This is where we can come to know him; this is where we learn of the personality and person of Jesus. This is the guidebook of life, the world's most practical pattern for living! The challenge is to pass this spiritual legacy through the family. A child cannot inherit the faith of the parents—God has no grandchildren. Each individual must accept the truth of Jesus Christ in their own heart, mind, and soul. However, we can instill the practices of faith within our family life—the habit of Bible study, prayer, church attendance, and service to others. The lessons found within the Bible translate into life activity that continues to feed the faith day by day. The Bible is not only a book of stories for children; it is a book of life to adults to be applied by the adult mind.

In the life of the family, we can foster a love for the Bible through reading and studying together. Modeling is important, and our children learn vast amounts through the behavior of their parents. This knowledge multiplies when we participate in activities together. Church attendance is most valuable when the whole family attends the service, the lessons, and the small groups for fellowship. In this way, lasting friendships are formed and are much more likely to translate into mature faith. It is vital to set the stage for a true conversion experience through camps and retreats, where there is longer exposure in the setting of memorable activities like campfires and storytelling. Ultimately, each individual has a moment of change of heart, and this occurs when the heart is prepared, ready to receive.

Here's Help
April 19
Luke 19:28–40

The human being is quite a marvelous creature. As an animal, he can be surpassed; there are other animals that are bigger, faster, stronger. Even so, as an animal, he has considerable agility, strength, and resiliency. What truly sets the human being apart, though, is his intellect. Through his oversized brain, Homo sapiens stands alone. He has amazing inventiveness, outstanding adaptivity, and surprising ingenuity. There is one thing the human cannot do. We cannot save ourselves! We were born to live in two worlds—this one and the next. On our own, we are unable to negotiate that transformation. It could feel quite hopeless. Yet just as we cry out in fear, Jesus Christ answers and says, "I am the way, the truth and the life" (John 14:6).

Jesus doesn't simply tell us how to get somewhere, he takes us by the hand and walks along with us. He doesn't tell us about the way; He is the Way. He lived in a body just like ours and experienced life like we do. For those who know Jesus and seek to be like him, life is transformed.

Christ also personifies truth. He was the messenger and the message. The truth is that we are all brothers and sisters in Christ. We all long for peace; life is good when we follow his way. Life with Jesus as the sure center, the firm foundation; guided and empowered by our Lord is life indeed. It is life worth living.

Life by Immersion

April 20
Romans 6:2–11

One of the richest sacraments in the faith of the Christian is baptism. Baptism is the doorway into the church. It is an act that is more commonly practiced by those who acknowledge themselves as Christians than any other. Though many argue about the specific mode of baptism, the uniting theme is that it represents newness of life. It is actually uniquely related to the resurrection. As one goes into baptism, one dies to the old life. As the person rises again—whether from the knees or from the water—the person rises as a new creation in Christ. This is the hope, the prayer, and the whole desire of the one being baptized as well as the witnessing congregation. Baptism reminds all of us that we are dead to sin and alive to God in Christ Jesus.

If we are to be alive to God in Christ Jesus, we must first immerse ourselves in life. One way of putting it is to get out of the grandstands and into the game. This is life by immersion. Of course, the very activities we are immersed in do reflect our priorities. It is much too easy to simply get caught up in busyness and intense activity of life, so that we are drawn away from the significant activities of faith. Faith isn't something to be added to our other duties, making our lives more complex. Faith in God must be the center of life, and all else is remodeled and integrated by it.

Note that this is immersion in the *faith*, not simply the duties of the church. With the joy of the spirit of faith, we are able to live in the enthusiasm of being alive to God in Christ Jesus. In fellowship with God, we find reason for living, we find joy in sharing. We discover a steady peace down at the very depth of our souls, where all strain is gone, and God is already victor over the world. Already victor over our weaknesses.

Life or Death?
April 21
John 3:1–16

Have you ever noticed that much of our living is making decisions? Most of them are little decisions, like what to have for dinner, yet sometimes they can grow to great proportions. Of course, we don't always recognize the decisions as momentous, but in retrospect, we become aware that some decision, some occurrence, some turn of events, was a decisive moment in our lives. Such was the time described in the story of Nicodemus.

Nicodemus was a Pharisee who came to Jesus at night. He somehow recognized that he could not scoff at what Jesus had done, that there was something about Jesus that could not be lightly dismissed as his colleagues were doing. He had actually managed to keep alive the conviction that God was still speaking to humankind. To his ears, there was something in the demeanor and teaching of this impudent intruder that rang true and majestic … something that might well be God's voice.

Many people today have caught a hint of the truth of Christ and want wistfully to follow, who vaguely but yet gnawingly are hungry to grasp this glimpse of vital and unified life. Yet they furtively and hesitatingly come by night, or read on philosophy and slip in the back door; afraid of laughing friends, scoffing relatives, even family. They are those whose hearts are weeping inside to give in and believe but who cannot quite do it. Who, like Nicodemus, think to themselves, *I'm too old. My ways are set. My fight is over. How can a man be born again when he is this old? This is for vigorous youth, not tired old men.*

The whole point of the Christian message is that God can give life to any age—child, adult, senior—the kind of new life that puts a spring into the step and a glorious purpose to living. We stumble at this new life because we have grown fond of the way we are. It's not too painful or too demanding. It is such an effort to change. Jesus was saying that life in God requires sensitivity, willingness, eagerness, and a measure of disregard for conventions and cautions.

Jesus was proclaiming that *new life was available*. He was saying, "If men see me and keep looking at me, the heavenly things that are all dark to them will storm their hearts and bring them to their feet whole men, ready to live a fuller life than they have ever dreamed possible." Such a life, Jesus said, is eternal life—beginning now. Christ showed us the difference between life and death. Despite the difficulties and responsibilities, choose life. Life can be forever changed with the beauty, challenge, and peace of Christ.

On Being Realistically Optimistic
April 22
John 13:31–35

Jesus had just finished washing the disciples' feet. All the disciples, including Judas, whom he knew would betray him. Peter, on the other hand, was enthusiastic as always, yet Jesus tells him that he, too, would betray his leader. Jesus then gives the well-known command: "Love one another. As I have loved you, so you must love one another. By this, everyone will know you are my disciples" (John 13:34–35). Despite the coming betrayals, Jesus encouraged the disciples with love. The tension between optimism and pessimism is a constant. Jesus was able to pull off the optimism by knowing the vision of what was to come of his sacrifice.

Christian faith is essentially optimistic. Our dynamic of faith is a trust that our God will prevail for good even through our misunderstandings. God can redeem the pain and fear of any situation and restore us to wholeness of spirit. Faith is dynamic, holding that our God takes us where we are and calls us forward to a victorious conclusion. We know that we will stumble along the way, but we also know that God is less interested in condemnation than in redemption and restoration. We are encouraged to arise, dust ourselves off, learn from our mistakes, and go on to a higher calling.

Realistic optimistic faith is a way of seeing. Jesus knew of the ultimate victory. So do we. We encounter our difficulties knowing that we are the ultimate victors. Whatever befalls us is temporary, because we see beyond to what yet can be. Realistic optimistic faith allows us to see that hardship and pain may actually be a gift. It can lead to growth, motivation, and forgiveness, deepening our relationships. Ultimately, realistic optimistic faith recognizes that God is always concerned for us personally and individually. He knows us more intimately than we know ourselves. God yearns for us to be in harmony with him and with one another. In partnership with him, we can cope with a real world, nurturing the beauty of what is yet to come.

Prepare for Action!
April 23
Acts 2:14, 36–42

One of the first things we learn as we begin to go out to do anything on our own is to be prepared. This is true for scouting, boating, camping, even for war. For the disciples, they had been prepared by Jesus Christ himself. They had gone out on short missions prior to the death and resurrection. This is still true for each of us. To witness in our communities, we need to be prepared physically, mentally, and spiritually.

In the Acts passage, Peter says, "Repent and be baptized, everyone, in the name of Jesus Christ for the forgiveness of sines and you shall receive the gift of the Holy Spirit" (Acts 2:38). The Holy Spirit armed them, and us, with the fruits of the spirit: love, joy, peace, patience, kindness, goodness, faithfulness, gentleness, self-control. Shortly after this precious list comes the admonition, "and let us not grow weary in well-doing" (Galatians 6:9). The well-doing kind of goodness must come from a secure and joyous heart, firm in the love of God and confident of the power of the Holy Spirit. Then the well-doing is not a chore and a drudgery but a joy and a privilege. We can actually find ourselves thanking others for the privilege of being given an opportunity to be of help!

Of course, some might say that this desire to help others may be taken advantage of. Yet it is not possible when you want the needy one to become full and no longer needy. Only so, can that one also begin to care for others. Think of what would be the result in our communities if we were to deliberately and steadfastly carry out the gifts of the Holy Spirit. It could be transformational! So, prepare for action using the fruits of the spirit as your means.

Retreat and Return
April 24
1 Thessalonians 5:17

Many people who are living outwardly normal lives are really living lives of quiet desperation. Along with those, there are many others who are obviously complaining that surely something can give them a more meaningful life or a more purposeful existence. What can be done about this? Jesus gave a great example in his own life: retreat and return. Drop out of each day's hustle and bustle at least once for meditation and directed positive prayer, then go back with your cup filled for the needs of the day.

Jesus gave the disciples some guidelines to follow in the Lord's prayer, but that isn't quite the full answer for how to get the kind of peace he experienced. One significant requirement is discipline. Valuable results generally require discipline. We see this in studies, sports, music; even gardening and cooking require experience. Discipline translates into regularity, humility, and a positive, receptive attitude. Next is to retreat. Retreat from the business of the world is as vital to the spiritual life as sleep and food are to the physical. Such retreat empowers and even propels return. The human soul is like a pot with a hole in it. It needs to constantly be refilled, or there is nothing in it to pour out into a hurting society. For faith is action. Prayer can change your life—anytime, anywhere, and at any age. It can heal your diseases, renew your mind and body, and begin to calm the storms of daily living.

Salt and Light

April 25
Isaiah 58:6–10; Matthew 5:13–16

Salt is intriguing in that a pure crystal of salt can be drawn out from impure water. Somehow the things in the water—bacteria, dirt, chemicals—are drawn out by the evaporation of the water. So it is with us; we live in the swirl of thousands of others. The work of the Holy Spirit in us draws out our impurities to make us an instrument of God's divine purpose. Within our hearts we want to belong to Christ and be all that Jesus would want us to be. But we have competing calls: things we want to do, things we need to do, work, family commitments. How does it all play out? Will we be able to become a pure crystal of sharp saltiness able to accomplish that for which Jesus calls us? The purpose of salt is to penetrate, to permeate, to flavor all it touches. God calls us to be the salt of the earth, to flavor the world around us with his presence.

The next image Jesus uses is that we are to be the light of the world. Light is similar to salt in that it penetrates the darkness. The specific kind of light Jesus refers to is a gentle, useful light. One that draws others to it. Our personal spiritual lives are nothing, and we will surely not get to heaven if we are not carriers of the light, lifting high daily and constantly and consistently. Jesus is calling us to reach out. He is appealing to us to be God's agents, to penetrate into the lives of our friends and neighbors and coworkers. To bring them salt and light. These images are meant for our salvation. They are meant for the saving of those around us. They are meant for the fruition of our world. Let us be that salt and that light.

We Offer Unto Thee
April 26
Romans 12:1

Life can truly feel like a treadmill sometimes. We get up, go to work, hit it all day, and then come back. Day after day after day. What is it all about? What gives it all meaning? The celebration of Communion can give us some ideas. Communion brings the life of Christ into our actual lives; it reminds us that he loved us enough to give his very life for us. That has to be worth something! If you have ever had the opportunity to serve Communion to others, there is a sense of privilege associated with it. As each person shares the bread and the cup, there is a recognition of the mutual support in the community of faith. One of the prayers in the traditional service of Communion states, "although unworthy … here we offer and present ourselves unto thee." That's it! Life is an offering.

When we get up in the morning, it is our life blood we are spending. For those of us that have given our lives to Christ, that means that every day we work for him, not ourselves. In return, our lives have purpose. There is more stability, more fruitfulness. With Christ's help, we learn to comfort the sorrowing, bind up the brokenhearted, visit the sick and imprisoned. In so doing, we develop a harmony with God that brings deep down joy. This joy makes a vitalizing impact on the world around us. This joy leads our youths to serve as missionaries and ministers. This joy brings light into dark places.

When we offer and present ourselves to God to be used, life goes from being a treadmill to being an adventure.

What Difference Does It Make?
April 27
Luke 22:28–46

Picture two men, both pastors, sitting over a cup of coffee. One of them is obviously disturbed. He has been pouring out his feelings to the other. There has been a torrent of words, a futility of appearance, a heart-rending struggle. One Sunday, during the pastoral prayer, he had the overwhelming sensation that he was out of place. What was he doing here? Why should he be praying to God? Is there a God anyway? What difference does it make? Thankfully, after much agonizing soul-searching and prayer, his hungering and thirsting received the filling of God. He doubted and fought through to faith. The kind of faith that cannot be shaken but which is sympathetic, understanding, and only wants others to learn, as he learned: it does make a difference.

Holy scripture has ample testimony that to struggle is no sin. Doubts are not wrong. In fact, the satanical face of a cunning demon called doubt can very well be the fire that tempers the metal. Consider some of the great struggles: Abraham when called to sacrifice Isaac (Genesis 22:1–18), Jacob with the angel (Genesis 32:22–32), Jesus in the Garden of Gesthemane (Luke 22:39–46), Peter and the crowing of the rooster (Luke 22:54–62). Each of these persons of scripture struggled mightily as they hammered out a faith of their own.

We may be encouraged to believe in the dynamic qualities of the Christian faith because of the perspective it gives us, the power that is available to us, and because of the open ear of God as our struggle bursts forth in words of prayer. God lifts us out to help us demonstrate the love of God. He helps us avoid the mistake of making people things not persons. He gives us new perspective as we find the limit of ourselves as we attempt to render service to others. Further, God grants power to redeem and build and overcome doubt. This power comes through the gift of prayer. Prayer is not for things; it is for spirit. The plain fact is that if we have to do without God, everything adds up to nonsense. The perspective of people through the eyes of Christ, the power of God that comes through service, and the communion with God through prayer adds up to the difference between nonsense and the eternal.

What Does It Take?
April 28
John 10:22–30

The self-appointed protectors of religious orthodoxy, the scribes and the Pharisees, have been shaken by the healing of the man born blind. Finally, they ask, "Are you the Christ?" His answer, "I have told you and you do not believe me," kind of stings. Here is Jesus, having done everything needed to open out the beauty of faith, plainly saying that he is the expected Messiah, and they still do not believe!

What does it take? What does it take to believe? It is a tough question. Interestingly, scripture suggests no less than four routes by which to come to believing faith: heart, mind, action, and sacrifice. I am convinced that it takes all of these routes.

First, it takes an open heart. God is love, and we love because he first loved us. Our human family, as imperfect as it is, is the closest human parallel. It is a partnership not of legality so much as a bond of blood, the bond of love. However, the mind also has to be convinced. Faith simply cannot be a fantasy based on wishful thinking. It has to be reasonable. It must make sense to intelligent, sensible, reasonable people. Not only in the intensity of heartfelt emotion, but also in the logical cold light of day. One ought to be able, with the mind, to find confirmation everywhere in the truth the heart conveys. The heart and mind come together with the soul and will for a unanimous decision. And when that happens, one has a faith with power and wisdom, with joyous length and strength.

No belief is real without action. One must be willing to get up and receive. It is easy to sit back and consider an idea. It only becomes real when you act. For us, this means to help the needy, share the word, and be bearers of love. Action leads to sacrifice. Helping, sharing, and showing the love is not necessarily in line with today's society. Jesus said that to be identified with him would mean separation from society, persecution, ridicule. With heart and mind together, the actions of faith follow, and the sacrifice seals the deal, knowing that we are identified with our Savior.

Who Am I?

April 29
Mark 8:27–38

Each one of our lives began in helplessness and will end in helplessness. The time in between those two points will be spent, many times, wondering about the purpose of our existence. The queries haunt us at times and bespeak our never-ending struggle to know ourselves. We struggle to establish our own identity. One answer in this quest is finding a faith of our own, a faith that meets our needs. Some persons have such a faith now. They have learned to live life well; they can say, when all is figured up: "I have sought to be faithful." This is a shining hope that will carry us all our days into a holy eternity.

On the journey to such faith, a good start is to accept that "I am a creature of God." Someone has figured out how many chances to one it would take for the world to have happened by chance, and the figures go around the world thirty-five times! The world doesn't make sense without God, and we are his creatures. Furthermore, if we are his creatures, then he is our God. A creature of God finds his true self in complete submission to the will of God, and real freedom by serving the one true Master.

An important aspect of being a creature of God is living well with one another. A child born in isolation, without human input, would not develop personality, socialization, or language. The secret of knowing our true selves is serving our fellow humans. That's when we're happiest; that's what gives the greatest joy. Nothing feels better than doing something good for someone. The greatest tool to remaining faithful is to become a disciple. The disciples were learners. They were persons like you and me that made mistakes. They needed forgiveness, but they were powerful. They were powerful because they were dedicated to the Lord, who so inspired them, who gave them the only life worth living. If we are Christians, we are disciples of Jesus Christ, and there we find ourselves.

Yeast
April 30
1 Corinthians 5:6–8; Matthew 28:20

Yeast is a very common commodity. It is that which causes things to ferment. It raises, it impregnates, it imbues, it permeates with a transforming element. We, as Christians, are yeast in the community. You can't put a package of yeast in bread dough and have it work only in one corner of the loaf. It is in the entire loaf. Either the spirit of Christ works at the office and in the home and on the job, or we're kidding ourselves.

The essence of what God has done in Jesus Christ is that he came to *us*. Christ came to change anger to gladness, darkness to light, frowns to smiles, tears to laughter, hate to love. The gospel has liberating power. It lifts horizons, gives new perspectives, breathes in hope. God shows no partiality. It spells out that every person is valuable, not just a privileged few. Each person has the freedom to respond or not to respond to the gospel. We literally have the freedom to go to hell if we want to. But Christ came to tell us that while we have the freedom to go to hell if that is our choice, we do not *have* to go.

If we make the decision for Christ, we are also responsible for the decision. This means that we must treat other people as if they are responsible too … that they too belong to God. When God came to us in Christ, it changed everything. God had a plan, and we are a part of that plan. The plan has an ultimately successful and righteous conclusion. God is at work even while we don't know it. He calls us now to a self-conscious purpose to do his work of mission. The mission of bringing the liberating gospel where it can lift horizons, give new perspectives, and breathe new hope.

Always One Friend
May 1
John 14:15–21

We human beings are truly social creatures. Even though we often like our aloneness, we are greatly pained by being cut off from one another. Being alone and being lonely are entirely different. When we suspect that our loneliness is a result of some act of our own where we have gotten angry and unjustly broken a relationship then it is even more devastating. There is no more desolate punishment than solitary confinement.

The disciples were torn apart by the announcement of Jesus that he must ascend to the Father. He was not only their best friend and mentor; they had come to see that he was the Word of God, the embodiment of truth. Humans have shown a passion for worshiping throughout history. Jesus promised the Holy Spirit would abide with them forever.

It is still true. There is always one friend standing with you. Even when we don't perceive it, or when we feel unworthy to receive anything. The Holy Spirit comes to us as a comforter, a counselor. He is beside us when we need aid. He also comes as a teacher, to help us remember and understand the sayings of Jesus. With the Holy Spirit beside us, we are never alone.

An Inward and Spiritual Grace
May 2
Ephesians 5:21–6:4

Have you ever noticed that we wrap ceremony around our most precious moments? Its purpose is to preserve and enrich those moments and give them more than passing meaning. Two central ceremonies in the church are baptism and matrimony. Baptism is a sacrament, meaning it is commanded by Jesus. Both ceremonies have a symbol that is an outward and visible sign of an inward and spiritual grace. Without spiritual grace, the act is meaningless.

The home is a place where emptiness reigns unless the outward and visible actions are undergirded by an inward and spiritual grace. The core of the spiritual home is husband and wife. Marriage requires sacrificial love. The kind of love that thinks first and most of the other. The kind of love that gives itself away—like Christ did for the church. The love needs to build one another up, to show particular care. It is so easy to take each other for granted. Furthermore, in the Christian home, our Lord is always present. In that case, there are not two partners, but three—and the third is Christ.

The relationship between parents and children is next to observe. Children are a twenty-four-hour-a-day responsibility that requires the inward and spiritual grace. The struggle to raise a family is evident on both sides of the relationship. The parents want to impart every bit of wisdom they can, and the children mostly want to "do it my way!" There are many rewards throughout the process, but sometimes we need to remember that this relationship is also in "sickness and in health, and for richer or poorer!"

The thing that wraps the family together is the relationship between the family and God. Here is where the resources for loving one another come. God gives us conquest of circumstances and strength for the long haul. Much of family life is covered by "outward and visible signs." But it is God who sees the "inward and spiritual grace." It is he who also will supply it.

Blest Be the Binds that Tie

May 3
John 10:10

A solid, whole, loving family is a tremendous asset. Children who grow up in such homes have been given lifetime bonuses. They are given roots that allow them to handle difficult situations and know that after all of it, they are loved. This does not mean that they are idyllic homes. In real homes there are both good times and bad. The parallels between family and faith are clear. Jesus is often referred to as the good shepherd. Sheep and shepherds were common in Jesus's day. The sheep were often kept in a common pen at night. In the morning, the shepherd had only to speak to the sheep, and his sheep would follow him and no other.

In every family there are problems. We cannot escape that, nor should we. Instead, we need to take those binds into which we get and let them become the means by which our lives are tied together in a common bond. The cross is a good example. We see it both as a crucifix, with Christ's body still hanging on it, and as a resurrection cross, empty and victorious in the defeat of death. The first reminds us that when humanity was in a bind, it took the sacrificing of the closest of human ties to bond us to our God. The victory of the resurrection cross was no cheap, bloodless victory. Such faith is sacrificing, committing, giving unstintingly. Without that ingredient, the empty resurrection cross becomes almost meaningless. On the outside of Catholic churches, there is always a resurrection cross, showing the unbelieving world victory. On the inside, there is the crucifix, to remind the faithful of the cost, and the validity of our own sacrifices, which grow from our gratitude.

Come and See

May 4
John 1:35–51

"Come and see." These are intriguing words. They are a call to action—like a child beckoning for your attention, or a telephone ringing in the other room. In the context of this passage, it is Jesus who is speaking. Can you imagine hearing those words from Jesus? This is in the beginning of his ministry. He has attracted the attention of the disciples of John the Baptist. "Rabbi, where are you staying?" "Come and see" (John 1:38). They accepted the invitation, and spent the afternoon with him.

Perhaps most important is what happens after you "come and see." In this case, Andrew immediately ran to tell his brother that he had found the Messiah! We often feel we need to go far away to proclaim what we have found in Jesus. Here we see the appropriateness of reaching out right where we live. If we cannot share our good news to our local brothers and sisters, how do we expect to proclaim it to those of a different culture?

How did Andrew see that Jesus was the Messiah? Just as we do. When we come into the presence of one who knows our troubles—and has answers to them. Someone that exudes the genuine love of God and guides us to live life abundantly, in harmony with God. Although we cannot physically be present with Jesus Christ, we can study his Word and proclaim it to our neighbors—through our lives, our thoughts, our words, and our actions.

What will you do when you are called to "come and see?" Will your eyes be open and ears be able to hear the true message of Christ? Will you then go and proclaim it to those around you? When you truly *see* Jesus, deliverance through salvation becomes a reality, and he will give you life.

Depth
May 5
Ephesians 3:14–21

Of all human relationships, none are more vital and enduring than those of home and family. Paul speaks of this in the passage, "May you be strong to grasp … what is the breadth and length and height and depth of the love of Christ, and to know it" (Ephesians 3:18). It has been said that the breadth and length and height and depth are the four arms of the cross and represent the wholeness of the truth. The two outstretched arms—reaching for the sinners crucified beside him—are the breadth and the length. No person can so foul up their life as to go beyond the reach of the truth of God, for everywhere one looks, there God is beckoning that person to join him in fellowship. The post, then, is for the height and depth. It is to the depth of hell, even there God seeks us … calling us to join him in the joy of the heavenly relationship.

It is to the strength of the inner self that one ought to turn in order to grasp this depth. The inner self meant something specific to Paul. It meant reason, conscience, and will. He was praying that Christ would so dwell in our hearts that one would not only know the right and feel the "ought" of the right, but have the will to do the right. It's funny. When one is young, one knows everything. When one gets older, one grows to believe he knows nothing. That's why it is so good to touch base with things like the family and the deep places of the inner self. It provides a sureness that come what may, there are some things that count, which are eternal—like the love of Christ, which surpasses knowledge, and like being filled with the fullness of God.

Faith Is Joy
May 6
John 15:11

Consider those words. Faith is joy. An all-time favorite hymn is "Joy to the World." We associate it with Christmas, but if you take the words out of that context, it opens up a whole new perspective. There is no mention of the Christ child, or baby in the manger. There is no star in the sky, no angels on high, no shepherds watching their flocks by night. In fact, the words promise that the Lord comes to make God's blessings flow! He removes sin and sorrow and brings truth and grace—what joy!

John 15:11 says, "I have told you this so that my joy may be in you and that your joy may be complete." This sentence sums up the story of the vine and the branches. We are the branches, put together with Jesus—the vine—because we are to bear fruit. The fruit is joy. Joy comes from the joining of the branches with the vine. Without the vine, the branches die.

How do we capture joy in daily life? One way is to open your mind to think in prayer. We are in constant conversation with ourselves. Prayer is conversation with God, which opens up the channels to a marvelous perspective, just as the words to the hymn allow us to see the broader image of joy. Life has nothing to offer that can begin to compare with the peace of conscience and the fullness of joy that comes from fellowship with Jesus Christ. Pope John Paul II put it this way: "For me, the great fruit of belief is joy. There is a God, there is a purpose, there is a meaning to things, there are realities we cannot guess at, there is a big peace, and you are part of it." What joy!

Feeling Sorry for Yourself?

May 7
1 Kings 19:9–18; Romans 12:1–2

Elijah was one of the great prophets of the Bible. He showed the power of God to the worshipers of false gods through a great display of fire. The false gods were completely powerless, and God showed up. Sadly, this great victory led to a threat on his life by the queen of those gods. Elijah ran for his life. He ran until he could run no more, then he collapsed. God even sent angels to take care of him. Ultimately, he stops, and God says, "What are you doing here Elijah?" (1 Kings 19:9). Elijah answers that he is the only prophet left, and feels completely conquered.

Most of us have experienced that feeling. Abandoned, excluded, feeling sorry for ourselves. There are so many circumstances in life that assault us—work, relationships, health, loss. It can seem like there is nowhere to go, and you're not sure you want to go on anymore. It is always helpful when the Bible shows us how God uses broken, disobedient people like us. For Elijah, God said, "Go stand before me on the mountain" (1 Kings 19:11). He told him to get up and get going, and that he would be with him, and show him important things to do. That is exactly what God says to us when it feels like there is nothing more: "Get up; I have important things for you to do, and I will be with you." We are never alone.

Giving Life
May 8
1 John 4:7–9

The moment of birth is indescribable. The first breath, the first cry, the first look, the awe. It is a natural thing, the moment that a human best understands natural instinct. Amazingly, that is the easy part. Having life is a completely different thing. To have life is learning to live by God's guiding light. The act of putting God first in our lives is absolutely crucial to be able to do this. Does God come first because he is some kind of egomaniac? Why bother with the commandments? The commandments are there to free us. God is the only true giver of life—our creator. We are made in his image. The laws of the commandments are actually hardwired into our beings. When we follow them, we are living life in the direction God meant for us. When we don't, nothing goes right. When Adam and Eve sinned, they short-circuited that wiring for all of humankind. All our interactions with God are aimed at solving the problem of sin.

Finally, gaining life is the acceptance and understanding of John 3:16. Jesus came so that we would have everlasting life. Jesus is the answer to the problem of sin and separation. Life on earth is not our final destination. God has a bigger plan. He has made better provisions. Accepting Jesus as the Lord of your life and God's guidance as freedom to have life is pivotal. Gaining the assurance that God holds us in the palm of his hand is to have life abundantly.

God Enters
May 9
Colossians 3:1–17

When God enters your life, things change. The truth of this is unchallengeable. The practice of acting upon the principles of Christianity is more difficult. Many Christians have simply not truly allowed God into their lives. This is evidenced in their behavior. They may have accepted Jesus as their savior but not experienced the indwelling of God—the Holy Spirit. God cannot enter our hearts until we are ready and willing to accept him. Once God enters, life gains a new perspective. Clearly, all problems do not cease, for we are still imperfect, and we live within a world that is imperfect. But there is much in the serenity of our pulse to putting our problems in their proper perspective.

It is easy to be distracted by the man-made rules and regulations of organized religion without experiencing the heart change that occurs with an intimate experience with Jesus. Jesus spoke regularly of the risks of becoming swayed by the human interpretation of God's guidance. When asked which is the greatest commandment in the law, he responded, "Love the lord your God with all your heart and with all your strength and with all your soul and with all your mind. This is the first and greatest commandment. And the second is like it: Love your neighbor as yourself. All the Law and the Prophets hang on these two commandments" (Matthew 22:37–40). The clearest example, aside from the Pharisees, is Paul. He was full of knowledge and zeal and hate, persecuting Christians prior to his encounter with Jesus. After coming face to face with Jesus, he became equally zealous for Christ, and showed a love for others that is unsurpassed. When God enters your life, you willingly lay aside your own will, and follow the path of Jesus.

Good Things Come in Threes
May 10
Psalm 8; John 16:12–15

We are always reaching for something ... something more. With the psalmist, we ask, "What is man that thou art mindful of him?" (Psalm 8:4). What does the God of the universe know or care about our little joys and triumphs? We are as insignificant as a grain of sand. Yet our God proclaims otherwise. We are made with a longing for meaning and purpose, love and belonging, to know and understand. In our creation we are made for oneness with our creator. We experience this oneness with God the Father, Son, and Holy Spirit.

The word *father* means "orderer"—bringer of order out of chaos. God the Father gave us the law and the prophets. The law was to be a beacon of truth for the wandering. But we did not use it well; we sought to define every moment and regulate every possibility. What was to be a beacon became a burden. So, God sent his Son: God the Son. He sent his Son to give us a new agreement. The truth is received from the Father and revealed by the Son. The primary persons to transmit the Word of the Son, his disciples, were common, everyday folk, just like us. In fact they were hardy, working men who could tell the truth when they saw it. Their report is a believable one. Their proclamation transformed them, their world, and us. They experienced the Word made flesh, the Word made into a person. But, being of human flesh, even the Son of God could not be among us in that form always. So, after his death, he sent us the Holy Spirit. God the Holy Spirit would comfort us, teach us, and guide us into all truth.

Whenever we learn something, the insight bursting upon us is the Holy Spirit. Whenever we enjoy something of beauty like a rose, a sunset, or an act of kindness, we experience the Holy Spirit. Whenever we have a loss or hurt, we experience the comfort of the Holy Spirit. It is God in three persons, blessed Trinity.

Hi, Mom. Have You Been with Jesus?
May 11
Acts 4:13

Parenting is one of the hardest and most rewarding things in a person's life. There is undue stress on the marriage with all the wants, needs, and discipline. There is also considerable stress on the children, especially when they become teenagers. Suicide has become the leading cause of death among individuals between ten and thirty-four. There is such pressure on these kids, and they lack the experience and awareness of true mortality. What can turn all of this around?

Placing Jesus at the center of your heart and home. After Jesus's death, the disciples were discouraged and without direction. When the Holy Spirit descended upon them at Pentecost, their lives were transformed! They spoke with such command and confidence that those around them were shocked. This occurred because they had spent time with Jesus. With Jesus and the Holy Spirit behind them, nothing could stop them—not prison or hunger or loneliness or even physical beatings. We have access to this power.

Jesus gives confidence to parents and children alike, a safe place to grow and learn in the heart of the loving Christian community. The support of the community gives consistency, so that words match actions, and truth wins out. True acceptance beats out the false friendships of the secular world. Finally, putting Jesus in the center of your life gives purpose; we are created with a huge need for the love and guidance of our creator, we were made in his image. With Jesus in the driver's seat, your path will always be true, not easy, but true.

Holy Armor
May 12
Ephesians 6:10–20

We don't think much about armor these days. Although, there are many parallels. Consider a bike or motorcycle helmet, a jacket, special footwear. All these physical things protect us from the physical elements that we face. Spiritually, we need exactly the same items as were needed two thousand years ago. First, we need to protect our minds from risky thoughts. It is so easy to allow your mind to drift. Oddly, left without conscious protection, we seem to get into dreaming—about a better job, bigger house, complaints about those around us. How do we protect from that? By intentionally redirecting our thoughts, to think instead about blessings, to pray, to praise God. When we fill our minds with spiritual things, there isn't as much room for the negative ones.

How do we protect our bodies? This is about what we do. Jesus has clothed each believer in his own righteousness in order that we may face God. This occurs when we accept him as our savior, but it does not keep us from sinning. We are all born sinners. The protection we do have is the Holy Spirit. The Holy Spirit causes us to recognize wrongdoing, admit it, and stop it! Without the Holy Spirit's guidance, the natural tendency to do things that are not pleasing to God may run rampant.

The only weapon in the spiritual armor is the sword, which is the Word of God. At this time in history, we are in a huge spiritual battlefield. We have been armed to fight. Satan cannot stand up to the Word of God. Knowing the word allows us to protect spirit and soul. So, we protect our minds, remain aware of our actions, and study the Word of God, which holds it all together.

Keeping Close
May 13
Psalm 22:25–31

Keeping the faith can be almost a catchphrase. Yet keeping close to God is the absolute core of being a Christian. The trouble is that faith requires constant attention. It is like a garden. If you plant a beautiful garden then walk away and never water, trim, or weed, it will become a dry patch of weeds in a matter of weeks. We want so much to have a vital faith life, so how can we be steadfast and productive?

One element is to be down to earth. Psalm 22 is a cry of separation. It is the scripture quoted by Christ at the cross: "My God, my God, why hast thou forsaken me?" (Psalm 22:1). Most of us have prayed yet felt we didn't connect. God's answer to this problem was Jesus Christ himself. God came to earth in the form of Jesus so that we could *see* his love for us. Jesus lived as a man and experienced all the challenges life has to offer. He still remained pure and sinless in order to redeem us from our sins.

Another method to keeping the faith is not to wait to be loved before loving others. God loved us before we ever turned to him. Waiting for the other person to break down first is a pride issue. Somehow it seems stronger to respond than to reach out. Remaining close to other people is not easy. Far from it. Yet the vulnerability of close relationships is critical to remaining close to God. Separation from others may feel safer, but in fact leads to hard-heartedness due to self-centeredness.

Keep the faith—stay down to earth, love others, keep close connections.

Little Tin Gods

May 14
Matthew 6:5–14

A little tin god is when we try to play God—when we think we can call all the shots. Things may look good on the outside, but under pressure, tin crumbles. Ultimately, little tin gods have things upside down. They (we) don't know who's really on top. Ultimately, we realize that we need to seek a better god—the real God.

The disciples knew they needed to seek the real God when they asked Jesus to teach them to pray. A key phrase in the Lord's prayer is "lead us." How often do we rattle right past that part and go ahead and do it our own way. The amazing thing is that God has given us the free will to *be* led … or not. God's love is such that he won't make us follow; he won't make us love him. However, when we ask God to lead us, he comes alongside us. He gives us teachers, preachers, friends, nature, and our own minds and hearts to realize that his leading is exactly what we need.

At some point, we realize that his way is the right way. Living according to God's will feels better than following the path of playing god. We begin to share concern for others, to live out our faith on a daily basis. Then, and only then, do we enter into God's kingdom here on earth. Then we feel the power and the glory of God right in our own lives on a daily basis. At that point, we become saturated with God's love in Christ and have no further need for the little tin god of our own will. Let us pray with all our hearts that God would lead us into his will today and forever.

One Flock, One Shepherd
May 15
John 10:11–15

Religion is a funny thing. It is based on faith and trust, and it is not possible to prove either one. Is religion just a matter of speculation and human need for security? Some believe so. But the Christian has other things to believe in. We have Jesus. It is a fact that Jesus lived. On the basis of what he did and what he said, he is the most impressive human of history. Every evidence points to Jesus as embodying God in human form. Furthermore, there are a host of witnesses. There are those who were eyewitnesses and who wrote about their experiences and observations. There are also the faithful who lived with us, who show us that following the way of Jesus is to live life well. It is to live it so well that it must be due to something beyond this world's power, which we identify as Jesus Christ.

The biggest thing that leads me to trust faith is that the claims of faith are confirmed in my own experience. Jesus says God has a purpose for me, and I function much better with a purpose than wandering around. Jesus says that love has the highest value, and I find that when I am in harmony with those around me, my heart feels full, and I am happy. The Bible grounds eternal things in specific images and experiences. The picture of Jesus as the good shepherd gave his hearers a sense of his true relationship with them. They knew that the true shepherd stands with his sheep when the predator comes. God gathers all of his children, all of his creation to himself. To bring about his purpose, God sent Jesus. Jesus gathered the church. We are the church, and our purpose is to fulfill the purpose of Christ.

Our Birthday Presence
May 16
Acts 2:4

The beginning of the Christian movement can be pegged at many spots. We could say it began with the creation. We could justifiably say it started with the birth of Jesus, or with his baptism, crucifixion, or resurrection. The church in its universal form has come to think of Pentecost as the day on which the church received a life-giving gift. A present, yes, but better to say a presence, because that's what it really is; the day of our spiritual birth. It is the day when we have, as our birthing gift, the presence of the spirit in every cell of ourselves, every day of our lives. If a person is to have a significant spiritual life, it is necessary for that person to wed the mind and the heart. There are limitless ways in which that power-filled experience can take place. Unless there is some kind of an electric, dynamic, unforgettable experience that unifies the intellect and the emotion, the life of faith will always be less than powerful for that person. It is experiential faith, like most of our deeply felt convictions, and it is the day of our spiritual birth. It is our birthday presence.

It is the dynamic presence of the Holy Spirit of Christ moving powerfully within the people of God. It is a dynamic presence that is needed throughout the whole church throughout the whole world. The love of God in the hearts of the people of God is what enables the church to be in ministry. The Holy Spirit's purpose is to build up the whole body of Christ, the church. The presence of the Holy Spirit is also personal. It will transform your life in a gentle, loving, fulfilling power for each moment. The Holy Spirit is expressed in the Hebrew and Greek as the word for "wind." It is like the blowing of the wind; it cannot be seen, but its effects are obvious. The inflowing of the Spirit is an outpouring of faith. It is our birthday presence.

Practicing the Presence
May 17
Acts 4:1–13

You may have been asked how you can believe in a God you can't see. Yet we act on things we can't see practically every moment. When you speak to someone on the phone, or send a letter, or even think of a loved one while you are apart, you are practicing that person's presence. It is just so with Christ. We can't see him, but we can read his letter to us, talk with him at any time, and experience the comfort of his presence everywhere. In our busy lives, it is easy to think that we don't have time to pray, study the Bible, or go to church. Practicing the presence of Christ is how we can easily strengthen our relationship and draw on his unlimited power.

Of course, one tool is knowing the Bible and learning the characteristics of God. It is like getting to know a friend. The more time we spend together, the easier it is to imagine that person and even consider how they may react. The world around us can be so negative—the news, books and movies, even the casual conversations at work or school. How can we put all that into the context of the presence of Christ? Paul said it better than anyone in Philippians 4:8: "Whatever is true, honorable, just, pure, lovely, gracious, if there is any excellence, if there is anything worthy of praise, think about these things." If we can truly think on these things and spend time with God and his people around us, that is practicing the presence.

Reality in Religion
May 18
Micah 6:1–8

There is more controversy over religion than any other subject. This is true primarily because people feel deeply about their faith. Who has not had some religionist or another at his door seeking to say, "You're wrong; I'm right"? We must be cautioned not to throw over the Christian faith because some misuse it or misrepresent it. There is reality in religion. The Christian faith is vital, valid, and real. It allows us to be honest with ourselves and God. Clearly, life full of hate reaps a hateful life, whereas the life of love reaps loving returns. Many people think they can break the law and get away with it. What they don't seem to see is that they don't break the law; rather, they break themselves upon the law. The law is not simply the rules of society enforced by the police. It is the truth that when you destroy other things and mar other people, you are also destroying yourself. The universe is created in such a manner that it sustains honesty, integrity, and fellowship.

"What does the Lord require of you, but to do justice, and to love mercy, and to walk humbly with your God?" (Micah 6:8). Justice in the daily relationships of life, kindness to one's fellows, and walking humbly before God is a trustworthy guide to live by. The doing of justice requires our interest and our support of the good things in our society. The definition of faith is action. Faith is a willingness to act upon what we believe. If we don't, we're kidding ourselves—we don't have faith. Justice is conscientiousness on a social level; mercy is justice on a personal level. Mercy is loving kindness—a cup of water to the thirsty or a loaf of bread to the hungry. Much of what is involved in loving mercy is our attitude toward possessions. All we have comes from God and therefore should be available to share with those in need.

The final requirement refers to our relationship with God. The power behind all that we may do for others is trusting in God alone. This goes back to our attitude toward things. So often a priority on things or status destroys our relationship to persons. Through confession and dedication to God, we can avoid getting stuck in our own ignorant darkness. Justice, mercy, and humility bring reality to religion.

Rocking Chairs
May 19
John 14:23–29

One of the happiest places on earth is in a rocking chair. It is even better if there is a comfy lap to sit in, and solid arms to hold you. Jesus speaks of peace and a comforter. As he was preparing to leave his place on earth with the disciples, he told them that another would come to be with them. They would never really be alone. God is not only a God who calls us to account, but who also rocks us and comforts us.

Jesus and God come and make their homes *in* us. Not just next door, but in our very hearts. This means that wherever we are in the world, the comfort of home is always right there with us. The thought of home brings out so many of the facets of life. It is at home that we discover both joy and sorrow, comfort and pain, understanding and misunderstanding. The uniqueness of home allows those lessons to come together to draw us into deeper relationships and reach out to others in need of relationship.

What allows Jesus to make our hearts his home is our obedience in keeping his love and his Word in our hearts. If we know the Word of God—and the words of Jesus—peace will always be there, beyond our capacity to understand. The Hebrew word we translate as "peace" is *shalom*. It means more than just the absence of trouble. It also means all that makes for the highest good. It means, "come unto me, all who labor or are heavy laden." It means, come into my arms, into my lap, for the deepest comfort of all.

See Far, See Whole

May 20
Acts 2:1–21

The day of Pentecost must have been quite a day. The normally stoic and somewhat discouraged disciples had been touched by flames and were changed forever. Everyone was of one mind! They had become convinced, heart, mind, body, and soul that what God had done in Christ was the unifying event of history. That is why today we call Pentecost the birthday of the church. God wants humanity to be unified and to be one people in their love of God and of peace.

Christ promised this day would come. The assignment of the Holy Spirit was and is to keep you alive in the faith. Whenever you read the Bible or attend a class, the Holy Spirit is there teaching you. Whenever you are puzzled by the faith, the Holy Spirit is there guiding you. Whenever you get mad at God, the Holy Spirit is there bringing you back. That's what Christ promised. And that's what Christ delivered to the group on Pentecost Sunday. That's what Christ delivered to you when you decided for the life of faith.

Life can be difficult. While the problems of life can be very painful, it is in the process of meeting and solving problems that life has its meaning. Problems call forth our courage and wisdom. They strengthen our character and provide an avenue to glorify God. Our tendency is to want the feeling of closeness with God and the warmed heart like we want fast food. But without seeing to the future, it is only momentarily productive. In the long haul, the Holy Spirit keeps us on the path toward Jesus.

Seeking First Things First
May 21
Matthew 6:33

We are made human—thoroughly in this world; thoroughly enamored with the things of this world. We are also made with that flicker of the divine in us. Our humanness has a dependency on things. Our spark of the divine draws us to the beauty of the spiritual dimension. It comes down to what we want versus what we need. What we desire versus what is best for us. Jesus knew this double pull very, very well. It seems that as people become more prosperous, they begin to lose the fullness of their spiritual life. How can this be avoided?

Whatever you have to do, whatever you have to set aside, whatever it requires, seek first a relationship with God/Christ. Nothing else is more important. Next, seek Christ's body for support and accountability. We all need support. The church is the body of Christ in the world. There is no doubt that it is not perfect, but if all were to put each other first in this way, the church itself would be transformed as well. Finally, seek God's righteousness. That word sounds so pompous, so intellectual. But it is really so simple. It means to be right with God and to be right with one another. It means living a moral life. When we seek first things first, we are within God's will, and receive blessings with power. We are blessed.

The Common Good
May 22
1 Corinthians 12:4–13

The Holy Spirit gives the body of Christ—the Church—gifts for the common good. Specifically, each person who accepts Jesus as Savior receives the Holy Spirit and his gifts. These are such as knowledge, inspiration, and unity—all for the common good of God's people. Knowledge is light, which can grow throughout one's lifetime. There is a connection between the mind and the heart. The mind gives direction, the heart empowers with ardent energy. Either without the other is incomplete faith. We all require the energy of each other to keep going in this world. It is so easy to become involved in the tasks of living, to get preoccupied and forget the source of it all: the Holy Spirit. The world can get us down; it is the gift of inspiration through others that brings us back together. God's people are called to share joy in their faith, caring for one another and being willing to reach out and draw others into that joy.

Unity is the cement of the body to hold us together in serving the world. Paul uses the example of the body. Each individual part has its own job to do, but without the support of one another, the entire body fails to operate. Jesus cared for us before we even knew him. It is our task to embody Christian caring and service for the common good.

The End Is the Beginning

May 23
Philippians 1:3–21

There are many events in life that appear to be endings but are truly beginnings. The most obvious is graduation, or commencement. One is finished with twelve years of formal education, yet it is just the first step toward adulthood. For many, it means further training; for all, it means a new way of life. A much more difficult perspective is the recognition of tragedy as a beginning. How can one say that losing one's job, home, family, or health is a beginning? Regardless of what humans may think marks the finale for them, it may be turned into a beginning in the hands of God. At the intersection of humans and God, the difference is that humans are always beginning and ending, while God is *the* beginning and *the* end. "I am the Alpha and the Omega, says the Lord God, who is and who was and who is to come, the Almighty" (Revelation 1:8).

God gives completeness to our view. He does so by taking us beyond ourselves. When I am limited to only my own resources, I find them alarmingly small. Even then, I realize that what little resources I have are not really mine, but were given me as a gift of God. Suddenly, I come to the realization that I am only truly myself when I am fully given to him who is the Beginning and the End. With this perspective, we can view life as not some insignificant number among millions, but as a participating agent in the whole plan of God. From the eyes of God, if we will let completely go and trust in him, the leap of faith into his hands is not long.

God has promised that our end is the beginning, and demonstrated that it is so in the cross and the resurrection. Fellowship with God in love is the root of all that is good in life. When we put ourselves totally in his hands, we can accept the promise that all things may be begun, continued, and ended in him.

The Inner Man
May 24
Ephesians 3:14–21

At the time of acceptance of Christ as your savior, God's Holy Spirit comes and fills you. Yet throughout our lives, more of the richness of God's love is revealed to us as we are able to understand it. This growth is not within our own power but in the power of the Holy Spirit. Through his presence, we learn more about God's grace, ourselves, and our relationship to others. God's grace is really the fulfillment of his love for us. One element of it is a unity of our minds and our emotions. He works within us to strengthen and guide us. We are drawn into a relationship with God partially through the love of others. God does not force us into relationship. It is a decision we make every day. Once we allow God into our inner selves, he grips our lives with an abundance of fullness that transforms life because we become grounded and rooted in love.

This transformation cannot help but spill out to others. Within the community of faith, we can revitalize one another without some of the barriers of selfishness and pride that are so much a part of our selves without God. The spirit of Christ in the inner self gives us breadth and length, height and depth that surpasses our ability to take it all in. God can work within us more abundantly than all we ask or think.

The Spirit of Truth
May 25
Acts 17:22–31

Persons cannot live for long without the truth. Put in the negative, lying can and will destroy relationships. Truth and trust and honesty are basic to an ordered life and an ordered society. In the dilemma of knowing what is the truth, we have been given the Spirit of Truth—the Holy Spirit. In our normal dealings with the world, one way to find the truth is to look at the spirit of the action. Nothing is more complex than human relationships. We come to each contact with preconceived notions of feelings, ideas, and hopes.

The promises of the Bible can help sort out some of the confusion. First, Jesus promises us that we are never alone. He will never forsake us; we have become children of God. To feel abandoned, cast out, or left out is terrifying. The Spirit of Truth tells us that we are cherished, we are cared about. God is never far away.

It is easy to get caught up in relationships and things that creep in and take priority before God. They become "little g gods." It is important to make a living, to have friends, and interests and hobbies. However, without priority of worshiping the one true God, these things are empty and false.

Priority number one is to worship the true God. It is to love the Lord our God with all our minds, hearts, souls, and bodies … and our neighbors too. Worshiping the Spirit of Truth before all else will make us better; it will keep us free.

The World We Cocreate

May 26
Matthew 16:24–27

We have a lot to do with creating the climate of the world around us. This includes the people we come into contact with regularly, those with whom we work, our home and our family. We can make an impact on that climate, be it positive or negative. Just by our own optimism, we can create positive climates, but when we invite the Lord of life to be our constant companion, then we have a champion on our side. The words of Jesus sometimes seem like moral or ethical values, but in reality, they are truths of what actually exists. For example, we think we can save our lives by keeping them for ourselves; Christ tells us we have to move through the difficult areas to find the deeper right that inspires us. We want to create a climate of optimism and hope, but we often fall short of the mark in doing so.

Recognizing and accepting these truths requires a good understanding of ourselves. If we are unwilling to face the truth, and instead prefer to live in the shadows of our fears, anxieties, and insecurities, then we often unwittingly project hurt onto others. In fact, if we never examine the roots of unwanted outcomes, we'll never know ourselves, and it will be hard to empower anyone, including ourselves. That's not the way God wants it! That's not the way we want it! What we want is to cocreate a world with a little joy and a little cooperation in it. When we know ourselves, the Lord guides our hands in the shaping of the clay of our lives and those around us.

The final aspect is to look at cocreation. This means we have to acknowledge that we simply can't do it ourselves. It is easy to become a functional atheist—to function without God. To try to function as our own god. Thankfully, God desires to work through you and I. He does not need our help; he wants to direct our actions to become conduits for his ways. God always works toward the light, away from the darkness. So when it seems like things just aren't working out the way you'd like, try leaning into the truths of Jesus—the fruits of the spirit: love, joy, peace, patience, kindness, goodness, faithfulness, gentleness, and self-control.

Unless I See
May 27
John 20:25–30

The disciples of Jesus apparently found it easy enough to pick up and follow Jesus. Yet they had no idea what was ahead. It is possible to get a central idea straight, to truly believe in it, to be committed to it, and then to pursue it with all your might. It is possible—not easy—but possible. Once we "see" with our inner understanding and are truly captured by that inner insight, things are different. That is what makes dedication possible.

Thomas, of our passage today, came to that kind of insight, but it wasn't easy for him. We can relate to Thomas. He was not there when the risen Lord appeared to the disciples the first time, and he said, "Unless I see for myself … I will not believe" (John 20:25). That is something to which we can relate. We want proof! Of course, Jesus did come to him and let him see—and touch—his risen body. Then Jesus said, "Blessed are those who have not seen and yet believe" (John 20:29).

The thing is, the Christian faith is not based on fantasy and dreamland. The Christian faith is based on the eyewitness accounts of hard-headed realists like Thomas. To this day, the most impressive realities to a prove-it-to-me people are what happened to those common, everyday people who were the disciples. At one point, they were a hapless band, huddled despondently behind locked doors. Then, the next thing we know, they have a power that is nothing less than amazing. With no political position, no financial backing, no organizational wizardry, these common men transformed the known world. At some point, every one of those disciples would have said with Thomas, "Unless I see." The point is, they did see, and left us an eyewitness account of what happens when you truly see the amazing truth behind the risen Christ.

Weeds or Fruit?
May 28
1 Corinthians 3:1–23

I grew up on a farm. Despite the worn-out stories about city slickers and country hicks, I think it was a great place to grow up. It is also a great place to learn some spiritual lessons. As the farmer is concerned for the first fruit of the soil, so is the family concerned for the first fruit of the soul. Not only we but our whole society is dependent on the fruit both of the soil and of the soul. As the soil represents life, so the soul represents spiritual life.

First, about weeds. Weeds are a fact of life. It's almost mysterious how they get there. Like the weeds that get into lives, they come in stealthily, little by little, hardly noticed at first. In fact, often weeds start out looking like a plant. They are pesky, too, aren't they? Just when you go to pull them, the little seed pods pop open, kicking the even smaller seeds all over. You can just see hundreds of those weeds attaining immortality! In the soul, the weeds of human conduct and personal relationships enter in just as determined a manner. Day after day, we battle against weeds like the pull between wants and needs. Our children waver between the good fruit of respect and attention and the weeds of disrespect and sticking out their tongues. Selfishness, unwillingness to help, neglect, argumentativeness, and self-centeredness are weeds. The trouble with weeds is that they destroy the productivity of the fruit.

Now, about the fruit. How do we go about obtaining good fruit? First is the method demonstrated by Jesus when he cleared the temple of the money changers, saying, "Take these things away!" So, we must start by pulling the weeds when we find them. We must start with ourselves in the form of self-discipline. The next way is suggested by Paul, "Whatever is true, whatever is honorable, whatever is just, whatever is lovely, whatever is gracious, if there is any excellence, if there is anything worthy of praise, think on these things" (Philippians 4:8–9). Choose your friends wisely, fill your life with worthwhile things, say thank you, and build each other up in love. This is fruit. Finally, recognize that it is God that gives growth to the fruit. Start with a grateful heart, a faithful joy, and worship God, and you will give root to wholesome fruit.

Well, I'll Be

May 29
Matthew 3:13–17, 4:23–5:2

The vision of the disciples of Jesus was as limited as that of little children. They had little previous knowledge on which to base their beliefs. It was only with growing awareness that they came to any accurate conclusion concerning who Jesus was. The gospels speak with such surety because they were written like memoirs—after a perspective had been gained. Much can be learned through the eyes of the disciples. Their relationship with Jesus was one of constant awe and further understanding. One of the early revelations was that faith growth is characterized by striving for godliness. If one were to follow the beatitudes with earnest and honest effort at creating solutions and not being the problem, one would truly be blessed in this life and the life to come. What would happen if we were to consciously listen to the inner voice and ask, "What, Father, do you desire said? What, Father, do you desire done?"

Another area of awakening understanding was the recognition that there is a "higher law." This was expressed by Jesus's admonitions to observe the spirit of the law, not just the letter of the law. Some examples are to "turn the other cheek," and to "go the extra mile," and to "love our enemies." Our most real and lasting treasure is eternal. As Christian people, we want God to be seated beside us. And he can be. He came to us in Jesus. And Jesus lives. He is here now. He places a hand on a weary shoulder, he touches a heavy heart, and he lifts to joy the response of our souls. God is seeking to give us the beatitude of striving, to inspire us to the higher law, and to place within us eternal treasure.

Which Way?
May 30
John 14:1–14

Which one of us can get along our way without the guidance of another? Everyone who goes ahead of us breaks the trail. What we find ahead is usually found by going just a few steps farther than those before us. How does Jesus guide us? We can't see him. We can't talk with him like we can talk with one another. He may be right beside us, but you can't put your arm on his shoulder like you can your friend when you're hiking along a trail.

Jesus guides us by leading us along the way. He has already been where we are going. The Christian faith is truly unique. We believe far more than that some well-meaning person has had some revealing vision. We believe that Jesus Christ is the Word made flesh, embodied. We are receiving the very work of God. Jesus was the true representation of God on earth; in knowing him, we can know God.

Jesus assures us that if we ask something in his name, in agreement with his spirit, he will do it. How do we know if it is in agreement with Jesus? We must listen to him, look at him, and follow him. This means knowing his words. Jesus expects us to remember what he has said and to apply it to our current situation. He gave us the brains, a supportive community of fellow believers, and prayer. He expects us to put that to effective and productive use.

Memories
May 31
Isaiah 2:2–5

Few things are as precious as good memories. Even bad memories are enjoyable after the sting is gone, particularly if we are somehow the one who emerges victorious in the outcome. We Christian people cherish memories. We venerate bravery and godliness and the pioneering spirit. History is important because in the very realm of history, God actually took the form of one of us and came to dwell among us. What an amazing thing! This is one belief of history that changes the direction of our lives into worthy pursuits and pure interests. Memorial Day is not specifically a Christian holiday, and yet without Christ, death is without hope. Memorial Day is really a prayer for peace.

One very effective avenue to express a desire for peace is in overseas mission. Mission lifts others of humankind into self-dependence, independence, and freedom. World Concern trains teachers, improves health systems and schools, and assists people to learn trades that allow them to support themselves and their families.

Memories are useless unless they serve to teach us today for our tomorrows. We must learn to live together in harmony. We are now becoming what we will someday be. We have a tendency to try to live life on our own power. Acknowledging a greater power above and beyond ourselves allows us to achieve far greater goals. With God's strength, all things are possible. Memorial Day is a worthy day, reminding us that it is a prayer for peace, that memories serve tomorrow, and that today's actions become tomorrow's memories. May we come to walk in godly paths forevermore.

Am I Pleasing God?

June 1
Galatians 1:1–10

There is only one gospel. When we accept the gospel that Jesus died for our sins to make us righteous before God, we want to please God. In fact he is the only one that is important to please. Now that does not mean we will be perfect, but as long as we are working toward living by faith, by trust, and by grace—Jesus has got us covered. We can never earn grace; we simply have to accept it as a gift. We live with mistakes, and live by grace.

What does it look like to please God? First, turn your life over to God. Allow him to weigh in on decisions, to direct and guide your life. He knows what will lead you to becoming the best person you can be. Next, it is important to participate in the body of Christ. Partly it is important to give in to what you believe, but mostly it is because we need others around us to help us to stay on track. The third area is winning persons to Jesus Christ. The gospel *is* the good news. It is a gift. It is the only thing that makes life on this earth worth living. How could you keep that to yourself? This does not mean you have to become a preacher on the street corner. It means to reach out to those around you. We touch so many lives in each day on this earth. Most of the time, it is inconsequential. However, when you interact with another human being, you are the picture of Christ. Responding with that filter in mind to those around us could change the world.

Either/Or
June 2
Acts 2:1–21

The disciples had been living in fear huddled behind locked doors. Jesus, the resurrected Lord, came to them and said three things. "Peace be with you." "I send you." He breathed on them and said, "Receive the Holy Spirit." From then on, the disciples took amazing courage and began to risk their lives to witness boldly and openly about what God has done for his people. It was the birthday of the church. It was the moment when the disciples caught the new vision of God. Either a body of God's people lives with that vision, daily implementing it, or, they huddle inside the walls of their buildings, calling that the church, and never going forth.

The Holy Spirit empowers, guides, remembers, and teaches. But for those not in the household of faith, the Holy Spirit of Jesus needs embodiment. We become the visible embodiment of the Word of God. We become the mouth of Jesus, sharing that eternal word that he gave. We become the feet of Jesus, carrying that eternal word everywhere. We become the hands of Jesus, caring, healing, tending, helping, building. Furthermore, we need Jesus as our empowerment, or we drift from our birthright—we wander from our charter. Jesus is the model for our obedience to God. Christ is God's instrument of action; the church is Christ's instrument of action, and we are the church's instrument of action. We must represent, as nearly as possible, the ultimate power. Our source of meaning must be fidelity to the God of creation.

Either we faithfully carry God's message by God's grace or that word of loving, forgiving empowerment languishes.

Encouragement for Battered Christians

June 3
Philippians 3:1–16

Christians have been "battered" in the last several decades. It is hard to know exactly what has been the cause. The attack has been subtle, insidious. People seem to think the church is irrelevant, outdated, opinionated. There are too many other activities vying for our attention. Sundays have become "me" time, instead of God's time. Churches are declining in membership and striving to regain a place of relevance in society.

One challenge is that a life of faith goes against the status quo. Jesus himself warned the disciples that they would be hated in the world because they were not of the world. Faith requires a person to live in the world but not to be swallowed up in the values of the world. There is an element of discomfort for many people when they are faced with the struggle of the poor, the fight for justice, caring for those who are outsiders in society. We want to be comfortable, safe.

The vast majority of people come to believe in Christ due to the influence of another person. It is not the church that draws them in; it is a friend that invites them in. As individuals, we are called to reach out to those who don't yet know the Lord of life and truth and wholeness. We are not only to feed the hungry but to help them learn to feed themselves. There are many who don't want any part of this type of outreach, and there are many who are disparaging of the cause. Yet these are the things that are truly worthy of giving our lives for. Let us "hold true to what we have attained" (Philippians 3:16).

Father, Son, and Holy Spirit
June 4
Matthew 28:1–20

How can it be that we can say God is one and yet maintain he is three persons? First, let us look through the eyes of the apostles. They knew the God of the Old Testament through their study. Their very lives were based on this knowledge. Every action they took was rooted in this knowledge. Yet when they came to know Christ, everything changed. The apostles recognized that they had not truly known God before Christ. In living with Christ and seeing his nature, they gained insight they had never had before. In fact, Christ himself said, "No one can come to the Father but through Me" (John 14:6). Further, the apostles experienced the presence of the Holy Spirit after Christ's death and resurrection. The Holy Spirit brought them power and confidence they had not known before. The Holy Spirit was acting within them. The experience of God had taken a threefold viewpoint. The work of Christ here on earth was and is the work of God, and the Holy Spirit was and is an expression of God's immediate and continuing activity now.

Only through the reality of faith may we truly understand. God, the eternal Father, Creator and Judge in whom all order, the very being of the world, the moral law, and all truth are grounded. The Son, the God who humbles himself in love for his children speaking at definite times in history—both the messenger and the message. Finally, the Holy Spirit, the sacred presence within ourselves binding us to him and to our fellow humans with cords of love, opening our eyes to the evidences of God and reminding us of his revealing acts in history. God cared for us so much that he gave his only Son for us and continues to guide and lead and help us in our daily lives. God came to us in terms we can understand and use. He is close and wants our fellowship in rightness. God: the Father, Son, and Holy Spirit—blessed Trinity.

Get Out of the Rat Race

June 5
2 Corinthians 12:9

Life sometimes feels like a rat race: like chasing after the wind with no real purpose. When we feel like that, it is a clue that we have wandered away from the source of life. It seems like it is all too often that we have the sense of working our very hardest and feeling like we haven't made a dent. When we go to bed realizing that there were too many things left undone and dangling. When it feels like if we gave it all, it still wouldn't be enough.

When those feelings begin to take over, it is a clue that something is missing. One possibility is that the prayer life has been neglected. This means we are trying to do it ourselves, forgetting to rely on the power of the Lord. Prayer brings intimacy with God, opening us up to his power and strength and guidance in the day-to-day things. It changes all kinds of things.

Other possibilities are that we have lost connection to the community of faith, where we can rely on each other like family. And, likely, we have wandered away from the Word. When the focus becomes set on the things immediately around us, we forget to look out for other perspectives. God has given us his Word to do just that—to remind us that the point of life is larger than we are. It is the hope that he gives us in prayer, support, and the Word.

God and a Fishing Rod

June 6
John 21:1–14

The biggest fish story in the world is in the Bible. It involved a fellow who wanted to get away from it all. Then he got so carried away with it that he got swallowed up in his subject! It is surprising how many fish stories there are in the Bible; the first three disciples were fishermen. The truth is that God is everywhere. Jonah found out. He was headed the opposite direction as fast as he could go. When he woke up, they tossed him overboard! Peter found out—when the cock crowed for the third time. Paul discovered it when he was struck blind on the road to Damascus. Each of us has our own experience. This truth spells out that no deed done or contemplated is ever finally hidden. God is in our deepest despairs as well as our greatest victories. To make God a significant part of our lives is to live coloser to his creation and more surely toward eternity.

Wherever we are, as Christians, we are ambassadors of Christ. As ambassadors, we must witness to that fact. The ways of doing this are myriad: being a good citizen wherever you are, telling others about Christ where the opportunity exists, inviting others to join you in prayer and worship. Gathering together is vital to our faith. While God is everywhere, we need the presence of other Christians to refuel each other. It can be lonely out there! God sent his Son to tell us that he longed for us to be reconciled to him again, to become sons and daughters by adoption, to become fishers of men in partnership with him. His Son told us that such a partnership was rich and abundant, significant and meaningful, rewarding and precious. God has the fishing rod. Have you been caught?

Holy Expectations
June 7
Acts 2:1–12

We all have expectations constantly. Many are appropriate; some are off target. When expectations are not met, disappointment follows. Human expectations often fall into this category. In fact, unmet expectations are the basis of many of our troubles at work, home, and in relationships.

Holy expectations are something else. We can truly count on them to be fulfilled. God always lives up to his promises. After Jesus's death and resurrection, he told the disciples to wait in Jerusalem for the "gift my Father promised" (Acts 1:4). They followed this instruction, and joined together in the upper room, praying. This is where they were on the day of Pentecost. Now Pentecost was one of the three annual festivals of Judaism, so Jerusalem was alive with people.

We can hardly envision what came upon them on that day. There was a violent wind, and they were touched with tongues of fire. They were filled with the Holy Spirit, never to be the same.

From that time, they spoke with boldness, empowered by the Holy Spirit.

What is your expectation of the power of the Holy Spirit? As Christians, we are told that the Holy Spirit fills us from the time of the acceptance of Jesus Christ into our lives. Why, then, do we struggle to feel the power described at Pentecost? Perhaps the problem lies in these expectations. The disciple expected to be changed—transformed—as we should also. Once we are willing to receive this transformation, God will not disappoint us. The Holy Spirit will enable us to do the work God has laid out for us. Whether it is teaching, ministering, caring for others, we do not always know. With expectancy, we seek the guidance of the Holy Spirit within us, and the way will become clear.

Holy Wind
June 8
Acts 2:2

Pentecost is celebration of the day that the Holy Spirit descended on the new Christians. It occurred on the fiftieth day after the resurrection of Jesus Christ. On that day, a rush of wind came through the group of Christians and transformed them from a raggedy band of misfits into a true force to be reckoned with. On that day, they stopped being afraid and began to witness boldly about the resurrection of Christ and what God was doing for the world and in their individual lives. The experience could not be captured in words, but the empowering of God's Holy Spirit can be experienced today. Each of us can have our own experience with the Holy Wind.

The Holy Spirit has real power to drive our lives. When we are in the Holy Spirit there is awakened in us a freshening sense of caring and compassion. It is only by growing in God's grace that we get pleasure out of helping others to prosper. With the Holy Spirit, our human gifts can be directed, channeled, focused. When we let God direct our lives, we are in the Holy Spirit of God. The primary power of Christianity is the unique ability to win others to Christ. That means giving our friends the chance to save their lives—for Christ, for life, and for eternity!

Salvation is opening our lives to the wind of the Spirit that clears us out and lets us breath again.

I Love Jesus, But ...
June 9
John 17:20–26

A comment that is heard all too frequently is, "I love Jesus but not the church." Jesus is appealing; he can truly change your life. After all, he is everywhere, even in our hearts. Why go to church? Isn't the church filled with stuffy people, hypocrites, and crazies? The church is just another big building, an institution constantly asking for time and money. To many, it is a place of control and heavy expectations. Besides, the church is man-made.

In reality, one of the core messages of Jesus was to go out into the world and share about his ministry—his intervention into the brokenness of the world. The source of the church is the creative love and reconciling power of God in Christ.

Many also believe that God, the church, will ask them to do more than they can do. They are afraid that they simply aren't good enough. Indeed, what God calls every baptized Christian to do is demanding. It is always greater than we can accomplish, but he calls us only to labor alongside, and he will give us strength for each day and each moment.

Finally, the church is full of hypocrites and needy people. Just like each and every one of us. The church is to be the body of Christ. It is to hold one another accountable and to hold one another together in faith. Without the body of Christ, any one person can easily be swept away by the demands and promises of the world. Together, we can serve both God and one another—just as Jesus commanded us to do. If we love Jesus, we also love his body—the church.

Invitation to Inspiration

June 10
Galatians 5:22–6:12

I have come to feel that our world needs not so much guns and bristling backs and hot tempers, as an inspiration to higher living in God's name and for his sake. Such inspirations are all around us. In fact, those about us inspire us to do something about ourselves. Usually good conditions inspire us to higher goals; even poor conditions can—if used rightly—inspire us to better ourselves. This is most likely if we will look with eyes that see and think with hearts that feel. Working together with God, we are able to help broken homes to be united, help youths channel their energies into constructive paths, help tortured minds find peace, and help men and women gripped by enslaving and degrading habits find rescue and self-respect. Seeing such possibilities inspires us to come to life.

As we recognize the gracious power of our God, we are inspired to seek his power. It is easier to seek his power than it is to find it. Wherein does God's power lie? And how may we appropriate it? God has chosen to work through humans in the power of love. Paul speaks of the godlike love that shines forth in gracious power after which we seek in all its fullness in the life of Jesus Christ. "Love bears all things, believes all things, hopes all things, endures all things." (1 Corinthians 13:7, RSV). If we were to read this thirteenth chapter of 1 Corinthians thoughtfully and prayerfully on a regular basis, it would change the tenor of our days and ultimately transform each of us. This is the kind of thing that can inspire us to see the gracious power of our God and allow him to act through us in all his majesty and power.

I Was There
June 11
1 John 1:1–2:5

There aren't many words filled with more suspense and portent than, "I was there ... I can tell you what happened!" Some of the greatest stories of literature are simply someone telling what had happened in some unusual or tragic event, some struggle for survival. It is this quality of the eyewitness that has made the letter of 1 John so appealing. Here was one who lived with and walked with Jesus himself. He was with him from the beginning of his ministry, he saw the feeding of the five thousand, he saw healings, he heard the Sermon on the Mount. John was one of the inner-circle of disciples, it was to John's care that Jesus commended his mother. He preached, he taught, he lived the new faith through days of doubt and rejection, persecution, and heresy. He wrote the letters of John as an elderly man.

John knew that Jesus was real. He knew that Jesus embodied God himself. God sent Jesus. God came in Jesus, his Son. To say otherwise is to miss how God loved us and loves us so much that he reaches out to us even in our separation. Furthermore, he saw him when he rose from death, before he ascended to God. This says something to us today. If Jesus really is real, then he is the test of reality. We get fooled a lot in this world. Jesus is the real bread, the real vine—to Jesus belongs the real judgment. John was telling us: check realness by Jesus. If it doesn't stack with him as a guide, it won't stack.

Everyday relationships provide the test of truth. If our relationships don't build one another up but tear one another down, then they are false ways. The test for John is a test we can use ourselves: "If any one says, 'I love God,' and hates his brother, he is a liar; for he who does not love his brother whom he has seen, cannot love God whom he has not seen" (1 John 4:20). When we are truly baptized by the spirit, we become one of those who gives instead of asking what he can get. John the Beloved, who was there, would have us love one another so we can know God's love.

Kid Stuff

June 12
Matthew 18:1–14

There are innumerable reasons people give for not wanting to attend church. They are too busy, too tired, too sophisticated. Some even say it is "kid stuff." When it comes to children, there's no question about God. God just *is*. A child is wide-eyed, absolutely certain of the existence of God. Jesus said, "Unless you become like little children, you will never enter the Kingdom of heaven" (Matthew 18:3).

We should receive God like a child. The capacity of children for wonder, receptiveness, and innocence is what Jesus saw. In the world, we seek greatness through power, materialism, knowledge. Yet children seek none of these things. A child lives in constant wonder, making toys out of trash and finding life a high romance. We, too, can become trusting once more. Faith can become an instinct again. We can receive forgiveness and depend entirely on a trust in God. We can have a new beginning.

When we experience that openness to the gifts of God, we are able to receive blessings. When the focus is on what we can get out of a situation, this gift is lost. The greatest gift given to children by Jesus was that of blessing them. He didn't offer coins or candy; he laid his hands on them and blessed them. Each of us has that power in us. Whenever we come alongside another human and pray with interest and concern, we share that gift. You don't have to be ordained; you just need to love the Lord!

Let Us Be Enthusiastic

June 13
Ephesians 1:3–23

The species Humanus Americanus is a breed of contrasts. We make more money now, in America, than humankind has ever made for so many people. Yet it feels like we just scrape by. Our youths are taller, straighter, yet we are told we are not physically fit. We're supposedly healthy, yet we take handfuls of vitamins anyway. We've never had it so good, yet somehow many are vaguely discontent. There is a reasonable cure. It is found in personal renewal in Christ. True enthusiasm is contagious.

One element of true enthusiasm is inspiration. Enthusiastic people are in demand everywhere. It is needed throughout society—in our church, in our homes, in our schools, in our workplaces. To be inspired is to be given new life. The original translation was "breath of God." Inspiration brings new dimension to our lives, new possibilities to our days.

Another element of enthusiasm is to be interested. Asking questions about details always brings new light to a situation or relationship. Take the next step to find out the reason for a decision; it is bound to pique your interest. At that point, it is time to become more involved. This can feel a bit scary, but with enthusiasm, there is great reward. Consider Christ. He became so involved with his disciples that he washed their feet. Now that's an act of true enthusiasm. There is infinite power in humble, inspired action.

Live by the Spirit
June 14
Isaiah 6:1–8

If one were to ask what the most important aspect of successful living was, you would get many answers. There are answers that run all the way from simple single words like money or love or even God's grace, to slogans, to statements running for entire volumes. One answer is to live by the Spirit of Christ. This is a valid principle because it provides both flexibility and firmness. Living in the Spirit of Christ is both personal and congregational. Individually, one can follow private disciplines like prayer, study, and meditation. The congregational aspect provides accountability and group formats for the disciplines. Under circumstances of constant change, what serves us best are principles, a source of supreme power, and a trustworthy guide by which to live.

In areas of Christian suppression, people are not permitted to gather, sing hymns, or own Bibles. Yet somehow, the faith grows under such circumstances. Christians recall scripture from memory, snatches of hymns from childhood, and worship secretly in homes. The Spirit of faith grows strong under persecution. Somehow, it allows people to focus on what really matters. It helps to weed out the physical evidences of power and influence.

Isaiah recognized his unworthiness when he saw the vision of the Lord in the throne-room of heaven. God purified Isaiah with a coal from the altar and gave him forgiveness and grace. Through that grace, Isaiah was then able to say, "Here am I. Send me" (Isaiah 6:8). That purifying grace is available to each and every one of us through the Spirit of Christ. Living by the Spirit of Christ means living by forgiving grace, godly hope, and the Word.

Minting a Likeness
June 15
2 Corinthians 13:14

Most coins have a face or image minted on them. We know that in Jesus's day, the image of Caesar was on the coins. This process of making this image on a coin is called minting. In the Sermon on the Mount, Jesus stated that since Caesar's image was on the coins, they belonged to Caesar. As humans, we carry the image of God, as we belong to him. When a person makes a decision to follow Christ as savior, a process begins to conform that person to the likeness of Christ. The disciples didn't come to Jesus already made in his likeness. It was a long process. We know from the stories about them that they were doubtful, prideful, and hotheaded. We do not start out looking much like Christ either. Actually, to the Christian, it is a relief to see the flaws and the worldliness of the disciples.

In the letter to the Corinthians, Paul was teaching them how to become more like Christ. He used words like grace, love, and fellowship. These are the things that draw us to Christ. Our deepest, most heartfelt need is for grace and love and fellowship. We would like to be able to earn our way into the kingdom of heaven, but it doesn't work that way. This comes only as a gift, freely given and freely received. One thing we can do to enhance the process of becoming more like Christ is to ask for eyes to see and ears to hear the signs, wonders, and mighty works of God. The wonders of God are all around us, but it is so easy to get caught up in the wonders of the world, like money, popularity, bigger and better homes and cars. It is critical for each of us to carefully examine our actions to see if we are moving in the direction of becoming more like Christ. This means loving God with all our hearts, minds, and strength. This means giving of our time, money, and service. As we rise to that which God is calling us, we will find that we are being minted in Christ's likeness.

Planting, Always Planting
June 16
Mark 4:26–34

The parable of the mustard seed is the kind of wisdom nugget that permits any of us to ponder and apply the truth: "Be mindful of the power of tiny beginnings." It is a truism of life that most of us underrate ourselves. Most of us think—at least some of the time—that our little voice, our little one vote, our opinion, our presence, our contribution doesn't amount to much. In response to that very prevalent human condition, Jesus does not berate or deny it. He simply says, "Look at this little mustard seed. Not of much account. Yet it becomes large enough for birds to nest in!"

Perhaps your tiny beginning is the wisp of a desire that there be fewer fights and more love in your family. Perhaps someone has a problem at work and needs a way to let God make an appeal through us. Whatever our circumstance, it is God's gift to remind us of the mustard seed, and to be aware of the power of tiny beginnings.

There are several ways to maximize our opportunities. First there is careful preparation. When sowing a seed of a new idea, it is critical to have prepared the soil and to plant it properly. Next comes waiting in faith. This is not idle waiting but careful, subtle attention to the details of the growth environment. In our personal lives of faith, the time of waiting can be bolstered by fellowship with others in the same position. Finally comes the harvest. That is the hope, and it is a time of gratitude when it arrives. To grow in the faith calls for all these things. They are so simple, so obvious, yet what wonderful gifts. If our own minds and hearts were well cultivated to receive God's good truth, the harvest is harmony and love and joy in our relationships. So let us be planting, always planting. What we are about to be, we are now becoming.

Right Roots
June 17
Ephesians 3:14–21

Each of us has our own experience with the soil, whether our reality is a farmland or a window box, whether it is a heritage or a potted plant. It is fundamental to our faith to be strengthened in our inner selves, to really know Christ's love, and to be rooted and grounded in that love. The emphasis by Paul is knowing Christ's love in such a way that we will be filled with the perfect fullness of God. Isn't this just what we need in this world? Whether you suffer loneliness, confusion, business challenges, or broken relationships, what could be more powerful than to be rooted and grounded in love? Unless there is a deep rooting and grounding in the love of Christ, so much seems to make so little sense. All of us have a need to catch a new sense of the sheer vastness of God's love.

It is broad. No-one is excluded. The love of Christ includes every person of every kind, every age, in every world. There is no exclusion for sin, wealth, power, or suffering. It even includes those who don't know they stand in need of the means of God's love, and those who willfully and knowingly oppose that love. The love of God includes the obedient as well as the disobedient.

It is long. He will go to any length to win me over, to convince me of the wholeness of committing myself to him. In fact, he did. He suffered a torturous death, not so much to prove his love, but in the process of doing it. His love never, ever runs out. Its height is beyond our imagination. We will only know the true height after seeing it from the other side, in heaven.

It is deep. It is deeply knowing and understanding. It is the kind of love that has a master plan for our lives that will make those lives come out well. As the architect of our lives, only he knows how it all fits together. As we work toward knowing the fullness of God's love, we experience it and give it out as we know it. Those are the right roots. Roots that are deeply grounded in Christ's love, roots that bear good fruit, and of which we will never have to be ashamed.

Sometime But Not Now!
June 18
2 Corinthians 5:17–6:13

There is no question that the human species has a tendency to procrastinate. Procrastination is the enemy of the faith whether one has or has not decided for Christ. The question is why do we do it? Fear is the basic reason. We put off what we are afraid of. We delay what we don't know about. The consequences of putting off decisions on important things are something we would rather not look at. Now is the time to decide to settle your eternal destiny. It is entirely possible that tomorrow may never come for you. Now is the acceptable time. Now is the day of salvation.

If you have already made the decision to be a faithful believer, the question is about the fruits you bear. It is not about what you get out of your faith, but what you are giving to God and his people. "We are ambassadors for Christ, God making his appeal through us" (2 Corinthians 5:20). It is incredible! God has chosen to be in partnership with us, using us, making his appeal through us! Yet it does no good to decide for Christ if we don't do anything about it. There is a fear that we don't know what to say, to risk revealing our faith. What are we waiting for? Too many of us are almost Christians. We want what is right and good. We just don't want to grow into doing anything about it. Now is the acceptable time. Now is the day of salvation. It is up to us.

So You Have It Tough, Huh?

June 19
2 Corinthians 4:7–5:1

Sometimes, life is tough. There are hard thing to bear—pain and losses and death and injustice and unfairness. We can feel deeply alone, lonely and fearful. Those are real feelings by real people who are looking for help. To a lesser degree, all of us need our share of assurance. What can we do? There are biblical principles that can guide us in meeting those tough times. St. Paul was realistic. He did not deny his pain, but he had something more. He knew that though we are human, God can sustain us. So we do not lose heart; though our outer nature is wasting away, our inner nature is being renewed every day.

As Christians, we know something others do not know. We know that the kingdom is within and lasts forever. Eternal life—oneness with God—starts right now and outlasts everything, anything! Given this, we are called to be optimistic. The Christian faith is basically optimistic, basically world affirming, basically nurturing. Jesus Christ was God's proclamation that ultimately, life is victorious. We get into this life not by denying our hurts and difficulties, but by affirming our daily spiritual renewal. That means we release our burdens to the Lord of all life and turn our attention, instead, to what we can do as evidence of our spiritual renewal.

You may have it rough. It is important to be sensitive to that. You may very well be in deep spiritual or emotional pain. There may seem to be no good solution, no reasonable way out. But the good news today is: "We do not lose heart … we are being renewed in our inner being every day" (2 Corinthians 4:16). God is very much with us.

Synergistic Living
June 20
Romans 8:12–17

Synergistic is a bit fancy, but it truly expresses the message for today. It means working together, cooperating. Synergism is the joint actions of agents, or processes, which when put together increase each other's effectiveness. The body of Christ is a perfect model of this type of synergy. In order for a force for good to survive and be effective, cooperation is required. There is a common goal to live within God's will, and this common goal extends beyond the bounds of individual churches and denominations to the entire body of Christ throughout the world. Together, there is an energy that cannot occur individually.

Becoming involved in the body of Christ gives energy and meaning to each person. Involvement results in friendships, relationships, drawing others into the action to grow together. Another aspect of synergy involves the Holy Spirit. People need to respond to the Holy Spirit to experience the constant emergence of new life—regeneration. Synergistic living brings possibility and promise beyond ourselves. It will draw you into everlasting life.

The Growth of God
June 21
Ephesians 3:7–21

Many people are indifferent to the Christian religion because they have not been presented with a God adequate to the needs of a modern world, or themselves. Also, many sincere Christians hold an immature and small concept of God. How much time do you spend thinking about what you believe about God?

One way to begin to define our beliefs about God is to identify false gods. One such false god is our own conscience. The conscience can easily be perverted. Most likely, it echoes the taboos of childhood, with rules and restrictions that are no longer valid. In this way, a grown man may reject church simply because his conscience reminds him that he was unable to live up to the requirements of his parents when he was a child. At best, conscience keeps us rather negatively on the path of virtue, and if that is what we define as God, we are unlikely to be moved to worship, love, or serve such an inner, nagging voice. This view may also tend to lead one to see God as impersonal and distant.

A second false view of God is "God-in-a-box." This perception results from trying to force God into one's own ideas of him, and all else is wrong. Of course, one size does not fit all. We cannot control God by our little formula and prescribe his ways with our own set of words.

The God of the Bible is not only adequate, but strongly meets the need of humans in a swiftly moving time. The human mind cannot bring the true nature of God into focus. He is the Creator of the universe, the Primary Causer, the height of value, of truth, of beauty, and of goodness. Our clearest experience of God is God in Christ. Here, God slipped into the stream of history as a baby. Jesus allowed humans to see God expressing himself in human form. Further, one's concept of God must come from personal experience, not simply secondhand knowledge. When a person comes "face-to-face" with Jesus, a clear response is required—to believe or to deny. Let us seek this direct experience of Christ, which will lead us to find the fullness of God.

The Impossible Possibility

June 22
Matthew 28:1–20

What would you do if someone gave you $1 million? If you ask this of very young children, they might come up with seventy-five cents worth of that million dollars. As the children get a little older, the tab comes up to maybe several hundred thousand. By the time the teenager grasps this question, most of the million is spent in yachting, estates, travel, even investments. To the adult, however, while the question is a mental teaser, it is not a serious consideration. Mostly because we reckon it to be impossible to be given $1 million! Yet … it is still a possible impossibility.

In faith, we have a core impossible possibility. It is the doctrine of the Trinity: God the Father, God the Son, and God the Holy Spirit. God in three persons, blessed Trinity. This is not easy thinking. However, the triune God is the center of the Christian faith.

The disciples experienced the Trinity several times during their walk with Jesus. Most notably at Jesus's baptism, where God spoke; Jesus was there with them, and the Holy Spirit descended as a dove to confirm his identity. Even now, each of us has the Holy Spirit dwelling within us as the divine expression of Jesus's everlasting presence. The Trinity is not a mathematical equation—merely an attempt to fashion in human words the truth experienced by the soul. The words themselves are feeble, but the truth they are intended to convey is soul shaking.

When Christians affirm, "I believe in God the Father Almighty," have seen his impact on history as "Jesus Christ his only Son, our Lord," and feel the power of the Spirit in their lives and everyday decisions; this is no simple proposition. This is a faith in eternal truth—a conviction that this is the way our universe is made up. It is indeed impossible that God is "mindful of us," as the psalmist puts it, but he overcame that impossibility and became human flesh to dwell with us on earth. He rose from the dead to be the Holy Spirit within our hearts every day.

The Kingdom Is in Our Midst

June 23
Mark 1:14–39

Prior to the ministry of Jesus, the conception of god by all peoples was a god of demands. It was an idea of God as angry, wrathful, vengeful. God was a destroyer, one who had to be placated; to whom one makes sacrifices on an altar. The whole world, in fact, was a tragic place of the battle of humankind with the elements—both natural phenomenon such as weather, and the elemental spirits of evil.

With these things true, Jesus calmly and mildly says: "The Kingdom of God is at hand" (Mark 1:15). If this word from Christ is taken seriously, it means that the ultimate meaning of the universe is something in which we can have a part. It means the ultimate meaning of all time is something for us and not against us. To the pagan, life was the road to death, but Jesus came with the good news that we are on the way to life!

The fact that the kingdom of God is in our midst means two things. The kingdom is within us, and the kingdom is among us. For this to be true, we must have our hearts and minds right. We must understand that this good news means *truth, hope, peace, promise, immortality, salvation*. God's power is at work within us. However, the kingdom of God is not only within us, it is among us, next to us, and residing in each person we meet. This is where the work of the kingdom is to be done. Part of what Jesus brought with his ministry was the healing of the spirits and the bodies of the people. No act of faith can be complete without both belief and action.

The Power of Forgiveness

June 24
Galatians 2:11–21; Luke 7:36–8:3

A forgiver is not a pushover. Forgiveness breaks the circle of getting even. Anyone, then, who forgives is no pushover. Instead, they are the beginners of new possibilities. Forgiveness works a change, in both the person who is forgiving and the person who is forgiven. Hate and anger are great destroyers. Revenge often leads to an unhealthy obsession that ruins the life of the one pursuing justice. It becomes a terrible burden, choking out joy and the future. The stories of those who have been overtaken by the desire for revenge are endless. Sadly, they end as poorly for the one who has been driven to revenge as for the one in need of forgiveness.

Jesus told his disciples that they should forgive seventy times seven times. Of course, it really means infinitely, continuously, without end. Seven is the Hebrew number for perfection, symbolizing perfect unity in diversity. There are seven colors in the rainbow. Multiplication intensifies the meaning, so when Jesus said seventy times seven, he meant perfect forgiveness endlessly. Interestingly, the human response is to ask, "But will it work?" Has any other rule worked? Has anger, reprisal, or revenge worked? By forgiving, we are freed. Freed from anger, and resentment, and guilt.

Ultimately, forgiving is the condition that permits God to forgive us. God's forgiveness is limitless. He can forgive even us, and our response should be gratitude. The only one who cannot be forgiven is the one who is not forgiving. In the story of the woman who washed Jesus's feet with expensive perfume, he said, "I tell you, her sins, which are many, are forgiven, for she loved much; but whoever forgives little, loves little ... go in peace, your faith has saved you" (Luke 7:47–48).

Through or Around
June 25
2 Corinthians 5:17–20

God can go around us or through us. Whatever he wants to accomplish will happen. Being used by God is a gift he offers us; he doesn't need our help! God is constantly at work bringing about good things all around us—signs and wonders, miracles and new beginnings. God may be the only one left in the universe who still has a childlike excitement about his work. If you take a child and toss him up into the air and catch him, the first thing he is going to say is, "Do it again!" When was the last time you felt that way? Consider a field of daisies. Maybe God had so much fun creating the first one that he kept going, saying to himself, "Do it again, and again, and again!" He gets just as much pleasure with the millionth one as he has with the first one. God delights in what he does.

The funny thing is that when he calls us to his work, we are often unresponsive. There is always something else going on, another obligation or desire that gets in the way of accepting the challenge. Rather than catching the excitement that God has about the mission, we grumble about having one more thing to do. How much are we willing to pay to be responsive to God's calling? God can go around us, but he invites us to be used and useful in Christ's name. Those of us who know the Lord of all life, the higher God of all people, possess the greatest thing on earth and in heaven: the love of God and an offer of partnership.

Weeds

June 26
Matthew 13:24–30

Think of the dandelion. Such a pretty flower, and then that puffball! So artistic. One little parachute can go from one lawn almost across town—to yours. And each puffball has hundreds of those beautiful parachutes. Under each parachute is a seed. Fertile, vital, and vibrant, just waiting for a spot to touch down. Weeds are amazingly sturdy and prolific. There are weeds in life. The seed sown in today's parable was a particularly crafty weed. It looked just like wheat until harvest time. Jesus wished to show that the real world contains real problems and real threats. How many good people just need to ask to not be disturbed, to be left alone, to skip church and have a good weekend for the barriers to be let down and the winds of sinister power change lawns into weed patches or societies into chaos?

More specifically, there are weeds in the lives of each one of us. They cause us to want to fool ourselves into beauty or success or being better than someone else by putting something on rather than by changing something within. Thankfully, God is a God of second chances. In his infinite patience, he calls us, beckons us to recognize the difference between the wheat and the weeds. Then we need to root them out, with God's help, so that we may bear good fruit.

What If ...?

June 27
Revelation 22:6–7

We all love to speculate, to dream. Actually this tendency is behind the whole sweepstakes idea. It is why people line up to buy lottery tickets— sometimes even when they don't have enough money for groceries. When we think, "What if," we forget the hard reality in front of us. After all, everyone with a ticket is a winner until the drawing!

What if comes into play in faith as well. Part of faith is that Jesus is preparing a place for us and that he will return. Revelation is dedicated to preparing us for that reality. Prophecy points to it. Christ himself assured us that he would return. But, "What if...?"

What would Christ say of your life today? Are you living as you would want him to witness? Further, perhaps even easier to imagine, what if you were to die tomorrow? Most of us haven't even made a will. Yet death is as much of a certainty as life itself.

What if we were to serve him truly, *now*? This has all sorts of meaning today. It means letting him be in control, to having peace, to loving our neighbor, to seeking the right way, to taking on the mind of Christ. What do you need to change to live in this way? Christ guides us clearly in scripture. Despite this, it remains so difficult! Even in prayer, we ask that his kingdom come. Let us live this way: for his will to be done, to forgive as he forgives us, to seek his power and glory forever.

Wholly Prayer

June 28
Genesis 32:22–30

Prayer is something for all people, not just pious people. Jacob was a bit of a scoundrel, weaseling away his brother's birthright and inheritance. In this scene, he is transformed through prayer. He became a different person; he became a better person. This is important, because prayer is so vastly misunderstood and so often misused. It is easy to be like Jacob—to rely on our wits, then to resort to prayer only when we're in trouble. Those become prayers of desperation. Or, it is easy to think that we can simply plug in our prayer, and out comes our request like a vending machine.

Consider a revolutionary way of living. What if life became wholly prayer? Not simply holy prayer, but constant prayer. Prayer isn't something to be added to our other duties, making life more complex. God is the center of life, and all else is remodeled and integrated by it. Life with Christ in the center is peaceful, focused. It is not about us; it is about his influence on our lives minute by minute. Our deepest need is God. We become distracted by the economics of life, forgetting that God is truly at the helm. When we have done our part, we may lie down quietly in peace for, profoundly, all is well.

With God in the center of life, prayer is natural. He knows every detail of our lives, including our thoughts! Imagine talking with your best friend who knows all about you. There is nothing to hide, everything to gain by sorting things out. Things do not always turn out as we had hoped, but we can certainly know that God is in control.

Wide, Long, High, and Deep

June 29
Ephesians 2:19–20

As God's daughters and sons, we belong to God—body, heart, mind, and soul. Our bodies are God's temple. To do the work of God using the temple of our bodies, we need a continuing flow of God's love. That love from God is complete. It reaches every corner of our experience.

His love is wide enough to cover the breadth of our every experience and still reach out to the whole world, leaving no one out. The only condition is our own yes. The harvest of God's love cuts a wide swath. God's love is long. It begins when we begin, and continues for as long as we live. With the length of God's love, we have hope. His love will never run out. His love is very high. It encourages our celebration of life. If you ever feel shut out or isolated, remember that we can never be lost to God's love. Finally, God's love is deep. If you feel like you have fallen into the pit of despair where life can seem hopeless and discouraging, remember that no matter how deep the hole that we may at some time dig for ourselves, God's love is deeper.

Wider than the world, longer than life, higher than any barrier, and deeper than any hole, our God is awesome. He is our peace.

Patriotism with Judgment
June 30
Luke 20:20–26

A patriot is defined as a person who loves, supports, and defends his country. Patriotism involves an elemental love of the soil that bore us—and a desire to leave things better than we found them. This sometimes seems like a lost quality. It is a value that requires some encouragement. Unfortunately, as human beings with an inborn sin nature, it is not necessarily natural to do that—to leave something better than we found it. In the context of love, however, it becomes much more doable. Somehow, when love is involved, the desire is to improve. At its root, then, patriotism results in a desire to make things better.

Patriotism also involves a kinship to one's own people. One of the values of travel is a new appreciation of home. This is true both of distant travel— outside the country—and simple travel outside one's own personal borders. It is always heartwarming to run into someone that truly knows what you know! Someone who knows the landmarks, customs, and quirks with which we are familiar. We all experience the pleasure and bond of mutual experience, like hearing the voice of an American in a crowd of people speaking a different language.

The flip side of patriotism is judgment. It is so easy to generalize our own experience and think that everyone should be alike. The phrase, "When in Rome, do as the Romans do," comes to mind. It is easy to judge anyone that is different—in looks, customs, and behavior. How does one find and maintain the balance? It is found in the true root of our heritage— the common bond with our Creator. When we look at patriotism as a quality of God's kingdom, suddenly the landmarks, customs, and quirks become more universal. We are ultimately responsible for our actions before Almighty God himself. We are called to labor for the larger good. Patriotism is a great thing, not only in our country, but in the kingdom.

America, America
July 1
Matthew 11:24–30

America, America! God shed his grace on thee, and crown thy good with brotherhood, from sea to shining sea! So goes the vision we have of America. A vison of possibilities. A vision of dreams coming true. A vision of peace and brotherhood, liberty, justice, and freedom. The dispossessed of other nations seized their opportunity of free land, and with the sweat of their brows, they hewed out a place for themselves in America. It was a dream of the people to finally have a chance to have a space of their own, and a chance for something better for their children. It was a dream of generosity, of the common sense of the common people governing their own affairs.

Liberty is one of the great words of our Declaration of Independence, our Pledge of Allegiance, our Bill of Rights, and our whole frame of thought in America. Liberty is not unlimited. The concept is a great and truly inspiring thing. But the practice involves a deft balancing of liberty and conditions, exceptions, qualifications, and limitations. Freedom is the ability to do what we want to do. Yet no one is free. No one has ever been free, no-one will ever be free. Freedom must fall within the framework of safety and the smooth and efficient functioning of society. Freedom comes with responsibility.

The Christian concept of liberty centers on what brings fulfillment to life rather than on the rights of persons. For Christians to be free, we must become servants, we must humble ourselves, we must submit ourselves, we must commit ourselves, we must decide to be bound. Our highest happiness can be attained only if we freely choose to live in accordance with the purpose of our Creator. We hesitate to give ourselves away to God. We fear that God will have us do something we don't want to do or something we are afraid we can't do. Freedom is an opportunity for choice; it gives no guidance as to what the choice should be. Doing the will of God is not becoming a slave but discovering that in God's service is perfect freedom.

Freedom with Responsibility

July 2
John 8:32

Freedom is a great ideal. It is so great that our most severe form of punishment is not physical brutality but solitary confinement. The desire for freedom is so great that it never dies even though long lost. Interestingly, complete freedom is an illusion. We are not free, for example, to jump from the top of a building because of the restriction of gravity. We are not free either, to throw a twelve–pound weight farther than a few feet. These cosmic and biological limitations are easy to accept, as we recognize them as necessary and unchangeable. It is social limitations that grate upon us. The classic arrangement of freedom goes something like this: every person should be able to do whatever they wish to do, so long as it does not infringe upon the freedoms and rights of any other person, and that it does not interfere with the smooth and efficient functioning of society.

Based upon that, then, it is clear that there is no freedom without responsibility. Jesus himself said, "If you continue in my word, you are truly my disciples and you will know the truth, and the truth will make you free" (John 8:32). So, freedom is not so much a gift as a quality that must constantly be pursued. When I give my soul to God, then no person will ever own me! This freedom is the freedom to serve God, who will always have humans' best interest at heart.

Liberty in Law
July 3
James 1:25

Liberty is one of the great words of our Declaration of Independence, our Pledge of Allegiance, our Bill of Rights, and our whole frame of thought in America. Abraham Lincoln said in the Gettysburg Address that this nation is "conceived in liberty." In fact, America itself has become synonymous with liberty in the minds of people all over the world. But just what is liberty? Even this has its limitations. The practice of liberty requires a deft balancing of liberty and conditions, exceptions, qualifications, and limitations. There is a creative tension between liberty and law. Throughout history, there have been many demonstrations of the need to invoke conflict in order to allow change. There are examples in obtaining the right to vote for women, racial conflict, and the gay rights movements.

What about the individual and the Christian concept of liberty? The Christian concept of liberty does not so much center on individual rights as it does on a direction that brings fulfillment to life. Sometimes it seems that we equate liberty with "license" and law with "restraint." Yet Christian liberty involves becoming bound. For a Christian man to be truly free, he must become a servant, he must humble himself, submit himself, commit himself, and decide to be bound to the purpose of his creator. It is unsettling to commit ourselves, to give ourselves away to God. We are afraid that God will have us do something we don't want to do or something we are afraid we are unable to do. Experience shows, however, that obedience to God results in opening the scope of living, greater opportunities for vital activity, and greater enjoyment of all living things. Truly, the decision to "delight in the will of God" leads to the discovery that in his service is the perfect freedom.

Authenticity
July 4
Romans 3:22b-26, 5:1–11

Knowing that with God all things are possible—the idea that when one asks in faith, believing, God will provide—how could one ever doubt, ever fail, ever experience defeat? Yet each one of us does experience failure. Many of us feel the pangs of failure, inadequacy, and of being unimportant. There are disappointments in work, children, our level of happiness. We had hoped so much that it is hard to accept a reality that is less than our dreams. Sometimes, it is so hard to accept reality that we deny it. The truth is, every one of us has had to accept failure. Every one of us is a sinner. No one of us live up to our creation. None is perfect before God. Failure is the more natural state of a person's existence. The good news of the gospel is that God knows that condition and has provided for it! The reason for Jesus Christ is human, mortal failure. The reason Christ came is that we might have life again and not remain in defeat. The gospel is designed by God to deal with failure. Its whole intent is to make failure into reconciliation and reconciliation into realness and realness into authenticity. The opposite of authenticity is a fake, a forgery, a fraud, a phony. When we live as if we were supermen, in need of help from no one, we're phony. We are only fooling ourselves.

Failure hurts. But there is a good side even to failure. Pain can motivate to action. The pain of failure is the opportunity of the gospel for Christian truth. The healing medicine for failure is forgiveness. Forgiveness and support. God has promised that if we trust in his promises and hold steadfast to him through his Son, Jesus Christ, then he would receive us as if our sins were nothing! That's what justified by faith means. It means we learned to trust God's promises because we know Christ died for us. The promise is that even though we have failed in many ways, we're still precious, still valued, because we're his people. Authentic means worthy of acceptance or belief, trustworthy, genuine. If we can come to be that type of person, God will have had his way with us. Let our goal be authenticity in our personal lives and through the life of the church of Jesus Christ.

Exclusiveness
July 5
John 10:7–39

Exclusiveness is an elusive human nastiness. In its milder forms, it may pass as choice or competition or quality. In fact, there is much to be said for free choice, a competitive spirit, and standards of performance. Voluntary organizations rely on free choice for their memberships, and work to win the qualities of loyalty and faithfulness to the organization and its goals. But press the matter and it turns sour. Exclusive, meaning rare or special, is one thing, but in human relationships where lines are drawn and artificial differences are used to separate and cut others out, it becomes something else. Push exclusive to its next logical step, and it becomes superiority, snobbery, or arrogant haughtiness. It becomes the classic formula for unwarranted privilege, separation, division, anger, fighting—all the way to and including warfare. It is so easy to slip unknowingly into the error of saying "I am better than you." In athletics, one wins, and the other loses. In academics, one gets an A, another a C, D, or F. The A student is objectively better than the others. Better performance quickly and easily slips into better, period.

The painfulness of it all is that the next step is to degrade the other, to dehumanize the other, to discount the other. So, if one just pushes the idea of exclusiveness, it tends to reveal itself for the destroyer of the faith it really is. As usual, the question is balance. Loyalty has its place. Further, you are special, not better. Each of us is unique because God made us. We are God's children, and our importance comes from that and no other artificial differentiation. God's plan for us is unity in him. Our door is open to all, regardless of race, poverty, wealth, or station. Christ reaches out for all; *none* are excluded if they make their humble confession and walk in the pathways of Christ. We fail in the goal, but that is why we need to seek for understanding. It is why we stress the other and the blessedness of giving.

All Ye

July 6
Matthew 11:28

"Come unto me, all ye that labor and are heavy laden, and I will give you rest" (Matthew 11:28, RSV). These are beautiful words, and hit a responsive chord in every one of us. For which one considers that he does not labor, or carry a heavy burden, or need rest? *All ye* ... what wonderful words. They are the words of Jesus issued in an invitation to us to come unto him. This is the meaning of Communion, after all, that we come unto him. We take the initiative in response to his invitation; we rise and come. We kneel in humility and contrition. In the simple elements of bread and the fruit of the vine, we partake in his very nature. He offered himself and asked us to offer him as often as we shall in remembrance of him.

No one is excluded except by his own unwillingness. No one is forced either. Rather, Christ beckons, woos, wins, beseeches, loves. Christ establishes no limitation on who may come. He calls the discouraged as well as the confident, the defeated and the successful, the lowly and the highly placed. Will you accept the invitation and "come unto him?"

Being a Christian
July 7
Matthew 7:13–29

One of the hardest places to be a Christian is in church. There, Christianity is taken for granted, and it is easy to become what is called a Christian. In church, virtually everyone accepts the value of Christianity whether or not they call themselves Christian. When you became a Christian, did it cause you any hardship? Lower your position in the community? Put your life in danger? For most of us, the answer to these questions is no. In fact, in our society, the church is a place to network, to meet people, to get connected. One might even say that there are advantages to being in a church. It is so easy that it may become meaningless. How can we avoid this?

One way is to recognize that although we think we are self-sufficient, we cannot truly do anything apart from God. He supplies the very breath that gives us life. Pride and self-sufficiency can lead to a refusal to acknowledge that God is God. This is sin! It is an estrangement from God. It is sobering to think about how many times we deny God, lack trust in his way, or fail to speak in his behalf when we are nudged to do so. Sadly, sin is not simply denying God, but ignoring him.

Being conscious of God results in a conviction of our sin. When we compare our actions to the sovereignty of God, we must recognize that we are sinners and that there is no hope but to give humble recognition to God. He is the only absolute, and he calls us to him. Even on the cross, Christ died with the words, "Into Thy hands I commend my Spirit" (Luke 23:46). It is only with this humble recognition that we see our need for the grace God gives us as a gift. It is completely undeserved, completely unattainable without bowing before our God and accepting it.

Don't Kid Yourself
July 8
Romans 5:1–9

Most of us have heard the expression "Don't kid yourself." Usually it's kind of a soft way of saying, "You really don't get it, do you?" Yet, in our own little worlds, we do just that. It is easy to see the way when it comes to the big commandments—don't murder, don't steal, don't commit adultery. Yet people talk themselves into thinking wrong answers are right until the world is turned upside down. It's the less obvious things, when we cry out, "Lord, why am I so much like me, and what can I do to be the way I'd like me to be?" To avoid this trap, the only thing we can do is, "Don't kid ourselves."

There are eternal truths about which we must not kid ourselves. When the laws of eternal truth are broken, they bring inevitable results. True happiness comes in abiding with eternal truths. Consider a simple illustration: If a youth drives a car around a curve at seventy miles per hour when they should have been going forty, the car will not make it. It is irrelevant how great a kid they were; a law regarding the structure of the universe was broken, so the car will upset. Breaking the laws of eternal truths brings consequences.

Thankfully, abiding in those eternal truths brings happiness. True depth of serenity comes when we are right with God. On our own, we cannot become the person we'd like to be. When we say to God, "I give up, Lord. Melt me, mold me, fill me, use me," he will enable us to become that person. Don't kid yourself about eternity; this is the secret to glorious, challenging, and real living.

Don't Knock Fellowship

July 9
Romans 1:1–16

Anonymity is one of the realities that tends to destroy community. It tends to undercut a sense of personal responsibility. Studies have shown that in a crowd, people have a difficult time responding to need. When we are alone and obviously the only one who can respond, or if we know the person, the response is immediate and almost universally given. More and more, we are finding ourselves becoming a number on a card.

Fellowship is a community of interest. God, who made the human animal, also gave them the capacity to fellowship under many different circumstances and banners. Our commonness here is a community in Christ. There is history—we are part of the traditions, the experiences, the joys, and the sorrows of the past. That is why we are a people of the Book. The Bible not only provides us a sure rule and guide for living, it also tells us who we are. Our God is a God who interacts with his children in time and history, to draw us unto himself. Our remembering is also in the now. Right now, we are weighing whether the ancients knew what they were talking about and whether it applies to us. Our Bible tells of experiences that fill the heart and soul, yet we can only believe it if we have the connection with Christ in our hearts and souls.

Fellowship is found in the gathering together to worship. It is found in classes, in working together, and in common experiences. It is in fellowship that we find ourselves. We find renewal and new life. There we can accept our failings and our strengths. In a world of digits, punch cards, and computers; we need nothing more than we need fellowship—with one another and with Christ.

Doorways
July 10
John 10:1–15

Doorways are fascinating things. They each have a character of their own. They provide passage into and out of various places and can illustrate spiritual passageways as well. Through some doorways, we step into life more abundant, and through others, we step into features of life that degrade and debase the potential of God's creation of us.

The doors of a cathedral may bespeak the majesty and invitation of God. The doors of a government building may denote the power of the state. The doors of a home may offer sanctuary and peace, warmth and joy. Then there are barred doors, swinging doors, prison cell doors, each with their own particular story to tell. Doorways may be open or closed. They may protect and defend or imprison and hold captive.

The doorways of life are usually figurative and symbolic. These include such as the doorways to the heart, to the mind, to the soul, and to life's commitments. The doorways of faith are of this type. Consider the doorway of repentance and a right spirit within. "But, I don't need repentance," you might say. "I'm a pretty good person." May I suggest that repentance is a practice of real honesty? For if we cannot come before God in honesty, there is very little chance of success of finding him at all. To repent is to acknowledge where we have attempted to live without God, to satisfy ourselves with sin.

Now consider the doorway of faith. It is here where we consider the words of Jesus: "I am the door; if anyone enters by me, he will be saved." Jesus also said he was the way, the truth, and the life, and that he and the Father are one. Now doesn't that sound like a door worth going through? Faith involves an attitude and the content of the mind. The doorway of faith leads to prayer, Bible study, and fellowship. Likewise, it leads to the third kind of door: the doorway of action.

Action is really a shortened version of faith. It means we are willing to put what we believe into activity. Activity is such as supporting an orphan in another country, volunteering at a homeless shelter, or even providing a ride to church for someone that could not otherwise attend. Through the doorways of repentance, faith, and action, you can be assured that you will encounter the living Christ.

Faith and Laughter
July 11
Psalm 15; Luke 10:38–42

It is curious that in the life of faith we have both the serious and the light. On one hand, of course, the Christian faith is serious business. We're talking about our eternal souls. On the other hand, when we are right with our God, and as right as we can be with one another, there is a delightful joyousness and a glad-hearted happiness that spills over in spontaneous laughter and an abiding sense of well-being. We naturally take our faith seriously, but it is necessary to be able to laugh at ourselves from time to time. It is good for practical-minded realists to let go a bit and truly enjoy our God and truly believe in his amazing power. Present-day Christians tend to err on the side of being dubious about the power of God.

If we really want to understand life, and live life in faith, we will understand that to immerse ourselves in God's rich, abiding, fulsome, and joyously wise Word is to become a wholesome people of God. We will understand that we are partners with this powerful God in fighting what would undo his will, and in living what fulfills his will. It is yin and yang: yin is the silence, yang is the sound. The reality is that it takes both for wholeness. We must have sound to appreciate silence. We must have silence to appreciate sound. We must have faith to know Christ's laughter. We must have Christ's laughter to have faith. The wholesome people of God rely on God and therefore are able to cry with others and laugh with them too. Jesus knew great sorrow, and he knew great joy. Most of all, he knew what was truly important.

Footprints
July 12
John 1:43–47

We all know the story of footprints in the sand. You know, the one where two friends are walking side by side on the beach. Then one of the friends falters, and there is only one set of footprints, deeper, because one is carrying the other. This is the way Jesus is. Jesus is always there for us if we call for him and always nearby even when we ignore him. Jesus is always faithful. Jesus loves his precious people, and he will never leave us or forsake us. So, we want to follow Jesus, the one whose feet are in the lead.

Jesus called his disciples one by one, personally chosen by him. And they followed, for the most part. The disciples are such wonderful examples, because they are so like us! They made mistakes and were forgiven, they fell away at crucial times and were welcomed back. Jesus carried out his entire ministry on foot. His footprints led him to miracles and healings, to synagogues and casting out demons. Jesus goes on, one step in front of the other, carrying the love of God place to place.

Each of us will have our own stories of where the footprints have carried us. Our lives are set free to transform the world through using the fruits of the spirit God has given us, and following in the footprints of Jesus. Being a Christian means allowing ourselves to be shaped and formed by Christ. We must allow ourselves to be shaped in his image in order to become a brand-new person and to live in the world differently than we have ever lived. We are put on this earth not merely to "make a difference in the world." We are here to make the world different.

How?

July 13
John 3:1–21

Some of the most intriguing words of the English language are three letter words. For example, G-O-D, M-A-N, Y-O-U. These are intriguing enough and have occupied the minds of people for centuries in the fields of theology, philosophy, and every ingenuity of science. But words of the three-letter variety that may be more intriguing still are: W-H-O, W-H-Y, and H-O-W. There is no way of even estimating, I suppose, how many times we have used those three words in questions. I think the hardest of those words is *how*. It is easy to be critical, to tear down, degrade, belittle, ignore. When we are asked to be creative, to be constructive, to originate, and to provide for better ways and ideas, then we are reduced to "how" and that's a humbling thing. There is One who knew "how"; there is One who showed us "how." The light of his glory dazzles us, makes plain our path, warms our souls.

I want to know how to be a Christian … so long as it doesn't require me to give up my favorite TV program, so long as I don't have to change any plans in order to work it in, so long as it means I won't get involved in anything I don't want to do, so long as it's comfortable! We can't do it on our own power. Fundamental change in the direction of our being must come from God. The whole point of the gospel is that God can do just that for anyone—for you and me. It is not something *we* can do with our hands. It is our responsibility to respond to the breath of God's spirit … but it is God's spirit, now becoming our own doing. To find ourselves coming unto God is to discover that God started it, God continued it, and God brought it to conclusion. To believe in Christ's belief in us, we must be lifted above ourselves. Believe in the immortality Christ taught us was ours, and instinctively we use a new standard of measurement and a new scale of values. The specifics, God will show us once we have been born again.

How It Is Done
July 14
Matthew 13:1–13

Jesus loved to tell parables. Have you ever wondered why? The answer is that it is for those who do not understand. It has to do with coming to insights. If you give a person an order, they have a choice: obey or disobey. When you tell a story, the mind gets to work on it and comes to its own conclusions. In this way, the discovery is ours; it is something we know, not something we have been told, or something we simply repeat.

In the creation of people, freedom meant risk. In the midst of that freedom, people inevitably broke relationships. The whole biblical message tells of a people's call and fall and subsequent recall, time after time. Then a most wonderful thing happened. God sent what was the closest thing possible to sending himself: he sent his Son. It was wonderful, because Jesus was a person of flesh and blood, a person with a mouth and a mind, with a heart and soul with whom we could actually speak. Jesus brought true forgiveness. It almost seems too good to be true. We cannot earn it; forgiveness is purely a gift. We don't have to be good; we are forgiven. All of us are called to share the good news of forgiveness, reconciliation, and new life. In fact, if we don't share the good news, our faith-life will atrophy, as surely as an unused muscle will atrophy.

Sharing can be difficult, scary. It must grow out of the joy of the knowledge that we live not by law but by the love of God. It is not because we have value that we are loved but because we are loved that we have value. Our value is a gift rather than an achievement. We may not have all the answers, but if we share our personal experience with enthusiasm and joy, we can be secure in knowing that God will do the rest.

Is Being a Good Guy Enough?
July 15
Matthew 19:16–20:16

We all want to be well thought of by others. The problem with being a good guy is that it means pretty much going along with the flow. It means not always taking things to the next level. If one begins to be too "deep," you don't always fit in with the crowd. As children of God, we have to be more than just "good guys." We need to know deeply what we believe in and be willing to stand up for it.

The rich young ruler in today's story was a great guy. He followed all the commandments; he gave to the church; he even attended church regularly. Yet that wasn't quite enough. Jesus told him that to have eternal life, he would have to sell all he had and follow him. The man's response tells us that he loved his things too much to give them up. Now, Jesus didn't say that was the general rule, but he does require that we give ourselves unreservedly to God's will. The bottom line is, what do we love? Ourselves and our things or God and others?

It is easy to get wrapped up in the things of the world. After all, that is what is here in front of us every day. The responsibilities of work, home, and family can be all-consuming. The only way to rise above is to have the perspective of eternity. The lesson Jesus tried to teach over and over is that eternity is *now*. It is something we enter into now. The kingdom of God is an attitude of life for eternity. It gives us the sensitivity to the needs, feelings, hurts, and joys of others. Because the scars of tragedy as well as the lines of joy carry on through eternity. The children of God must have the depth of understanding of their faith, discipline to live by it, and an eternal perspective by which to enter into life. It takes much more than just being a good guy.

I Am Not Ashamed of the Gospel

July 16
Romans 1:8–17

The Gospel is not something to be ashamed of; it is the power of salvation for all humankind and will bring us into oneness with God and with one another. The word *gospel* actually means something that is regarded as true and implicitly believed. There are many gospels in this world. The gospel of power, which can extend to war. The gospel of money, which extends to greed. Pride, which leads to arrogance. Superiority, which becomes prejudice. Each idea is attractive in its offer but also has fatal flaws, containing only a partial truth.

The Gospel is the gospel of Jesus Christ. It is the gospel of God. His promises are true, as made known through Jesus of Nazareth. This truth is good news because it means that we, who are separated and broken, have a chance to start afresh! *But* the truth must win in our own hearts by the consent of our own minds. God does not force us into a new relationship with him. The very nature of love is that it cannot be gained by force. We can't be forced into loving someone; rather, we fall in love. The gospel must compete for our attention, our minds, and our hearts. It is a case of the truth being before us but out of reach unless it can be seen, heard, and put to use.

Why would we be ashamed? The truth did not bring Paul acclaim and prestige—rather it brought imprisonment, beatings, mockery, and loneliness. Certainly our own sufferings for the gospel are minute compared to what Paul suffered. There are subtleties, however. Somehow, we are ashamed to tell our coworkers or even friends about our Christian faith or invite them to church. Perhaps it is because we do not truly believe in the power of the gospel. It brings singleness of mind and heart, oneness of purpose, a sense of direction. Yet we ourselves fight within on giving up the diversions of time, which lead to a spinning of emptiness. Power comes from giving oneself without reservation to our Lord Jesus Christ.

Keep Your Eye on the Ball!

July 17
Ephesians 4:1–6

Keep your eye on the ball! Anyone who has ever played sports has heard this admonishment. It doesn't seem to matter what kind of ball (tennis, golf, baseball, football, etc.); if you are going to be in the game, you have got to watch the ball. Unfortunately, we are often content to watch from the sidelines and be entertained rather than doing the hard work and having the commitment of truly being on the team.

On the team of faith, it is critical to recognize that each of us is not here by our own design; we have been placed here by God. What a deal! We've been picked by the great I AM! Boy, if that doesn't give you a rise, nothing will. We are called to do something good. When we acknowledge that God is in control and has a plan for us, changes happen. Life takes a different spin. Now that is something to be grateful for. Ironically, it takes constant vigilance to let God have control. Somehow, we always want to take it back. The only answer is to keep your eye on the ball through constant prayer and communication with the Father.

It is so easy to get preoccupied with our own stuff and let our eyes wander away from the bigger picture. Faith is a team sport! We need to be aware of the part we play. This means staying in fellowship with others so that we all do the right thing. We trust that each one knows their part, and then we work toward doing ours. Together, we help each other reach the goal of communion with God and eternal life. Individually, we join the team; together, we make it great.

Label Libel
July 18
1 Corinthians 3:5–13, 16–22

In our busy lives, we have to make quick judgments. So, we need categories that sort things out and help us to assess situations and even people. What we tend to do with people is to apply *labels* to them. It is a little like the old-fashioned rolltop desk, where there are little cubby holes to sort things into. We meet someone, and they instantly are labeled: liberal, radical, Christian, atheist, nice, mean, and so on. Even in reading these words, a picture comes to mind, doesn't it? Unfortunately, that means we lump that person in with others that may or may not be similar. To avoid making a label libelous, it is critical that it is not a permanent label. It must be kept open for review.

Jesus had an amazing gift of seeing beyond external labels and seeing who a person might become. For example, take Zaccheaus the tax collector. Jesus called him out of that tree to eat with him, and he went on to become an important disciple! Even in our day-to-day lives, most of us can recall a person that we may have written off as someone we wouldn't like who later became a wonderful friend.

One of the gifts that comes with the decision to follow Christ is that people can have a dramatic change of heart. Only the Holy Spirit within a person can accomplish that kind of change. As Christians, then, it is critical to remember that every person in the world is susceptible to this miraculous change. If we can keep our minds open, we can cherish people not only as they are, but also as what they might become with Christ.

Life's Trusts

July 19
Psalm 8:1–9; 1 Corinthians 4:1–2

"What is man that thou art mindful of him?" (Psalm 8:4). Likely most of us reading this would agree that there is a God. But it takes more than belief in the existence of God to value Psalm 8. God is our creator, and he has given us dominion—trust—over many things. Truly, it is overwhelming to think that humans are responsible for all the works of God's hands! What have we done with them? Perhaps it is easier to consider one's individual areas of responsibility. There are three main areas: ourselves, our families, and our time, influence, and resources.

Looking out for yourself seems to be the most natural of all areas. There is some fine print, however. Primarily the fact that none of us exist in a vacuum. Our responsibility is significant only in relationship to others and for others. This goes beyond just our families to all those with whom we come into contact. God entrusts us to make the world around us a better place.

Family is a tremendous trust. The value of the family unit is critical in the home and in the community sense. A word that comes up here is stewardship. A steward is an administrator, manager, supervisor. A steward handles details for another, in service to them. Ultimately, in the Christian sense, it means the recognition of God's ownership of all material resources and of life itself.

These resources clearly extend to our time, talents, energy, and influence. We must be good stewards of these things. The world puts so many demands on each individual that we must determine, "What comes first?" We have just so much time and energy; to what are we going to devote it? This brings us right back to Psalm 8. All we have comes directly from God. If we can view each demand on ourselves—time, energy, money— through that lens, it becomes easier to prioritize. God has given each of us great responsibility and great reward. It is up to us to be trustworthy, faithful stewards.

Loyalty ... What Is It?
July 20
2 Peter 1:3–11

We admire loyalty a lot. When we say the pledge of allegiance, sometimes it is purely rote and routine. However, it is a pledge that could require the laying down of one's life. Closer to home, there is the loyalty of family. Anyone who has been married for any length of time knows that it isn't always about romantic love. Loyalty leads us to stand at one another's sides while falling back into love. From the faith perspective, loyalty almost defines faith, at least part of it. We are loyal to God, to Christ, to the Holy Spirit, and to those in the body of Christ with us.

This is important, because it really is counter to the current culture. Society encourages individuality over community. Take care of number one! Loyalty is about "all for one and one for all." How do we get there? Start with seeking to grow in God's kindness and peace.

A few pointers on getting there. First, learn to put aside your own desire. Then, "As you know God better, he will give you, through his great power, everything you need for living a truly good life" (2 Peter 1:3). Following the instructions in this passage will keep you from being ineffective and unproductive. Next, care for each other in mutual affection. Talk about being countercultural! It seems like society calls for less of everyone else and more of me. But where does that lead? Exhaustion and loneliness. Go for kindness and peace; the rest will follow.

No Strings Attached?
July 21
Luke 5:39–49

The choice to be a Christian is one we make completely of our own free will. God designed it this way. After all, if we are forced to love, it isn't love at all, is it? However, once we make that choice, it becomes a covenant. That means that I make a commitment to God, and he makes a commitment to me. My part of the commitment is that I love God with all my heart, soul, and strength, and love my neighbor as myself. Of course, that is a tall order! On my own strength, I cannot possibly do this. It is only through the Holy Spirit's guidance and strength that I can accomplish this type of commitment. A covenant takes two parties. What is God's part?

It is not that our lives suddenly become easy. In fact, Jesus promises that we will face trials in our lives of following him. God gives us the Holy Spirit to enable us, and, ultimately, he grants us eternal life through the grace of the sacrifice of Jesus Christ. The difference between a Christian and a non-Christian is that we actually live *for* something. Otherwise, what is the point—to live a life only to die into nothingness? Faith gives us purpose and meaning.

This is the second part of the commitment: to love my neighbor as myself. That means that I have also made a connection to others. Everyone becomes my neighbor; in fact, to go one step further, everyone becomes my brother. We are all united in the family of Christ. If we could really live this out, what a change that would make in the world. We are committed to law with mercy and mercy with law. Where there is the force of law, it must be tempered with mercy to avoid oppression, and where there is mercy, it must be armed with the force of law to avoid permissiveness and disorder.

Bear Fruit
July 22
John 15:1–8

Gardening presents several wonderful illustrations of the life of a Christian. As a gardener, one of the big challenges is pruning. It almost seems cruel to cut away the new shoots on a plant, but any master gardener will tell you that if you fail to do this, the plant will waste its energy on the shoots and not produce fruit. When Jesus says he is the vine, he means the trunk, the core of the plant, the part connected to the roots that nourish its growth. When you cut off the fruitless branches, they quickly wither and die—just as a Christian will wither and die in the faith if cut off from Christ.

When we look at our own lives, it is easy to feel like most of it is spent in hectic activity. How do you know you are spending your energy on the right things? You know by the fruit that comes of the activity. If there is no fruit, there is no value. Judging that can be difficult, no doubt; thankfully, the Holy Spirit guides us. Are you producing love, joy, peace, patience, kindness, goodness, gentleness, faithfulness, self-control? If so, you are on the right track. If not, you must consider that activity and determine if it needs to be pruned from your life.

Reaching back to the true vine, the source of life is the only way to continue to grow. Jesus, the vine, guides us through prayer, study, and faithful relationships in the body of Christ. God, the master gardener, will show the way to fruitfulness as long as we can remain faithful.

One Foot in Heaven
July 23
Philippians 1:19–2:11

When Paul wrote most of the letters that now make up the New Testament, he was in jail. It is amazing to think of his impact from his imprisonment. He realized, and helps us realize, that "to live is Christ, and to die is gain" (Philippians 1:22). For him, to die was to be immediately with Jesus and out of this world. However, he could no longer preach and teach, to help others find the way to Christ.

Today, there is no question but that we live in a time of conflicting values. There has always been the battle between right and wrong, but the circumstances are different in that there is little real agreement as to what direction to take. We need a reason for living. Many seem to do well without one, earning money to have a good time, but in reality, we need a reason to continue to put one foot in front of the other. Living in Christ gives the task to spread the word, the strength to accomplish the task, and the reward of everlasting life.

Living in Christ also brings unity of purpose. All Christians are tasked with bringing the message of salvation to those who need it. Christ gave himself up for all. Our heart in Christ is to care for one another. Having one foot in heaven, we catch a vision of the truth. Having one foot on earth, we have a place to apply the truth. Pray that if we are living in Christ, we will find the way to share him in our everyday contacts where we live and work and play. To live worthily, caring for one another.

Personhood
July 24
Luke 10:27

Norman Vincent Peale, who wrote the book *The Power of Positive Thinking*, stated that the most difficult personal problem among people was the lack of confidence. A lifetime of pastoral counseling underscores this idea. It is unclear why so many are plagued with a sense of inadequacy, but it seems to be true. Abraham Lincoln, on the other hand, observed, "Most people are about as happy as they make up their minds to be." However, the Bible is clear that God made us for joy and gladness. What has robbed this joy?

The power of the positive is biblical. Joy comes from the pattern of salvation wherein one admits fault, receives God's forgiveness, and accepts Christ's love and power. Just because a person is filled with joy does not mean they ignore reality. To be aware of the terrible human needs that surround us on all sides is not to deny joy. Certainly, gloom is not going to attack those human problems. It is joy in doing, believing that something can be done, and the will to bring about positive good that attacks human need. It is easy to worry about every event and drag every bit of bitterness out of it as possible, but believe me, positiveness is infectious and a whole lot more powerful!

Confidence is rooted in personhood. The Great Commandment can be boiled down to four words: love God, love humankind. God is for us, not against us. The God who made us calls us to set things right with him and to move out. God believes in you.

Seeds of Potential
July 25
Matthew 13:1–9

The parable of the sower is the first parable Jesus told. It is such a great visual—the seeds dropping on the path, eaten by birds, choked out by weeds. In short, Jesus was implying that three out of four people wouldn't get what he was saying! Those aren't exactly great odds. It is easy to see that there are many obstacles to understanding the Word of God. Anyone who has done a little gardening recognizes that the first step to success is preparing the soil. The soil has to be weeded, cleared of rocks, and broken up to be an inviting place for a seed to grow. Turning that around, in order for the seeds to grow, there has to be a gardener! The underlying message here is that God—the gardener—prepares our hearts to accept his Word.

The next obstacle is the birds. What is lying in wait, ready to take the Word from you? It is so easy to become disillusioned, disappointed, discouraged. In fact, it is hard not to be. One way to avoid this is to get closer to the gardener; the other is to be sensible about the fact that the evil one is looking for opportunities to steal the word away.

Finally, the weeds. What is choking out your time with God? What distracts you from spending quality time studying his Word? Think about those distractions. It is so easy to get caught up in the day-to-day life. The little things build up until no more time is left at the end of the day. Determine to clear out some space for study and prayer. This is the only way to grow those seeds of potential.

The Formative Power of Words

July 26
John 1:1–5

Words form who we are; they have incredible power. Think of what words can do! They can move us to fury, invoke fear, soothe, irritate, encourage, and empower. Words of scripture, learned early, sunk deep, leave formative impressions and make us what we are. Some of the earliest memories we have are songs learned in Sunday school. It is amazing how the words of those songs come back to us. "Jesus loves me, this I know …;" "This little light of mine, I'm gonna let it shine …;" "Jesus loves the little children …" From these simple songs, the early formation of our Christian faith arises. Scripture passages have the same effect. Who among us hasn't murmured the words of the Twenty-Third Psalm or the Lord's Prayer when frightened or lost?

The power of words is, perhaps, undervalued these days. They are often used carelessly, thrown about like they were worthless. The phrase we all have heard, "Sticks and stones may break my bones, but words can never hurt me," isn't really true, is it? In the dark of the night, those words come back to haunt you. Likewise, the positive words of the Bible come back to soothe you.

What words will you spend your time with? Are you sharing the study of the Word with others? Will you pray that the Holy Spirit will guide you to deepen your roots in scriptures and understanding? God's words, learned early—or learned late—and sunk deep, form us, motivate us, transform us, cheer us, sustain us, empower us, and save us.

The Power of Salvation
July 27
Romans 1:8–17

When we give ourselves without reservation to our Lord Jesus Christ, there is power. We are filled with the desire and the need to find ways of sharing that good news with as many as we can. For the faith of our fathers in Christ is the gift of God to the world. That salvation, new life, hope, is for *all*. It is the task of the household of faith to labor toward sharing it to all who will hear. Not all will hear; not all will understand. But the gospel is the good news for young and old, rich and poor, wise and not so wise, no matter the job, the color, the similarity to us. *All*.

To truly share, we must recognize the oneness with God. Through faith in Jesus Christ, we have his righteousness and will live. We get hung up on our own ability to stand before God in our own righteousness. There is no-one on earth that has never made a mistake. The only way to be right with God is to stand beneath the righteousness of Christ. He vouches for us to God, speaks to our repentance, gives us forgiveness, puts us right with God. That is what faith is all about—being set right with all that is true, honest, worthwhile, of good report, worthy of praise. Finding the freedom to leave off getting even, hating, being resentful, and taking up with openness, a glad heart, forgiving, and loving one another. This does not mean that there will never be another faltering or that we will never need forgiveness again. But there is the promise that one is on the road that leads to harmony and peace, joy and gladness, instead of the other direction. This is eternal life, starting now!

The Responsible Christian

July 28
Ephesians 6:10–20

Freedom isn't free. That is a statement frequently heard in this volatile day. It is fascinating to explore the roots of freedom, particularly from the perspective of a Christian. The earliest histories of Egypt and Babylon assert the sanctity of a man's home. In fact, the public and private rights of humans have long been seen to be determined by the most basic quality of relation, human to human: love. Seems pretty simplistic, doesn't it? First John 4:20 elaborates the best: "Whoever claims to love God yet hates a brother or sister is a liar. For whoever does not love their brother and sister, whom they have seen, cannot love God, whom they have not seen."

In the political arena, the expression of the basic relationship of love is through justice. Justice is love in action in the complications of an imperfect world. Therefore, the foundations of our freedoms stem basically in the creation: in how God made us, in what we believe about God, in how we worship him, and in what we believe he requires of us. Our immediate history is studded with religious acts: The Reformation, the Mayflower, the colonies, our Constitution. These instances were the result of basic theological and religious struggle. So, we find in the Constitution a recognition of the dignity of a person, the sovereignty of God, and the impact of religious conviction upon the life and morality of a nation. These freedoms also mean that we must actively see that they are applied to every human contact. The vigor of the Christian witness depends upon the person's capacity for interpreting their faith in the significant areas of common life. That means where we work, eat, pray, and sleep. As Christians, we are compelled to be responsible citizens—God being our helper.

The School of Jesus
July 29
Matthew 7:1–29

We are prone to using books and lessons about the Bible rather than the Bible itself. Many people hold up the Sermon on the Mount as their guide for conduct. Sometimes, they throw in the Golden Rule as well. Unfortunately, since one is within the other, these folks have probably never read the entire Sermon on the Mount for themselves. It has some puzzling sayings in it, like, "Judge not or you will also be judged" (Matthew 7:1), and, "Don't throw your pearls before swine, for they may trample them, then tear you to pieces!" (Matthew 7:6).

Jesus didn't teach as an end in itself; his school was simple, informal, spontaneous. He used some unique techniques, such as companionship—association with Jesus. Interestingly, such modeling is the way babies learn to walk and talk. The disciples learned how to love God and their fellow humans from Jesus, who made this his whole life. We, too, need to spend time with the master to learn his ways. Being with him allows us to begin to take upon ourselves his frame of mind—his attitude.

Companionship leads to friendship. Friendship involves giving of oneself in frankness and love. We can always be ourselves with him. What a joy it is to really be yourself with people—no need to pretend to be smart or clever or polite or thoughtful. The disciples were able to ask him questions and talk over what others were saying about Jesus together.

Finally, Jesus encouraged his disciples. As Christians, we're always being shown a goal that we must continually reach for, but which we cannot attain. It is easy to compare ourselves to others, seeing them as saintlier and more dedicated than ourselves. Of course, we never see the whole picture of another's dedication. There are also those who are desperately in need of the hope of the gospel but who continually reject both it and everything connected with it. God would not have put us here if he had not also placed within us the ability to know redeeming fellowship with him. Though we will stumble, we still stand more than we stumble. The stumbling is awful, but the getting up again is important. Living the Christian life is mainly about accepting God's sovereignty and his rule over us. The school of Jesus teaches us to place our hearts with the heart of Jesus and know that continuing to walk his path is the way to success.

The Stuff of Miracles
July 30
John 6:1–15

God's Word indicates that the stuff of miracles has two ingredients: an almighty God and his people responding to his will. Wherever it is with whoever it is, it takes our almighty God along with responsive people who have a firm faith to bring the miracle of God's convicting Word and God's blessing Word. With this, all kinds of miracles take place daily in the world of God's creation. We want visible proof for miracles, and there have been all kinds of explanations for the feeding of the five thousand. What impresses me even more is what it means. It means that even though I come into the presence of our Lord with literally nothing, my almighty God can fill my needs so abundantly that there is enough for everything and a whole lot left over.

Our almighty God is the creator of all kinds of life—life in the skies, life in the earth and on the earth. Life in the oceans. Plant life, animal life, human life. What is so incredible is how this almighty God created humankind with a mind, with a tongue, with a soul. Humankind is so incredibly sacred because God made us spiritual. There is a place that responds in the deep and quiet moments of our greatest insights and says its yes to our creator. Our God calls us to respond. God's purpose in our creation is to draw all things unto himself. His purpose is to unify the global community. Individually, our purpose is to sacrifice for the sharing of God's Word. The commission to reach out in the name of Jesus is not an option. It is God's holy will for us. Our response will bring joy; our lack of response brings our peril … eternally.

Win-Win
July 31
1 Corinthians 13:1–13

We all like to win fair and square. The possibility of playing the game of life and coming out on the winning end is one of the challenges of American life that we hold very dear. We call it competition. We are all familiar with the ideals of competition—that appropriate competition will lead to a better outcome—a better product, a better athlete, even a better student. Competition leads to motivation to better oneself.

The problem with competition is to keep it within bounds. If the pressure to win is too great, it can actually deteriorate the quality of the outcome. It can lead to cutting corners and trying to cheat the system. In life, it seems that the "game" is always to win or to lose. That is the only possible outcome. What if there were a better way? What if it could be win or win? The idea is that one can win by helping another person get ahead as well. Ideally, this means that not only is one not deprived, but that both parties are enhanced by the exchange.

The thrust of 1 Corinthians 13 is win-win. It calls us to love seriously. The characteristics listed here do not allow for a win-lose attitude. The love described is perfect love—that of God the Father toward us, his children. This kind of love never gives up, never goes away. If we were to take the list of qualities of love seriously and truly abide by them, we could change the whole environment of our lives. Self-respect is, in fact, built, not at the expense of others but in the process of building up one another. God calls us to live in the world to make it a better place, just as Jesus came, not to condemn the world, but that the world might be saved by him.

A Step toward Holy Creativeness

August 1
Colossians 1:3–14

Christianity is under attack, and has been throughout history. Sometimes it has been violent, sometimes it has been vocal, but mostly the attack on Christianity has been behind the scenes: subtle, whispered, secretive. In some ways, it is an attack of lethargy. Christians have the words of truth, the means of redemption, yet it appears that we hold them back, keeping them to ourselves. We must not undersell the power of the holy. When a person stops long enough to look into the face of God, he dies … to the old person and is born into a new person. The scripture has always contended that a mortal could not look into the face of God and live. To really know God is to die to the way of life that counts #1 as the only and the most important, and to be brought alive to the joy of others and the delight of giving oneself away. The power of the holy does that.

The power of the holy opens a person to God's dealing. It fosters the conviction that God is standing at the door and knocking. It promotes belief in the peculiar and special presence of God in Word and sacrament. When that kind of holiness works into the fiber of a man or woman, he or she begins to change: to become more gentle but stronger, to become more loving but more responsible, to become humble but tenacious in laboring for the well-being of others. What is needed is the knowledge that God has come *to us*, deep down in the core of our being. This is available to any and all. Once that knowledge is fully adopted, a spirit of thanksgiving will erupt in a way that cannot be hidden. What a great style of life. Surely it is a beautiful outgrowth of steadfast steps toward creative holiness.

By Faith
August 2
Hebrews 11:1–3, 8–16

Have you ever thought about how much we live by faith? Consider your car, computer, heat, air travel. Further, consider love and trusting one another. The truth is, we live most of our lives trusting in the reasonable predictability of our everyday activities. It is a good thing, too; we wouldn't even be able to get out of bed without a level of trust in the construction of our home! What is faith, then?

Faith is the result of reasoning. It is the knowledge of our own experiences. Since the car started every day for the last 365 days, we expect it to start this morning; we have faith in it. The Bible is like those 365 days. Throughout its pages, we see examples of how God came through. There are thousands of fulfilled prophecies and life-changing experiences. For that matter, the evidence is before us in nature—the sun rises and sets, the seasons follow one another—year after year after year.

Faith is the perfect antidote for fear. It is what gives us the ability to move forward. Jesus brings faith to a whole new level. He came to earth knowing his ultimate purpose, knowing the pain and shame that was ahead, and he persevered and is now seated at the right hand of God the Father. He is our promise of eternal life. By faith, we are able to run the race set before us. The race of our own lives, and the excitement to share eternal faith with others.

Caring Corrections
August 3
Psalm 119:33–40; Matthew 18:15–20

Warnings in this life are so plentiful. There are road signs, signs in the workplace, even notices on the foods we eat. Most warnings are givens, but the kind of warning Jesus suggests we give to an erring brother or sister, that's different. That's personal. Who wants to blow the whistle, especially personally and face-to-face? Being the bearer of warnings has significant danger. One must balance the need to warn and the problem of being judgmental or even vindictive. There must be a caring line between a warning and being a nice guy and saying nothing. We all recognize that the absence of discipline is not evidence of great love.

Jesus points out that it is the responsibility to warn—to attempt a redeeming discipline. Especially in the church, were we constantly work at truly caring about and for one another, and, by extension, for the world. The implementation is the key to fulfilling this responsibility.

The warning must be set in a context of future usefulness and support. It needs to be in the context of respect, appreciation, and hope for greater future usefulness. Often the error carries its own consequences. The correction is critical as well. The admonition to "not get caught" is not enough. An explanation that the action is wrong or risky, along with the understanding that the concern is due to love and the desire to grow together well into the next phase is vital to the outcome. Knowing that not one of us is without fault helps guide the action. The text is a recommendation of our Lord for caring corrections. He believed in us enough to know we would lovingly work on the caring as we all continuously correct our courses.

Daily Battles
August 4
Isaiah 40:31

Almost everyone on this earth finds themselves plagued with challenges. For each of us, there is, every now and then, something missing. We fight daily battles to quiet fears, to retain patience, to grope for spiritual solidity, to be happy children of God. Generally, we pretty much know the rules; we're aware of common ethics and the wisdom of accepted morality. Yet each day, with the best of resolve and intentions, we catch ourselves shouting at the traffic, even at our spouses and children. Sometimes, we wonder what is wrong with our prayers. What is wrong with our Christian faith, that we can't seem to live up to our ideals? We forget that there are means for recovery. We forget that there is power available. "They that wait upon the Lord shall renew their strength, they shall mount up with wings like eagles, they shall run and not be weary, they shall walk and not faint" (Isaiah 40:31). This is a steadfast promise of scripture. Yet do we forget how to use it?

A few keys help to unlock the power to fight daily battles. First is forgiveness. It has a transforming power to restore people and their relationships. The second key is faith. Faith means that there is help available to us over which we have no essential control. It helps to look back at times when you could feel the guiding hand of God upon you. Third is fellowship. We enter a fellowship with others who are trying to live lives that are open on all sides, lives that are inviting the grace of God. At its best, fellowship in Christ is incomparably richer than any other human fellowship. Finally, humility. This is recognizing that life is not self-dependent, self-created; all we do comes from God. Humility means lack of pretense. It occurs only when the view is on God, not self. We ask for God's help for the daily battles against the attitudes that would undo and separate us from the love of God in Jesus Christ our Lord.

Expecting?
August 5
Acts 8:26–39

When you come to worship God, are you expecting? Have you anticipated that God is here, that a great moment has arrived and is waiting for you? We want rest and relaxation, we need to be refreshed and inspired, but we need more than this on occasion. Once in a while, we need to be taken over! We need a new life, a new direction, a new commitment! The first thing that is needed as we approach worship is to be open to receive the faith. In today's passage, the Ethiopian said to Phillip, "Come up and sit with me." Jesus put it a different way: "He who has ears to hear, let him hear" (Mark 4:23). Jesus said or implied this over thirty times in the New Testament.

We must, each of us, be open to hear divine guidance. The divine presence can change our attitudes, relationships, and even make friends of enemies. As we become other-centered, we can honestly want the best for others and put our own heady ambitions in proper perspective. Living the Christian faith means honesty, integrity, sensitivity to the needs of others, unselfishness, personal discipline—all things we know are right and true. We cannot expect the Christian movement to spread unless we exemplify it ourselves. This does not mean we are saints; no, we make mistakes and have wrong attitudes and ugly moments. It does mean that we have a sure confidence that God is our light and salvation; a desire to seek forgiveness and to deepen our lives, and a genuine concern for others and their development as children of God.

It takes courage to speak up. The early Christians drew other people to themselves because they stood out as living upright and pure lives. Then, having made friends, they spoke of their best Friend and so shared him. There may be failures and rebuffs, but it is critical to share our experiences, our witness. A personal, vital, direct acceptance of Jesus Christ as the Master of our lives is the most exciting, amazing, and wonderful thing that can happen in our lives. It makes us eager to share, long to be of service, expectant and ready.

Following Jesus
August 6
1 John 4:7–5:12

There is no great and secret formula to living a life following Jesus. Of one thing we can be certain: it is not going to be a bed of roses. Indeed, it is a most difficult thing to be truly Christian. It is easy to say that Christ is the answer to everything. While this is true in the big picture, it is the day-to-day living that is rough. To what extent do you confess you are truly Christian? To answer this question, we must define a true Christian. Simple honesty, regard for truth and justice, and sincerity are not enough!

The good news is that God knows that we will all fall short of his glory. It is only in the strength provided by God that we can live in right relationship to him—to follow Christ. This involves faith, grace, and love. These elements make up the "how" of following Jesus.

Faith can most easily be seen in little children. A child can look into the face of even a poor parent and have a look of adoration. Children truly believe their parents can do anything! Our faith, too, must be as a child's in so far as it is complete in trust and confidence. This does not mean it will be unquestioning faith. Rather, it continues to seek further knowledge of God through prayer, study, and the fellowship of other Christians.

Once a person can feel a measure of faith, a second aid to following Jesus comes into play. This is sustaining grace—essentially God reaching down in his concern and helping us as we try to do his will. As we glimpse the tenderness of God, his love begins to take over, pushing out the selfishness and placing in his love and sensitivity.

Love for others is the test of true faith. This is not just for those we like but for the unlovable. Jesus calls us to exchange the treadmill of life for something with purpose and significance. If we have faith that he reveals real life, he will sustain us.

Fresh Bread!
August 7
Mark 7:1–8

The smell of fresh bread, right out of the oven, brings happy memories for almost every person. The smell is simply mouth-watering! Fresh bread is bread at its best. It is life sustaining, and every sense in our bodies feels it. The bread of life that Jesus was offering was just that good. It was marvelous bread. It is the staff of life now and eternally. Jesus himself is the bread of life. God draws us to him, and through into eternal life. It is offered to us by God but never forced upon us. God allows us the choice to know him as our one true God or to follow false gods.

The real question for us is am I just a lump of dough or am I fresh bread? Am I a Christian in the making, willing to be used? There is an element inside each one of us that makes us think we are self-made persons. We like to say we have done it ourselves. We take what others have done for granted, belittling their part and enlarging our own. But we will never be a useful part of the nurturing body of God's people until we give thanks—deep, heartfelt, humble gratitude for all that have tended us until now. Thankfulness is a basic ingredient for usefulness.

The next thing required to make fresh bread is heat. This means to use our faith. We must let the potter's fire work in the ingredients, bringing them to usefulness. God brought each of us to just this place for a purpose. He wants us to rise up, interact with one another, with him, and with his Word. This requires taking the initiative to put our gifts to work. In our country, we have so much bread that it goes to waste. Our faith can be like that too. Many have grown up with Christ, with the Bible, with the church. We must take the initiative to find ways to fulfill the spirit of the words of Jesus. That occurs with acts of kindness, words of encouragement, patience to bring reconciliation, and thanks to God for his grace to be the bread of life.

He Returned with Power

August 8
Matthew 28:16–20

To many in our day, the claim that Jesus of Nazareth is the Christ, the Messiah of the Jewish prophesy, the savior of all humankind, and the one to whom they should give all commitment and allegiance is a gross exaggeration. The belief that Jesus was raised bodily from the dead and appeared to his disciples seems to be a tad ridiculous, a trifle unbelievable. Many reject his claim upon them. It may be apathy, irrelevance, or even angry rejection. Where do we, then, find authenticity, verification, food for faith?

One of the characteristics of the New Testament is that it is so conservative. Only stories that could be authenticated would be included. A writer trying to perpetuate a fraud certainly would not have portrayed Jesus appearing first to women, nor would he have remained silent in front of Pilate, nor would the betrayal of one of the most loyal disciples be included. All it would have taken to dispute the claim of the resurrection would have been to produce the body! Instead, what is recorded is the appearance of the risen Christ to over five hundred individuals. Many of whom were readily available to give their own eyewitness account.

The most compelling aspect of the account of Jesus's return is the power and courage the disciples went on to display. They shared their witness whenever people would listen. They were so persuasive that the faith spread with amazing speed. So persuasive that the faith has now withstood the doubters of some eight thousand generations and persists with power in those who believe today. Personal testimony of a changed life is undeniable evidence of the power of Jesus within each believer.

Joy
August 9
Isaiah 61:3–8

Picture in your mind the last time you felt true joy. The kind that reverberates inside you. It could be the joy of success, the joy of falling in love, the joy of seeing a child discover that they can ride a bike or play a musical instrument. In a Christian sense, joy is a little different. It is a deep knowing, and it simply must be shared.

Christian joy is knowing in the total sense of one's whole being. It is a confidence, a certainty; it goes way beyond what is temporary. It is a conviction in the soul that God is not a philosophical proposition or a metaphysical maybe. God is as real as the morning dawning, the evening dew, the rain and the sunshine.

This deep knowing brings a joy that is irrepressible; it bubbles up out of you; it is contagious and abundant. Christian joy must be shared! Shared joy is a gift of God. Love is nothing until you share it. Every baptized Christian is called to be in ministry. Ministry is not a complicated thing. It is simply sharing our faith in a way that we can do it with energy and enthusiasm. It is witnessing to the joy we know. It is enjoying together our spiritual journey.

If Life Is an Upper, How Can I Be Sinking?
August 10
Matthew 14:25–31

The Christian faith is upbeat and positive. Without Jesus Christ, the world sees life as a circle; with Jesus Christ, life is dynamic. Life has a positive, successful, dynamic conclusion. A basic difference between Christianity and other world religions is that the Christian is world affirming. Other religions seek escape from the world. A Christian affirms the world as the place where we are set to live out our lives for the best. Yet it doesn't always feel that way. Bad things happen: business failure, bankruptcy, joblessness, homelessness, illness, death. We also live in fear. Fear is a universal emotion, and it is a terrible thing to be afraid. Fear can paralyze us. More things are made impossible by fear and doubt than by any obstacle.

It is easy to wonder how this can happen if faith is so good. The answer is that Jesus knows and reaches out. Through our hardships and fear, Jesus knows. He is able to unlock obstacles, resolve fear, and with him, anything is possible. In our humanness we are a mixture. We carry hope and fear, possibility and doubt, belief and unbelief. When you are walking in the storm and it is raging about you, Jesus can scoop you up and say, "Why did you doubt?"

I Won't Bow to Anyone!

August 11
Deuteronomy 5:1–22

The enemy is within. We know this, really. But we need the reminder, as well. The enemy is insidious. Its presence isn't suspected. It comes in the form of good, or at least, "not bad." On one hand, we say, "I will not bow down to anyone." On the other, we begin to be worshippers of money or things or our job or some partial idea or some false prophet. The biggest enemies are false pride and excess.

Pride. There is a kind of pride that says, "I can do it myself." That kind of pride rejects interdependence and a need for one another. The reason pride is such a sneaky devil, though, is that we need to take pride in ourselves, our work, our families, and our country. The person who has no pride is as useless as one with an overabundance of pride. The first step to faith is to take egotistical false pride and give it away for God to dispose of. To put God on the throne of our lives and not ourselves.

Excess. This is the definition of heresy. Heresy is to say that one part of the truth is actually the whole truth. Whether it is ultraconservativism or ultraliberality, excess eventually becomes untruth. It is an insidious and difficult enemy of the faith, for almost all of us could use more heat in the fires of our faith. But too much heat burns out the boiler just as too little gives no head of steam.

The commandments were never intended as a scolding finger. They were meant as liberating truth. And they are. Trust God that they are, and you are on the pathway to a full and wholesome faith, having defeated the enemy.

Living the Faith in the Heart
August 12
Deuteronomy 6:4–9; Mark 12:28–34

The Christian faith is a fascinating thing. It is at once the simplest of credos, and yet it can profitably engage the greatest intellect for a lifetime, with much more to discover. Living the faith in the heart requires a decision. It requires an experience of the presence of God. It requires someone to believe in and someone to believe in you. It is not so much a matter of ethics and morality as it is like falling in love. It pervades the spirit, transforms the personality, tips over our former set of values and sets a spring in our feet and a glow in our hearts.

It is possible to come to a personal acquaintance with Jesus. He is the living Christ, who is historical and who is real today. He is someone who has happened, is happening, and will happen. He is not only the central figure of history from which all else must take its cue, but he is both personal and individual. His life and teachings have inspired music, literature, laws, art; even our calendar is based on the time of his life. Somehow, someway, he makes himself known to every heart that yearns for him and longs for him and waits for him. Then he makes us new.

Once we know Jesus in our hearts, our lives naturally exhibit the fruits of his spirit. Sometimes this is true in spite of ourselves; sometimes we don't even know it. The fruits of the spirit of Christ don't come by accident or laws. They come as an outgrowth of a prior commitment. They come from a heart-to-heart talk with God. To live the faith in the heart is to approach the kingdom of God with outstretched arms.

Love
August 13
1 Corinthians 13:13

"Faith, hope and love abide, these three, and the greatest of these is love."

No other words encompass more of the meaning of the Christian life than these three words. Certainly, they each are common to the vocabulary of each person. More importantly, they are loaded with meaning in the Christian context. In faith, we look to the past with confident belief in Christ. In hope, we look confidently to the future. In love, we live in this present life. Love is the guide of every Christian. If there were to be a single word to encompass the Christian's life, it would be love.

Any discussion of Christian love requires at least a short foray into the Greek meanings. In the Bible, there are three words used in the place of the word love: (1) eros—a rather base form of love that is characterized by seeking its object for the sake of its own satisfaction and self-fulfillment; (2) philia—this is a worthy type of love characterized by kindness to others; (3) agape—the kind of love that shows its meaning in action. With agape love—only expressed through the gift of God—one helps its object rather than desiring to possess it for its own self-satisfaction.

Within our purely human nature, we are incapable of agape love. It is possible only because God first loved us so much that he gave his only Son to us for our salvation. By belief in Christ, we are enabled to partake of this love because he revealed it to us. In agape love, we help the down and out, we help those who need assistance, we help those who cannot help themselves, and we lift one another in the spirit and the bond of Love. This type of love requires something beyond ourselves to make it possible. Do we really think we can love our neighbor as we ought without help? If we are to live the lives of love here and now, we need the support of the church, Christian friends, the Bible, prayers, and God's grace. Now we have the capacity for sacrificial giving, sacrificial living, and self-giving love.

Will you be strengthened in this way? Study and pray and believe that you might. This is the better way, which is love.

On Peanuts ...
The Gospel in the Commonplace
August 14
John 3:16

Peanuts, the cartoon in the funny papers, is hardly a scriptural text, is it? Yet if there is any value at all in the "funnies" it is that they reflect life. The "funnies" mirror us as we really are—they reflect the ridiculous in our lives and help us to cure them by laughing at them. The point is that the gospel is in the commonplace—in the everyday. It is all around us. We all know this is true. We also know that we each fail to put it into practice as consistently as we wish we would.

One of Peanuts' cartoons has Lucy chasing Charlie Brown: "I'll get you, Charlie Brown! I'll get you! I'll knock your block off! I'll ..."

Next panel: Suddenly Charlie Brown halts, turns around, and stops Lucy with: "Wait a minute! Hold everything! We can't carry on like this. We have no right to act like this ..."

Next panel: "The world is filled with problems ... people hurting other people ... people not understanding other people ..."

Next panel: "Now if we, as children, can't solve what are relatively minor problems, how can we ever expect to ..."

Next panel: Lucy socks Charlie Brown and knocks him down. Then she explains to a friend in the next panel: "I had to hit him quick ... he was beginning to make sense!"

Too often that is just what we do with our gospel. It begins to make sense, and in our self-centeredness, we ignore it and continue on our way. The very thing that will bring all the fragments of the everyday into a sensible whole is to apply the gospel in the commonplace. When we make God the center of our time and talents, then all else is remodeled and integrated by him.

Snoopy also conveys the gospel. He loves to dance about, and hard-hearted Lucy can't stand it. She shouts: "FLOODS, FIRE, and FAMINE!" Charlie Brown looks quizzically at her as Snoopy continues to dance. Again, "DOOM, DEFEAT, and DESPAIR!" Snoopy dances happily along. Lucy sighs and says, "I guess it's no use." Snoopy is still joyously and obliviously jumping up and down as though for the sheer joy of living as Lucy concludes, "Nothing seems to disturb him."

The person whose singleness of heart is Christ is likewise undisturbed. His confidence comes from Christ alone. For now, we can say, yes, the gospel is as common as *Peanuts*. Yet this gospel is at the same time special—special because it is individual and precious. Let us live for the sheer joy of living, with the gospel tucked inside our very souls.

Peaks and Valleys
August 15
Psalm 23

Mountaintop experiences are spectacular! They are what often bring us to the truth. They are the very special moments when we truly feel God's hand upon us. They are the times of life-renewing insights of faith. Yet they must constantly be refreshed, or they die. Alongside the power of our faith is our forgetfulness. Alongside the strength of scripture for daily living is our capacity to make the sacred common. The worst thing about it is that we recognize the feelings fading, the warmth cooling, but we wonder how to overcome it.

One approach is to not be ashamed to start over. No one likes to start over, but in the spiritual life, it is another thing. The tough part about starting over spiritually is the image of self that must be dealt with. The first step out of the valley is to be humble enough to start over. Once we have begun again, the next step is to reach out for faith. We want to be self-sufficient. This is where the words of the Twenty-Third Psalm come in. When one reads these familiar words, one feels the quiet beauty and spiritual insight satisfying and possessing their soul. To put it a different way, when the going gets tough, help is available. This is why the church—defined as all of God's people—exists. To point to the God who can be with us.

In this attempt to live a vital Christian life, there are the continual new beginnings and the warmth of the help of the fellowship of Christ's church. The third way to overcome valleys is to remember the peaks. This may seem like a simple concept, but it is vital. From the mountaintop, one can see that the valley is not all darkness. Life is not always smooth, but there is a firm, steady, and sure presence that will uphold us in this real life.

See?

August 16
John 9:1–41

Jesus was quite a challenge to the Jewish leadership. He was trained in the church, but he didn't always follow the rules. The Pharisees were all about the rules. They had developed law upon law, decree upon decree; there was no grace. The weight of religion was heavy, crushing the spirit of the people. Jesus comes along and performs miracles. Nothing wrong with that, but there was always an edge. In this story, the simple part is that a man born blind now sees.

The back story is the interesting part. God is seeking to bring light and hope to the people crushed in the darkness of the law.

The man was born blind. To the disciples, to the public in general, this must be due to a sin by someone. Yet Jesus answers that no-one sinned! "This happened so that the work of God might be displayed in his life" (John 9:3). The healing initially seemed simple, but wait. There is now sight where there was no sight. Life where there was none. Light in the darkness. Jesus is the light! The previously blind man immediately goes about telling everyone of his miracle and the man who performed it.

Now the Pharisees are worried. Who could do such a thing? A sorcerer? That would be blasphemy. It is the blind man that recognizes God's hand in this miracle. The Pharisees remain blind to it. They (like we) become caught. If one recognizes the miracle, the only course is to repent and convert to Jesus's way. This is the ultimate challenge to the self-righteous, stubborn men—to let go of their prideful, empty ways and change is simply too much. Isn't it the same for us? What stands between you and the light? Blindness is like arrogance and self-justification. Confession brings sight.

Talents
August 17
Matthew 25:14–30

Most of us have had an experience like the one described here. Originally, the word *talent* referred to a measure of weight—therefore an amount of money in this case. Interestingly, the principle applies whether we insert that meaning here or the more modern meaning of personal gifts. One of the ways we use this is when we expect more of someone who has more. More importantly, it is what the Father expects of us in his absence. Now we know that he is never truly absent, but to the outside world, there is no physical presence. What do you do when no one is watching? Are you careful to invest wisely and nurture those around you? Or are you afraid that you might make a mistake, and thereby refrain from reaching out and helping others?

God desires the best from us. He is always present, but does not judge earnest effort harshly! With him, there is no error. When working toward God's purpose and will, we truly cannot do wrong. That is kind of a relief in this perfectionistic world, isn't it? If you reach out in love to another person, good always wins. You help that person and in turn grow yourself. The currency of people is vastly more important in God's kingdom than money. Unfortunately, we often forget that and work only toward the profits that the world recognizes. In the economy of the kingdom, richness is defined in relationships. In such, the risk lies in not reaching out. Relationships grow cold without constant nurture. Left alone, they wither.

As Christians, we are all family. We love one another even if we don't always like what the other is doing. The commitment to family is not a casual one; it is not a matter of convenience. It is true love, giving without expectation and receiving joy beyond belief. Let us reach for that ultimate goal of hearing our Father say, "Well done, good and faithful servant" (Matthew 25:21). There is no higher gift.

That's the Point!

August 18
1 John 4:9–12;19

Have you noticed that some people just seem to have the capacity to get directly to the root of things? Jesus was such a one. Very early on people who heard him speak were amazed. In fact, he knew firsthand what the eternal truths were. The disciple John highlights one of these truths: "We love because he first loved us."

No matter where you start, you eventually come to conclusions like the one stated above. Consider humankind; trace through to religious experiences and you come to: "We love because he first loved us." Start with life experiences, crises through blissful peace, and you see: "We love because he first loved us." Look at Genesis and the creation, through the law and all the prophets, and it is clear: "We love because he first loved us" (1 John 4:19).

In that loving, God gave us an understanding of himself so we humans could have assurance about eternal things. With that assurance we are able to live through him. God's love is an action word. He had to make a way to get through our arrogance and pride. That way was Jesus. It was in Jesus that God supremely moved. Jesus brought God's love to us in personal terms we can understand; so that we can have full, rich, abundant life through him. We must recognize that it is not on our own that we live but in God's power. God's plan for human life offers real life, and that's the point.

The Bread of Eternity
August 19
1 Kings 19:1–14

A freshly baked loaf of bread. Just seeing those words can almost make your mouth water! There are so many images and memories that are stirred with that thought. With it and water, one can live. Without it or its equivalent, one cannot live. Jesus told the people: "I am the bread of life, whoever believes in me will have life eternally" (John 6:35). Yet they couldn't understand. He was speaking spiritually, and they were thinking materially. He was speaking figuratively, and they were thinking literally. It is so easy to get caught in that trap—the trap of thinking only one way. It is easy to be stuck on what has been, such that one cannot adjust to what is becoming.

It is hard to keep a balance between personal faith and what must be the outcome of such faith, which is outreach into the world we live in. Each of us is on a pilgrimage of faith. We are always at some point along the way of that journey. It will bring us along the way of Christ to fuller understanding and more committed discipleship. We must always remember that we can never fully capture the experience in words. The journey will be different for each one of us and must be continually reexpressed with our new understandings as they emerge. The quality of relationship we have with God and with his Son, Jesus, is an eternal quality that begins now and does not wait for death. We can enter into the qualities of eternal life now, in relationships with others. Eternity, then, is a quality of holy bread that can sustain us in the now. It is something the we can have now. It is life eternal, beginning now, as it reaches into forever.

The Cathedral of Your Soul

August 20
1 Corinthians 3:10–11, 16–23

We are God's temple! God's spirit dwells in us. It is God's choice to dwell in us, but he will not dwell there if we do not want him. We build the cathedral of our souls by making Jesus the cornerstone. The building blocks are the many who teach us the Truth. The steeple is our praise and worship. The foundation of Jesus is the cornerstone. Without that, there is no cathedral. He is the only way to God the Father and eternal life. We get that through the teaching and example of our building blocks. Each of us can look back and think of individuals who have contributed to the cathedral of our soul. For some, it is a little chapel; others may only sense a heap of stones. Maybe, it soars with towers and steeples.

Who are your building blocks? They may be parents, grandparents, teachers, friends, mentors, camp counselors, and so on. It starts very early, bringing young children to church and showing the example of personal faith. Later, we need people in our lives that bring us to conviction. That seems like a strange word, but it means to know that we are lost without the Lord. We can each only be saved by our own faith in Christ. Truly, just as we have building blocks, we can be building blocks for others.

Finally the steeple. Worship is not just singing in church. It is marveling at the amazing gifts given to us by God and serving him in whatever way we can. It is a spirit of gratitude and service so that we, and those around us, can see that we are the temple of God himself.

The Fifth Gospel
August 21
1 Thessalonians 1:1–2:4

We now have a fifth gospel. There should be a blank space in our listing of the New Testament books: Matthew, Mark, Luke, John, and *me*. Each individual is a fifth gospel. The majority of persons outside the church see and know only one gospel—what they see in you (or whomever is leading them to understand Jesus). Each day's witness is another page in this gospel; it is a gospel in the writing process.

The beginning of this gospel is how we came to know and believe the gospel, and how one can receive it. We all came to be under the influence and presence of Christ through another person. As we mature in faith, we become imitators of the Lord, and an example to others. To be clear, some of the pages of our "fifth gospel" are smudged, some unclear, yet we can still be read for benefit through the power of God at work through us. To our greatest ability, it is important to remain open, willing to learn, and courageous to let go and really rely on God.

The fifth gospel grows as we continue to mature. This means that it is important to gain knowledge through study, and put it to the test through our actions. Knowledge alone is not enough; the truths must make their way into our hearts and behavior. Our gospel must show that we ourselves have walked with Jesus. One of the abundant characteristics of our faith is that it prevents our coming into disaster. We never know exactly what it is that keeps us from the breaking point, and what will give strength in times of misfortune. There is always a chance to share for the person who is interested in sharing his Lord, regardless of formal education or vocation. The secret of renewal for God's people is to learn the word, love the Lord, and share him.

Two Jobs
August 22
Philemon 20

One of the first questions we ask each other as we get to know one another is, "What do you do?" What we do has such a bearing on our lives. Work consumes a major portion of our time, interest, and energy. To succeed in work is an ardent goal. For many, we pretty much revolve around our work. As vital as that may be, we also have a second job—our vocation of witnessing in Christ.

Now that sounds a bit pretentious, to take on the witness of Christ as a layperson. After all, isn't that the work of the pastors? In reality, the pastors are simply too much in the minority! Think about Christ's sending out of the disciples. They were simple men—laborers—their only training was that they had been with Jesus. Yet they were to go out into the villages and towns and "preach the kingdom of God" (Luke 9:2). They were incredibly effective. They shared what was tremendously real, dynamically alive for them.

Apathy is the great destroyer of our time. Millions belong to the church—and never say a word. While we may agree with this theory—that we must all be witnesses—the chief impediment of witnessing is not knowing how. Often, if we just knew what to say, we would say it. A few tips.

First, we testify not to who we are, but to whose we are. This is crucial, for we are not trying to say how good we are, but how good God is. We all know that we are far from perfect. We make our lives as good as we possibly can, but at the end of the day, we are still unworthy and imperfect. So, we witness by saying to whom we are committed.

Second, we testify by being a friend. This means simply coming alongside the people we care about. Finally, we must realize that our work will be undramatic. The vast majority of people will report that the major influence on their faith was another person. Most of the encounters were relatively inconspicuous. That is, most of the people had made a significant witness without knowing it. Paul wrote to Philemon, "refresh my heart in Christ" (Philemon 20). That is what we are called to do. Not to preach a sermon, but simply to come alongside and share our personal experience.

Well Done!

August 23
Matthew 25:14–30

To whom much is given, much is required. That is one of the harsher truths within the stories of Jesus. In the parable of the talents, the servant that buried his talents (money) in the ground was told that he wasted them—not even receiving interest, and certainly not using the money to its full potential. Jesus was a gentle man, but he also spoke the truth, and sometimes the truth brings us up short. Here, the truth reveals a folly; withholding ourselves, our self, our being, our innermost from God, results in the loss of that marvelous, open, rejoicing relationship with the One True God. Withholding ourselves from God is so unnecessary, and the rewards of opening ourselves are so great.

The useless servant is the one who withholds himself from God. So, how do you use your gifts? Are they used to the glory of God? For that matter, are you using them at all? We all know that if we don't use a talent, we lose it. Every student of a foreign language, every athlete, and every musician knows this truth. Practice, practice, practice! If you do not expose yourself to failure, that is surely what will happen. Not to try is to fail.

In this parable, the master leaves, having given the good gifts. Eventually he returns, and then he settles accounts. What will you do—risk losing everything by putting it all out there, or bury your treasure from the world, and ultimately from God? Let us all strive to hear, "Well done, good and faithful servant!" (Matthew 25:21).

We're In ... or Are We?

August 24
Luke 13:22–30

Entrance into the kingdom of God is not by birth or status, and it is definitely not something someone else can do for us. The door that leads to life is narrow. It requires a distinct decision by each who would enter. Entry occurs one by one. On a tour of the cathedrals of England, it was interesting to note that they often had gigantic doors, so big that it took a huge effort to open them. Not surprisingly, they were rarely used. Most people entered through small side doors, just large enough for one person at a time. Once in, the cathedral stood open before you, in all its glory and grandeur. Another remarkable fact about those doors—you had to hold it open for the next person to get in.

Entry into the kingdom of God also requires ongoing involvement. It is not because of duty but out of desire. As in the cathedral, the experience of entering is only the beginning; the joy is in exploring. In kingdom life, there is an ongoing commitment. The exploration takes a lifetime. There are multiple aspects of this—relationships, understanding, and equipping.

Each person that enters the kingdom of God becomes a new door of entry for others. The joy of the experience invites others in. One can hardly hold back sharing the experience with newcomers. This leads to learning individually as well. It is said that the best way to learn something is to teach it. This is certainly so for faith—the more individual investment in study, prayer, and fellowship with others, the richer the experience becomes. So, walk through that door, get all the way in, invite others, and share the experience widely. Once you are truly inside, there is nothing like it.

What Is Holy?

August 25
Matthew 7:6

The saying "do not give dogs what is holy, and do not throw your pearls before swine, lest they trample them underfoot and turn to attack you," is a tough saying. Our natural response is to interpret this saying as revealing a truth: that there are those who are not ready to receive some parts of the gospel. That there are those who would not only reject it if offered, but ridicule and run it down, and you with it. They are not unfit but unable by attitude or disposition to receive. Perhaps the value of the saying is not so much as a guide to keep us from sharing the good news with the wrong people as it is a call to self-examination. The question is, "How open are you?" How closed are you? What do we trample, put down, turn and rend?

We are often the very ones who trample the truth. We, who act casually toward the holy, ignore and forget what is sacred. What will serve us well is to stop fooling ourselves, to stop congratulating ourselves that we've got it made, and recognize he is calling us to new depth, new commitment, new awareness. If we would win persons for Christ, we must be willing to live with them for a lifetime! We must be willing to suffer with them, forgive, and be humble enough to ask for forgiveness for ourselves. We need to become a friend and share the deep things. Share with them of he who stands the test of time—Christ himself. Jesus is a realist who says we need to treasure the holy and win by a genuineness that stands the test of time. We need to stop trampling and have the courage to develop new friends in his name.

What Would It Take?

August 26
Psalm 130; Ephesians 4:25–5:2

This question is asked in the Psalm passage and answered in Ephesians. If, indeed, the Lord counted all of our sins, big and small, against us, no-one could stand. Yet the Lord forgives, especially as we approach with sincere desire to love and give our whole selves to him. This sounds so simple, but there is a huge leap between the ideals and the actualities. As humans, we are prone to bending and breaking the rules. We tend toward self-centeredness and groping greediness. We respect the ideals and fall far short of fulfillment. We want to do God's will, but time after time, we miss the mark. How, then, can we close the gap?

The greatest hope we have is that the Holy Spirit lives within us. The Holy Spirit prompts us to perform an act of kindness, speak a work of comfort, and be gracious to one another. These are the simple, everyday activities that help us be more selfless and more like Christ. With the help of the Holy Spirit, God asks us to focus on what we can do, not on what we cannot do. Then, God will make it do! God takes our meager efforts and turns them into actions of true value. It is so easy to allow the difficult situations around us to simply follow their natural, destructive courses. With God's help, we can enter into the fray and turn the destruction into positive construction and love for those we can reach.

When Imitation Is Real

August 27
John 6:35

Most of us really don't like imitations. Especially when it comes down to things like butter or coffee or leather. Usually, imitation is synonymous with inferior. However, imitation can also mean the highest praise. It can mean to copy what is superior. In fact, Paul uses the word in Ephesians 5:1: "Be imitators of God, as beloved children." It is an incredible idea! Is it an impossible goal? God is, after all, infinite, eternal. We are, after all, finite, human, of earth.

What would it look like to be an imitator of God? One thing would be to avoid the pettiness in ourselves and ignore it in others. God is always calling us to get past the petty and get on with the big picture. Numerous parables speak to this goal: the Good Samaritan, the prodigal son, and Zacchaeus, among others. In each of these stories, one's initial impression or expectation turns out to be the opposite of what Jesus saw in that person. The Samaritan stopped to help an injured person that the pious priest overlooked. The father welcomes the wayward son with open arms while the obedient son sulks. The hated, tiny tax collector is chosen out of the crowd by Jesus.

Imitating God requires thoughtful observation of habits we read about in scripture. Actors will view dozens of films, read as many books as they can find, and listen to tapes of the voice of a real person they are going to portray in a biography. We, too, must spend time learning about Jesus and the Father in scripture in order to be successful imitators of him.

Why Go to Church?

August 28
Romans 8:1–17

All too frequently, we hear the opinion expressed, "I've never had much to do with the church. I've found it better to live my Christian life without the church and all its petty bickering over nothing." This attitude evolves mainly from a sense of rejection or ignorance. So, how can we reach out to the unchurched Christians?

First, we can admit our failings. The church is a human institution, where members have varying degrees of commitment. Yes, there are church members who are hypocrites. However, the life of the church does not come from the people but from the Holy Spirit within them. This fact is not understood by many people outside the church.

Fellowship with other believers is widely described and encouraged in both the Old Testament and the New Testament. The purpose of attendance is to hold one another up, as well as to spread the good news of salvation. A simple illustration is to watch what happens when a coal is withdrawn from the fire. It doesn't take long for its heat to die out and become black. Without the fellowship of other Christians, our faith, too, will die out.

While the church is imperfect, it is a place to come and be accepted as you are, for everyone in the church seeks improvement through the work of God, his Son, and the Holy Spirit that dwells among us. The benefits of belonging to a church are clear: worship, education, and renewal of spirit through fellowship.

Why, Daddy, Why?
August 29
Proverbs 22:6

The raising of children involves parents in many, many things they had neither anticipated nor prepared for. Like many things in life, it is a venture of faith. One of these times is the period through which all children pass—the "why" stage. Some children are more persistent and inquisitive in their "whys" than others, of course, but to most parents, the phrase, "Why, Daddy, why?" strikes a responsive memory chord. As the incessant "whys" come, a child will stumble on some of the most doggedly difficult questions of the ages. Our answering of these questions can either be a building block or a stumbling stone.

One important area of training is that the attitudes we express on Sunday, at church, are the same on every other day, in every other setting. These include attitudes toward life in general, toward others, toward church, and toward God. Parents who teach one thing and live something else can easily cause children to turn away from the church. To provide a foundation upon which our children may form a faith of their own, we must honestly attempt to live our own faith and to share our struggles to live that faith with our children.

Another critical lesson is that we are here for a reason. God has a purpose and plan for each life. It doesn't have to be in the missionary field or the ministry. It does mean an ideal of worth and value. One can't make the decision for children as to what that plan is, but we can keep before them a sense of purpose and direction. We can explore possibilities, hold up ideals, and most importantly, set an example. Discovering a faith of our own and helping our children do the same is the greatest thing we can give ourselves. We want to belong to God, for nowhere else do we belong!

You Are the Man!
August 30
2 Samuel 12:1–10, 13

One of the extraordinary things about the Bible is the use of flawed, ordinary persons to accomplish the supernatural work of God. King David is one of those persons. One of the most convicting stories about David is that of his relationship with Bathsheba. As you remember, David coveted Bathsheba to the extent that he sent her husband into the front line of battle so that he would be struck down and die. After Bathsheba's husband was dead, David made her his wife.

Shortly thereafter, Nathan, the prophet, came to David and told him a story about two men, one rich and one poor. The rich man refused to feed a traveler from his own flock and instead took the poor man's only ewe to feed his visitor. David immediately stormed that the man who did such a thing deserved to die. Nathan's response to David must have chilled him to the bone. Nathan pointed his finger at David and said, "You are the man!" (1 Samuel 12:7) David was one of the most powerful people in the world at that time, yet he had been caught in a trap of his own making.

How is this story applicable today? Clearly, the act of adultery is occurring all around us, but aside from that, the exploitation of the poor is raging to just as great a degree. Each of us has a lot in the broader issues of our time. The fabric of our society is made up of many individual threads. Do we vote in each and every election? Do we stand up for the right by giving our churches unstinting support and living our lives in rigorous discipline? Indeed, we are held accountable for our actions—large and small—in the kingdom of God. Paul reminds us: "All have sinned and fall short of the glory of God" (Romans 3:23).

Sin is not exactly a popular word these days, is it? Sadly, it has far-reaching results. First, it separates us from God; second, it produces evil effects in the world. Thankfully, we can be forgiven and restored to relationship with God, but the evil effects remain forever. These consequences reiterate like echoes down an empty hallway.

David's immediate response to Nathan was, "I have sinned against the Lord" (1 Samuel 12:13). Humble repentance is the response God desires from us. He knows we are of a sinful nature, and when we turn to him in true remorse, we are forgiven and clean once again.

What's Worthwhile?
August 31
2 Peter 1:3–8

Recently, we were in a group that played the game gossip, the one where you tell a story and pass it around verbally, then see what it becomes at the end. A great story was reduced to a few disparaging words! This is what we do to each other all too often, isn't it? It is so easy to adapt the truth to fit what you think you heard. Unfortunately, the more often a story is told, the shorter it becomes and the more inaccurate. Somehow, it seems that it is easier to elevate ourselves by lowering others rather than trying to lift others and thereby find ourselves being made more whole.

Faith in Christ helps us to be more careful to cherish and appreciate one another. For Christ offers eternal salvation, and when one has eternal salvation, there is worth and value. The world boasts of "salvation"—mostly through the acquisition of wealth, or the escape into such things as drugs or alcohol. The world is set on a path of self-destruction that can only be reversed by looking up to salvation by the Creator. "His divine power has given us everything we need for a godly life through our knowledge of him who called us by his own glory and goodness. Through these he has given us his very great and precious promises, so that through them you may participate in the divine nature, having escaped the corruption in the world caused by evil desires" (2 Peter 1:3–4).

With these promises, we are able to follow the rest of the instruction of Paul: "Add to your faith goodness; and to goodness, knowledge; and to knowledge, self-control; and to self-control, perseverance; and to perseverance, godliness; and to godliness, mutual affection; and to mutual affection, love" (2 Peter 1:5). When you possess and grow these qualities, "they will keep you from being ineffective and unproductive in your knowledge of our Lord Jesus Christ" (2 Peter 1:8). I couldn't have said it better myself! That is what is truly worthwhile.

A Cross for Everyone
September 1
Mark 8:27–37

What image stirs in your mind when you hear the phrase, "take up your cross?" It speaks of suffering and rejection, of pain and death. One even might think of being nailed up to a cross if you are truly Christian. This is likely one of the images that comes to mind when some are afraid to become too serious about Christianity. Surely taking up a cross must be unpleasant—even painful!

It is important to separate Christ's commission to be his hands and feet in this world from simply letting ourselves off the hook. All who have been called by God have their own pilgrimage, their own questions and doubts, and their own longing to do what is right. Until we sort out what it means to truly follow Jesus, we are unproductive servants. There are two factors in faith: conversion to Christ as our personal savior and conversion to productive lifelong discipleship. We are not called to die upon a cross as Christ did; his sacrifice was sufficient for all of us. However, we are called to accept that we will give our God-given gifts to others, sometimes at a sacrifice to ourselves. We are all given such gifts; it is up to us to be willing to use them. Some are prophets, pastors, teachers, healers, helpers; all are contributors and called to love one another as ourselves. Further, part of the daily cross is to do our work happily, grateful for work to do and for coworkers to work beside. It is our purpose—to carry the gift of our saving, sharing cross into a wallowing world.

Christian Faith

September 2
Hebrews 11:1–12:2

"Faith is the assurance of things hoped for, the conviction of things not seen" (Hebrews 11:1, RSV).

Faith is a word of many meanings. We have faith that when we turn the key in the ignition, our car will start. It is by faith that a farmer plants his seed, knowing there will be a crop to harvest. By faith, a businessman stocks his shelves. What is it, then, that makes faith specifically Christian?

Christian faith is not faith in material things. Rather, it is essentially communion with God. Faith has as its grounds, belief in the significance of a historical fact exacted by God. That fact is the resurrection of Jesus. Jesus is the author and perfecter of our faith. Additionally, Christian faith is biblical. The author of Hebrews states: "Without faith, it is impossible to please God, because anyone who comes to him must believe that he exists and that he rewards those who earnestly seek him" (Hebrews 11:6).

It is always easy to think that the apostles and Christians who were contemporaries of Jesus had to have less faith to believe in Jesus. They knew him, yes, but they knew the man. They saw his humiliation on the cross; they saw his humanness, whereas we know him to be victorious over death in his resurrection. Would we have followed him and had faith in him if we had stood next to him on Golgotha and not known that he would be exalted? We can find his loving power and strength through faith, by letting go, by finally saying, "Lord Jesus, you win; I believe."

Consider Your Conduct
September 3
James 2:14–26

There is a wonderful spiritual dynamic tension between faith and works. True faith shows itself in works and results in gratitude and significant response. Faith without works is dead, and works without spiritual foundation will soon die out. We need to consider our conduct, and to do so, need faith to be made new creations.

In this day of two-income families, being a good worker for Christ is quite a challenge. The family is stretched with schedules and activities and heavy stress. The dilemma is that believing in Christ is not enough; truly fulfilling God's will includes doing works in Christ's name. The only way to accomplish this is in the power of the Holy Spirit. Despite being new creations in Christ, we continue to live in a world where good is in contest with evil. We need to be continually filled with Christ's redeeming grace. Little by little, we learn not to dwell in our sin but to seek forgiveness quickly and thereby be healed and restored. With forgiveness and redeeming grace, God does not allow sin to have dominion in our lives. We will make mistakes, but we know in our hearts that we belong to the kingdom of Christ and are in partnership with him.

Faith cements this partnership, and the Holy Spirit changes our hearts to desire to work for the kingdom of Christ. The work actually becomes an outpouring of gratitude for this heart change, resulting in a change in the way we conduct our lives. In this light, we see that faith results in works—they go together naturally. The works actually come out of faith, each part dependent on the other for depth.

Family—Awareness

September 4
1 Corinthians 13

Falling in love. Few phrases can evoke the emotions that this one does. It reflects so much of what is right about human relationships—mutual regard, tenderness, sensitivity, gentleness, kindness, awareness. When one falls in love, every nuance of the other person becomes fascinating, a moment for growth. Think now of how the experience of falling in love relates to the religious experience. One becomes aware of the truth of God in Christ, and along the way suddenly says, "Why, this is it! This is the way my life has meaning. This is how I want to direct my life! This is for real!"

Love is patient and kind. This means patience with people. It is not always easy, because people offend us; they push our buttons. Yet think how God is patient with us. Think of how often we must offend him. Think of how we sometimes forget him or speak of him in vain. Yet he loves us and beckons us to him and asks us to be reconciled within ourselves.

Love rejoices in the right. It is all too easy to see another person's failures. We all know that bad experiences are much more likely to be shared with others than good ones. Yet when we get the idea of rejoicing in the right, of being glad in another's victory, of seeing how the joy of another can add to our joy, things begin to take on a different perspective. That is love.

Love has no limits. It bears all things, believes all things, hopes all things, endures all things. As humans, the limits are all too easy to reach. But God's love is limitless, you know. No matter how much we have done, no matter how far we have wandered, he still longs for us and reaches for us. In fact, as humans, we are more likely to pull away than to move toward God. When we allow the Holy Spirit to come in and touch us and remold us, that is a wonderful thing. That is very much like falling in love. Let us try to keep close this idea of falling in love. To cherish the awareness and newness of love—with God and with one another.

Family—Fidelity

September 5
1 John 4:7–12, 19–21

The most universal experience of humanity is the family. We were born into a family. The whole pattern of search, romance, marriage, and children is part of our attempt to re-create the love and security we either experienced or knew ought to be there in the family. For all our awareness that not all families provide a good soil for mature love and not all families provide wholesome experience for tender childhood, the family is the best training ground in what life is all about and how to live it well.

"We love because he first loved us" (1 John 4:19). That is the truth of the family! We children love because our parents loved us. It is not always easy, though. Sometimes it seems more difficult when you are really in the thick of family. Families are messy sometimes! Families forget to help each other out, to do their part, to remember what is important to each other. We must look to God to see the example of true love. God *is* love. He sent his Son to earth to help us learn what love is. God's love is not capricious; he cares what happens to us. He is not far removed; he broods over us, follows after us, tucks us in at night, thinks ahead for us, puts out his hand to catch us when we stumble.

This is the image of love for which we strive. This is the kind of love that brings out the best in one another. If we love God, then we must also love each other. There is no room for half measures here. Only with God, with the Holy Spirit, can we hope to love others as God loves us. He has given us families in which to practice this. It may not be easy, but it certainly is a beautiful thing when it all comes together. In God's love, we are complete. Love is the only way.

Family—Spontaneity

September 6
Philippians 2:1–11

Spontaneity is a quality in relationships that really keeps things fresh. It is something that happens on the spur of the moment, always good, happy, joyous. Spontaneity holds out hope to aid everyday family happiness and to show us the hand and the smile of God. In order for spontaneity to work, the people involved must be on the same wavelength. In Philippians, Paul says, "Be like minded, having the same love, being one in spirit and purpose" (Philippians 2:2). This does not necessarily mean that there will never be conflict; that, too, is part of what makes good relationships better. But to live in harmony with one another, the conflicts and disagreements must be settled. This might even mean to "agree to disagree."

Another aspect of a relationship that has to be present for spontaneity to occur is mutual trust. Only as we trust one another can we have joy together. Think of planning a surprise for someone. The first step is that you know that the other person will enjoy whatever you have planned. This requires understanding and empathy with that person. It really means that you have to know the person well enough to predict what might make them happy. If everything in a relationship is planned out completely, there is no room for spontaneity, and a very beautiful joy can be lost.

The key ingredients to good, loving relationships are these: awareness, such as we see when we first fall in love; fidelity, the act of staying true to one another; and spontaneity, which requires mutual trust. With these elements, the bond remains strong and fresh, and the goodness of God shines through for all to see.

Fathers and Sons and Prodigals
September 7
Luke 15:11–32

The parables of Jesus are so rich that you can read them over and over again and still learn something new. One way to look at the parable of the prodigal son is to try to see it from the point of view of each of the characters. Finding ourselves in a parable causes it to open right up to us. The point of the story seems obvious from the surface—we are all wayward, and will be welcomed back by God, the Father. The depths of truth become richer and more meaningful as we are able to apply them to our everyday life.

Put yourself in the place of the son. He is the younger son—always in the shadow of the older brother—constantly fighting his position. Finally, the day came that he got his way, and he went off in total ignorance. Soon enough he realized the wisdom of his father and had enough courage to turn around and come home.

The older brother has a different perspective. In his mind, he has always done the right thing and never been recognized for it. Of course, the "always" and "never" are from his limited point of view. This is the peril of the faithful. It is easy to lose sight of what we have gained in being faithful and therefore to look down upon those with newly found faith.

The father. What did he do to deserve this kind of treatment from both of his sons? He gave them everything they wanted, only to have them throw it in his face. He waited and prayed and analyzed until one day he saw his son returning. He must have seen the change in the boy's attitude, even from a distance, and "had compassion" on him.

If you have ever experienced the separation of broken relationships, loneliness, a feeling of being unwanted or unneeded, this parable says to you, "In the Father's house you are precious!" You can always come home.

Glad to Do It, God
September 8
1 John 4:7–21

What is church for? Do we go to do God a favor? Or is it for the forgiveness of our sins and the renewal of our spirits? Why do we serve in the church? To help God out ... as if God needs help. Why do we pray? To tell God what's going on ... as if he didn't know. This is really one of the central theological questions around: Which comes first, faith or works?

"Glad to do it, God." Christian service comes from an overflowing heart. Without the spirit of God empowering us, it becomes habit, or expectation, or duty, or community pressure. Too often in our Christian experience, a subtle reversal takes place. From serving God because of his love in our hearts, we begin to serve God for what it can do for us ... and then for what people think of us for what we do ... and then because we're so good! It boils down to the question of "What is the purpose of humankind?"

In general, the non-Christian philosophers say the real purpose of humans is to fulfill themselves—to develop the fullest potential as a person. The New Testament contends that a person's primary purpose is to glorify God. Now, this doesn't mean that God needs to be glorified for his own sake. He's no egomaniac longing for self-glory. Rather, when the New Testament calls upon us to glorify God, it is in the sense of exalting him as head above all. It is to accord him his rightful place as creator, preserver, redeemer. It is to call him Father. So, Christian service comes from an overflowing heart glorifying God. Glad to do it, God!

Groundwork
September 9
1 Corinthians 3:10–23

Building a structure has many parallels to building the Christian faith. So much work goes into a building—long before the first shovel hits the dirt! Likewise, persons are prepared for taking on their own faith from the beginning of life, though they may not reach their own decision for faith until much later. All of the people in one's life assist in various ways—parents, grandparents, teachers, Sunday school teachers, and many more. What we learn is vastly important in what we become.

The first visible progress on a building is the foundation. The soil must be prepared, the ground leveled, and the concrete properly laid. If the foundation is not sound, nothing built upon it will be either. Our tools, as humans, are the scriptures, the church, the sacraments, prayer, and Christian friends who worship and trust in God. Our foundation is Jesus Christ and the gospel teaching. The basic facts that Christ is the Son of God, that he was born on earth, lived and taught here, then was crucified and died as payment for our sins, only to rise again on the third day, and who continues to sit at the right hand of God as our great high priest are the only true foundation for solid faith. There is a Master Builder, who is himself the chief cornerstone. He can draw out our best and make us into skilled craftsmen. God provides the plan and the words that give and sustain life in peace and truth. It is up to us to remain true to these basics as we grow to full maturity in our Christian lives.

Walls
September 10
Amos 7:7–14

The plumb line is a basic tool in the building trade. It is used to get a straight wall. It is the simplest of tools, operating on the fundamental characteristics of gravity. The plumb line is a symbol of judgment. To place the plumb line against our lives as Christian disciples is to bring into line whatever is unworthy. The truth is not that hard to find. The plumb line is set at the top of the wall, with the weight that brings the string taut. Anything that varies from the line is incorrect, too far one way or the other. This illustration works in our lives as well. We need to set the plumb line of integrity, maturity, teachablilty, and responsibility. We need to check our relationships, values, and goals. To correct variations requires working with others, especially youths, as well as politics and democracy.

Another facet of the plumb line is to see it as God's love. The purpose of judgment and testing is redemption. God is calling us to the highest life we can live. He is calling us to purity, to uprightness, to love, joy, peace, patience, kindness, goodness, discipline, and self-control. He is calling us from darkness to light, from death to life. Let the plumb line be a daily reminder. God does not ask the impossible. He asks only that we follow after that which will give firm foundations, straight walls, and abundant life.

The Steeple
September 11
Isaiah 6:1–8

How carefully we set the foundations of Christian character, and how prayerfully we lay up the walls of our Christian experience together, and how sacrificially we raise the steeple of our worship will determine the quality, usefulness, and lasting character of our Christian witness. The construction of a home is a useful parallel to the construction of a Christian character. It is a parallel that has its reminders all about us in every home we enter, every house we see. The steeple (clearly, not on your average house) is a symbol of lifting our hands in prayer—of reaching for the beauty of godliness. We approach God in gladness, praise his name in adoration, and quickly recognize our own unworthiness. We'll never come to godliness unless we learn to submit our weaknesses to God's light. Thankfully, God does not leave us there. The purpose of confession is not to drag down. It is to lift up. Fact is, no one can be forgiven until he's confessed.

Worship is our highest capacity. It tends to follow an order that flows naturally. We approach God in gladness, praise his name in adoration, and recognize our own unworthiness. This leads to confession, forgiveness, and renewal. There is a natural sharing of concerns, then a realization that each of us is called to serve. We offer ourselves with money and time. Next is a part that many of us skip in our private worship—time of dedication and listening to the Lord. This requires a period of silence. How can we hear the still, small voice of God if we are never still? Closure again brings adoration and praise. How good it is to spend time in the presence of our God, our holy, holy, holy Lord.

Hold Fast
September 12
Hebrews 6:17–20, 10:19–25

In the days of Hebrews, persons who had become believing Christians were falling away from the original enthusiasm. The writer of Hebrews was calling them to hold fast. It is easy to waver in the faith. It comes from taking good things for granted, from not wanting to make any personal sacrifices, from being unwilling to suffer from hard work on behalf of others, and from purchasing our own comfort without thought to the world's total need. How does one remain steadfast?

It is first critical to really know and receive the truth about Jesus. God wants us in tune with him so much that he sent his Son to bring us back. Jesus is the best picture of God we could possibly have. He was God's only Son, of the same substance as God. He lives among us now, since death could not hold him. He reaches out to those who yet doubt; he walks beside those who believe, and he encourages all to win by helping others win.

Along with the presence of Christ, we have the body of believers. We are the church. By gathering regularly, we are able to care for one another, to nudge each other to love and good works, and to encourage one another. The strength we have together far outweighs the strength of any one individual.

How Misunderstood
September 13
Luke 19:41–42; 1 Corinthians 13:12

It seems incredible that Jesus of Nazareth could have been misunderstood. Yet he was. The Jewish community expected the Messiah to come in a blaze of glory. That he could come quietly seemed impossible. Jesus did not come on a white stallion with a band of soldiers to establish his kingdom. He came on a donkey to signify humility and to win the hearts of humans. Because men in position tend to look for that which will enhance that position, the scribes and Pharisees were blind to the vision, and the doors of their hearts were closed. The warning is clear for us. Jesus comes to us, too. He comes to win our hearts. But our image is that if we give him our hearts, he will want us to change our style of life, and we don't want to do that. We want to have him, yes. But we don't want him to change us. Secretly, we're a little afraid that if we let him in, we couldn't change. We don't give up anything to become one of Christ's. We gain everything. What falls away is because we don't need it anymore. He comes not to bind us, rather to free us. That is what he said, and those who have heard that have found it to be true.

Even the death of Christ was misunderstood. At the time, it looked like the end. We know that it is not; it is the beginning. Yet too many of us think that Jesus was an historical person. We classify him along with other great but dead men. The gospel is that he *lives*. He lives within each Christian, wherever you go. The resurrection changes everything. No one else in history has died and risen, living still at the right hand of God.

How to Break Hate
September 14
Matthew 18:21–35

We often think of Jesus as meek and mild. In reality, he was a working man. He worked as a carpenter for most of his life. He was a muscled man with a strong personality. No one wants to be bullied, or to be a bully. What we want is a quiet, sensible, controlled strength that is always used for good. It is so easy to bully when one is strong. Think of it in terms of nations. There are those who think of the United States as a bully. Our sheer strength terrorizes some smaller, poorer nations. In fact, if we are honest, our national strength feels good to us. It gives a sense of security. We need to be strong, as long as we are strong advocates.

On an individual level, it is natural to mistrust those who are different from us. The more different, the harder it becomes. It is interesting to note that the more one knows about another, the more similarities are found, and the differences begin to fade away. Being a Christian compels us to be as well informed as we can possibly be. That means we need to invite people to share as much as possible. God has given us a better alternative than hate. God has given us forgiveness and reconciliation.

Forgiveness breaks the circle of hate. If you are really angry with someone, the first instinct is to "get even." This leads to inevitable escalation; it breeds the need to be better, stronger than the other. Just because one forgives doesn't mean the other forgives. But the possibility is inserted into the exchange. Before, the possibility did not even exist. Forgiveness is a radical idea. But the way of Jesus has worked. When it is practiced, the outcome is peace, harmony, health, and reconciliation. Forgiving frees us to be forgiven as well. Hate ties us up in all the anger and energy of hating. Forgiveness frees us to get on with what brings the abundant life that God promised and that God wants for us.

Living Water
September 15
John 4:5–42

The vignette of the Samaritan woman at the well is easy to overlook. The picture seems normal. A woman goes to the well at noon to get water, runs into a guy who asks for help, and gives him water. The thing is that *no one* goes to the well at noon. This woman is like one of the people standing at the street corner with a cardboard sign. She is an outcast. Not only that, but men don't talk to women, especially Jewish men and Samaritan women. Once you put it into perspective, the scene is transformed. It is a drugged-out prostitute talking to the CEO of the company! He is *the one* who could transform her life.

Jesus knew exactly who the woman was. He also knew that he had something that would change her life forever. She offers water; he offers eternal life. When she hands him the water, he says, "Everyone who drinks of this water will be thirsty again, but whoever drinks the water I give will … come to eternal life" (John 4:13–14).

Part of what is astonishing about this story is that the woman actually sees Jesus for who he is. She becomes one of the first to recognize that he is the Savior of the world. She runs off to share the news like a little girl. How excited are we when we encounter Jesus? Will you run off and share with everyone who will hear that he is the Savior of the world?

Lost and Looking
September 16
Luke 15:1–10

Have you ever been lost? Think back. It was probably when you were small. At first, you might have been just wandering ahead a little, looking at something of particular interest to you. Then, there was the realization that there wasn't anyone around you that you knew. Then that panicky feeling—you didn't know where you were!

You darted a few steps one way, then the other; finally you stopped—lost. Capture that feeling—the emotion, the fear of being lost. See if you can get into the despair of crisis. You felt so helpless! Now, become a parent for a moment. The parent of a child who is lost actually experiences even greater panic; the "what ifs" begin to take over. The parent imagines all the worst possible scenarios.

God is the ultimate parent. He knows it *all*. God has personally written your name on the tablets of life. God feels the pain, understands the fears, touches the tears, and hears the moans that groan, "God help me." God weeps right along with you.

The lost make two mistakes. First, the lost believe that there is no way back—no return. Wrong. Second, the lost believe God doesn't care. Wrong again. Far from that! God is out searching for you, beating the bushes for you; God wants you. The parables of the lost coin, the lost sheep, and the lost son all illustrate these mistakes. More than being parables of lostness, they are really parables of foundness! They are parables of reunion.

Reunion almost makes getting lost worth it! Remember how you felt when you were lost? Now, remember what it felt like when it was over. You were flooded with relief, no longer aware of the petty differences between you and your family. You were flooded with love. It is the same with God. Foundness is simply that we truly, passionately, fervently love God. Then we are no longer lost … or looking.

Mighty Mustard
September 17
Matthew 13:1–9, 31–35

People who work their whole lives in the church and who earnestly strive to live by faith sometimes have a haunting fear that having given all to this truth, it may be, after all, nothing. The disciples certainly carried this fear. They had left everything, alienated their friends and relatives, to a cause that seemed to be fizzling out. Clearly, the kingdom of God was not what they expected. We, who have seen the success of the church rise and fall, may also question where things are going. Evil abounds in our world today; in fact, its influence seems to be growing! Enter the parable of the mighty mustard seed. It is easy to miss the significance of this seed at this time in history and in this country. The mustard seed in Palestine, however, grew to be twelve to fifteen feet tall in a single season! This is, indeed, an impressive feat.

So many of God's greatest happenings begin so unobtrusively that they seem no more important than planting a mustard seed. Great things come from small beginnings—mere sparks of ideas. From each sermon, camp retreat or interaction can come the seed of potential that God will use for greatness. Each good step is a step toward redemption. Not all seeds grow as hoped. Without the proper nourishment, water, and light, seeds may become stunted. Here is the responsibility of the day-to-day Christian. Do we water the seeds of faith that we have planted? Do we give the light of love by sharing our personal faith? Do we provide ourselves with the nutrients of devotion? These are our responsibility; the growth is God's. If we give the seeds of God's Word within us and those around us free rein to grow, they will. Our lives want to be God's, to grow and bear fruit. With total commitment and trust in the promises of Jesus, we will find the heart overflowing with courage, strength, peace, and kindness.

Mind Minds
September 18
Philippians 2:1–13

Mind minds. Take care of your minds. Tend young minds. Cultivate the minds of youths. It is our duty, our privilege, our future. What tremendous things can happen if we will let the mind of Christ be in us. What a wonderful thing the mind is. Ten billion nerve cells, by which we are able to learn and remember; we are able to recall in color, including surroundings, and smells, and how we felt at the time. A mind able to distinguish between dream, hope, and visionary thought, while planning what next and doing something specifically now. A mind capable of imagination and inspiration; capable of controlling the body's muscles, chemistry, and attitudes. Theologians have determined that the location of the soul is in the mind. It is said we have a heart language too. We fall in love, and our hearts beat faster, feel warmed, and grow soft. But it is the mind deciding. The mind is the all-important determinate of life. There is where our will and drive are centered. It is what makes humans unique from all other fauna of the earth. The highest quality of the mind is the ability to understand and to worship the almighty Creator.

The model mind, Paul states, is the mind of Christ. What is implied is that the Christ mind can be put into anyone. The mind grows through the wisdom of the scriptures, the counsel of trusted Christian friends, and by endeavoring to pattern our thoughts and actions after those of Jesus. That is the goal—to move toward the mind of Christ. Action is the proof of change. Our minds are the instrument that employs the body to do our heavenly Father's will.

Attitude is the key. People say they are burned out. Not usually. More likely uninspired, out of ideas, out of imagination. People say they are tired. Sometimes. More likely bored, poor thinking. Let us move into a new mind. The mind of Christ. To see the world through the eyes of Christ will surely bring about a change of mind.

Patches on Old Cloth
September 19
Matthew 9:1–17

Jesus infuriated the Pharisees. Thye spent their time creating complicated rules for simple situations, while Jesus broke huge concepts into simple ideas. In this passage, Jesus clarifies his purpose. Everything is made new in his presence. Jesus is the bridegroom; we may be festive. The fullness of God's real love renders old brittle ways useless and new supple ways necessary, like new wineskins for new wine.

The temple curtain was torn in two—we pray directly to our heavenly Father. We worship in the simplicity of pine trees and rough-hewn benches, or the beauty of a carefully wrought sanctuary. Our prayer is free and open. The Holy Spirit is close in his guidance. Christ makes all things new. Christianity is not a patch; it is a new robe altogether.

To know the newness of life in Jesus, we have to experience his presence in our hearts. This requires a full decision; there can be no standing on the sidelines. The gift of God's Holy Spirit brings a new power in human lives. We are the vessel for that power, yet there was only one perfect vessel—he who broke that vessel upon a cross for us. We do better, often, than we think. We have a tendency to so idealize what a Christian should be that we despair that we can accomplish anything. We can know the joy of Christ shared, the depth of our common life, and the blessedness of our unity in our Lord. Jesus transforms our lives, our loves, our selves.

Promises, Promises, Promises

September 20
Luke 18:1–8

Promises are everywhere. We are bombarded by promises day after day. How many of them do we believe? We feel deep down that somehow, sometime, some way, promises should be kept. When we pray, we expect results. It's easy to get down on God, if you think about it. You feel like you have been faithful, giving, praying, then something happens that seems to be completely wrong. A friend dies unexpectedly, a job is lost, the bills go unpaid. Is prayer for real?

Consider the promises we make to God. "You will be my God, and I will be your people. God, you love us; we'll love you and worship you and serve you and adore you," we promised. Only the fulfillment hasn't quite run the cup over on our side of it. Actually, we'd rather the cup run over in our direction. We want our promises fulfilled, our dreams to become reality, our wishes to become true. How much time and attention do we give to God?

What is the will of God, and how can we know that will? These questions begin to get at the real answer. We would like a "slot machine" God. Plug in a prayer and out pops our heart's desire. Prayer isn't a magic wand. It is a two-way dialogue. Fervent, consistent prayer begins to change the heart of the person who is praying. Deep, meaningful and continual prayer changes our outlook on life; it changes how we see people and how we deal with them and with ourselves. The purpose of this story is to show that it is necessary to pray and not to lose heart. The answer is in the prayer, not necessarily in the outcome.

School Days
September 21
Matthew 7:1–29

A dilemma all too often expressed these days is that people believe in the Bible, believe in God, believe in Jesus, and in Christian ethics and morality, but their faith is vague, and their information is incomplete. It is time to go back to school! The school of Jesus, that is. The Sermon on the Mount is full of phrases that are in common use today, like, "Judge not that you not be judged" (Matthew 7:1), and, "Turn the other cheek" (Matthew 5:39). We've all heard not to be anxious about tomorrow, and love your enemies, and pray for those who persecute you. Yet these are phrases thrown about casually. What can we take from the Sermon on the Mount today?

The first critical lesson was in companionship. The disciples literally spent all day every day hanging out with Jesus. Jesus was the greatest teacher the world has ever known. Companionship involved learning how to love God and their fellow humans from Jesus, who made it his whole life. They learned that it was a serious undertaking—it could even cost their lives.

They also learned through friendship. Jesus interacted with them, and the disciples with each other, in frankness and love. With Jesus, we can truly be ourselves. No pretending or false affection needed. It is important to ask questions and consider the answers. This means to be honest and open, and to spend plenty of time with him.

Finally, Jesus was a great encourager. The goal of becoming like Christ is a high one. Sometimes it seems impossible. We must remember that God would not have put us here if he had not also placed within us the ability to know redeeming fellowship with him. We stumble, of course, but we also are encouraged to get up again. There is no need to be "religious." We seek companionship as we walk alongside him, friendship as we pause to learn of him, and encouragement as he puts upon us his attitudes and deeply believes in us despite our weakness.

The Discount

September 22
Ephesians 4:1–16

We all like a good bargain. We even like to think that we got the better end of the deal! A bargain discount increases value to us. However, in another sense of the word, it decreases value. Ideas are discounted because of the credibility of the source, or information altered its impact, decreasing the worth. The human tendency is to discount others. To devalue or impersonalize them. This tendency has gotten us into trouble historically. Most notably during World War II and ongoing instances of racial discrimination.

We also tend to discount others personally. It is all too easy to make a harsh, critical judgment on another based on some superficiality. Stereotyping occurs when there is a lack of personal knowledge, particularly where there are obvious physical differences. If there were communication, each would probably be closer together and could learn some valuable lessons from the other. So many times we find that the very person we once disliked becomes a friend when we get to know them.

To cherish, uplift and revalue others is one of our chief Christian commitments. To be a Christian is to be diametrically opposed to the discounting of persons. To gather together in Christ is to secure our forgiveness, set us right again, and revalue us. When we appreciate that we are children of God, the next step is to know that another is a child of God also. In the words of Paul, "Live a life worthy of the calling you have received. Be completely humble and gentle; be patient, bearing with one another in love. Keep the unity of the Spirit in the bond of peace" (Ephesians 4:1–3).

The Four Rs
September 23
Romans 12:1–21

The most common and vivid memories we can share together likely involve our school days. Of course, most of us remember the three Rs— reading, 'riting, and 'rithmetic. Four Rs that are central to Christian faith and life: receive, revive, rejoice, and respond. How very fortunate every Christian ought to feel. We are inheritors of a great line of splendor. We have received grace upon grace. No one can receive the blessing of God for us. No one can be a Christian for me. The faith is offered, proclaimed, shouted, even, but it can only be received individually and personally. What a blessing when it is received. It's not a once and for all thing; we fall short regularly. Christ is ready to revive us when we fail. We are encouraged by Paul to "never flag in zeal" (Romans 12:11). This is critical, because faith is not a guarantee that we will never get tired or weary with well-doing; rather it is the promise that in the midst of our weariness we will be lifted up through the discipline of the faith and made fit for what God may give us.

The third R stands for rejoice. We are privileged to rejoice together with our Christian brothers and sisters. Of course, those who rejoice together also weep together, and both serve to cement the relationships, leading us to love one another, to share hopes and dreams and visions of the future. This also gives us a springboard to bring those who weep outside of the life of the church back into a state of rejoicing. The right response comes naturally. To "overcome evil with good" (Romans 12:21). This is the essence of the faith. This is our hope and confidence. This is our work to do.

The Stone of Stumbling

September 24
1 Corinthians 1:20–31

There are many stones of stumbling in this life; these may also be known as obstacles. They represent that which holds us back and detains us from reaching some desire or object. What causes people to stumble today? One area is the desire to give allegiance to some person as supreme authority. William Penn once said that man would obey either God or the tyrant. Basically, all philosophies fall into the category of believing that salvation is of God or believing that salvation is of humankind. As Christians, we must exercise the prerogative of thinking. For no man can become our superman; we owe our first and primary allegiance to God.

Another area of stumbling is the delusion of power. Power is a reality in this life. However, power can be a means of losing freedom just as it can preserve it. Power can shoot people down or lift them up. It can be used to prove a political point by bringing people into submission or to upbuild the dignity and worth of each person. There was only one man in history who could be trusted with any kind of real power. He made it perfectly clear that power belongs to God and can only be used under his control.

A third obstacle can be the desire for all to conform to a set pattern. It is easy to think that only teenagers are subject to peer pressure, but a quick look at one's lifestyle shows the desire to "keep up with the Joneses." Unfortunately, those who want to avoid being different above all else are in danger of tyranny. Vital Christianity doesn't come from conformity. It comes from an individual encounter with the person Jesus Christ. Christ called his followers to be transformed to be like him, rather than to be conformed to the world. He warned that Christ followers would not be the same as the world but would be subject to persecution, just as he was. Christ is the solid rock upon which we can stand. In him all stones of stumbling can be surmounted.

Times of Refreshing
September 25
Acts 3:1–21

Think of some times in which you have experienced physical and spiritual refreshment. In the busyness of the daily tasks that occupy so very much of our waking hours, it is important to give thought to restorative reflection. This allows us to settle on what it is that we value and cherish most. What we would be willing to give up our lives for.

Times of refreshing come through pointing ourselves Godward. We have to want that refreshment. We must get in tune with the center, in touch with the nature of God's creation. Such things as harmony, rather than disharmony; building persons up rather than tearing them down; affirming instead of finding wrongs; nurturing as over against being toxic. This means that we will work on being centered in the presence of the Lord. The presence of our Lord is our greatest asset. It means looking at a situation through his eyes, his priorities, rather than our own. The source of strength for the Christian is our Lord. It is worth the effort to seek and do what the Lord likes. God being our guide and stay … it is truly refreshing!

What He Said
September 26
Matthew 5:1–16, 22:34–40

Jesus said that the summation of all the law and the prophets was, "To love the Lord your God with all your heart, and with all your soul, and with all your mind," and "Love your neighbor as yourself" (Matthew 22:37–39). So simple and yet so deep. There are really two critical dimensions: relationship with God and relationship with people. Only when we have established a rightful relationship with God can we hope for stable and shining friendships with others. But how? Human friendships provide a dim parable. To become friends takes time, getting to know one another, sharing deeply, giving of ourselves. So, we must seek God's company. We try to trace his mind by searching the scripture. We develop eyes to see the working of his hand. This is good, but it requires one thing more—the love of Christ, which brings the presence of the Holy Spirit. We can't succeed on our own; we must receive the gift of Christ.

The horizontal dimension is truly a challenge. The world is our neighbor. We know in ourselves that when we don't see others as children of God, we are capable of almost any savage brutality. A quick look at history underscores this reality. The real issue lies in the need to see value in our highest self, which is self in God. Shakespeare put it clearly in *Hamlet*: "To thine own self be true. And it must follow, as the night the day, thou canst not then be false to any man." All are children of God, and therefore of the highest value.

What're You Doing Here?
September 27
Genesis 1:31–2:3

In the creation story we are confronted with the basic question of our purpose for existence and find the answer in our response to God in fellowship and witness. Without an answer, life is hollow and aimless. Genesis tells us that we are children of God. The Bible is not a book of science. It is a book of witness, of faith, of proclamation concerning the acts of God. It hews to historical fact and is thereby historical. In the Bible, history is incidental, God's act and human's response is primary. What a tremendous thing to be able to say, "God is my creator!" Furthermore, we are created in the image of his spirit. Sometimes our lives get about as scrambled as the puzzle in the box. But if God is our creator, we have a place. We have a part.

Humans are creatures fashioned by God—made in his image. But they are not, thereby, God. They are still creatures. They were made of the stuff of mortality—the stuff of the earth, the dirt. God gave us dominion over all the earth, made us responsible to the rest of his creation. While all humans are created by God, those who have become reconciled to him by faith are his sons and daughters. A decision is necessary to become sons and daughters. God limited himself. He said we could say no to him. If we deny his laws, his fellowship, we will suffer the consequences. But we do have that choice. It is a choice that is constantly kept before us throughout scripture. This is what the fascinating story of Adam and Eve and the apple is about. For, having picked the apple, humans now must be reminded again and again, they are never true to themselves, and they can never really be content until brought back to the great thoughts and lofty impulses that were planted in them as their heritage from God.

Who Is He?
September 28
John 1:1–18

The world population is rising at an alarmingly fast rate. It took humans two hundred thousand years to reach one billion, and only two hundred years to reach two billion. We are becoming increasingly identified by numbers and codes instead of names and faces. The whole computerization of masses of digital information has made possible a higher standard of living because it increases individual productivity. So, does it matter who we are? World War II and the Holocaust helps to demonstrate the importance of the individual. Hundreds of thousands of people simply disappeared from their homes. How did this happen? Because a belief was fostered that some human beings were inferior to others. Given that belief, the world is better off without them. In some ways, the attitude is not even that surprising. We don't throw away things we cherish! We don't take our best things to the dump! Those that become devalued actually begin to lose track of their own value; they forget *who they are*.

As Christians, we are children of God. This fact has intrinsic value. God sent Jesus himself to save us. John states, "In the beginning was the Word, and the Word was with God, and the Word was God … the Word became flesh and dwelt among us" (John 1:1–2). If this is not true, then we have been duped! If it is true, it is the most startling, magnificent, and important thing to ever happen in the world! If you accept that "Who is he?" can be answered, "The Son of God, the Word of God embodied in a person," then at least three exceedingly important things happen: (1) he speaks the Word, (2) he speaks to our minds, (3) he speaks to our hearts. The beautiful thing about our Lord is that he is *person*. Not thing. Not just idea or concept. Person. Jesus is a living person, and believing in him is the most important thing we can do in our entire lives. It is the true definition of who we are.

Why Stand Out There?
September 29
Matthew 20:1–16

Parables were never meant to be timeless models for universal application. They were meant to illustrate spiritual truths by letting us find ourselves in the midst of our everyday surroundings. This parable speaks of a situation where workers agreed on a wage at the beginning of their work, and were all paid the same amount regardless of how long they worked. The pay was at the discretion of the owner. Many possible meanings have been proposed. There are several key contrasts.

First is the difference between labor as a contract versus labor as love. This is a reality of our faith. Salvation cannot be earned. If so, it would only be the fulfillment of a contract. The earthly ministry of Jesus was to draw us away from legalistic self-righteousness into a humble and contrite heart and a right spirit within. A second contrast is that between living by comparison and living by grace. How often do we cripple ourselves with embittered comparisons? The point is that the Lord is generous. God is gracious and merciful and forgiving. But we hold back. The banquet table is spread, but we stand outside. Why? Because no one hired us; no one saw our hidden talent; no one sought us out hiding behind the pillar. Why stand out there? Come in. Rejoice. Repent. Be forgiven, and enjoy the labor of the vineyard. Where are you in this parable? How many times have you identified yourself versus thinking of someone you know it applies to? Consider looking for ways to win our neighbor to the joys of the faith instead of waiting to be fed. Try to find a place of service in which to rejoice and give, without seeking a reward. The parable is a parable of comparisons. It highlights the difference between our thinking and the thinking of the heavenly Father. It calls us to adjust those attitudes so as to be more in line with those of the Father than the world. Come in; the gate is open. The Father's arms are wide.

Wisdom Comes One Notch at a Time

September 30
Job 28:20; Mark 9:33–37; James 3:13–18

It would be quite a good world if we were all wise. It is unfortunate that wisdom has to come one notch at a time. Wisdom can be right, and wisdom can be wrong. So much of our worldly wisdom comes from common folklore. It can be found in Proverbs and in the book of Job. Many of the old sayings are true, but what happens when they are not, such as when practice does not make perfect? What happens when wisdom fails you, and you get hooked on the world's lures? When the disciples were caught by Jesus arguing among themselves about who would be the greatest in the kingdom, he brings them a little child. Probably about two. Beautiful, energetic, innocent, accepting, loving, unpretentious. We need the little children among us. They can drive us crazy, true, but they do teach us grace. They do not live among us because they have earned the right or because of status and standing, yet we know that they are the most precious among us. Because of the children, we learn the need for a childlikeness within us. We learn that the wisdom sayings are both right and wrong. They teach us important things to know, but they do not help us when we stumble and fall.

We cannot earn our way; we cannot be good enough to storm the gates of heaven. True wisdom is knowing that. We are not let off the hook. We still need to be wise in the traditional sense. The sheer brilliance of the Ten Commandments is that they codify in a handful of words acceptable human behavior not just for then or for now, but for all time. There is wisdom, and there is grace. They reside together. Wisdom comes one notch at a time.

American Dream or Christian Hope
October 1
Exodus 3:1–6; Acts 7:51–8:11

It is easy to confuse the American dream (having more) with the promises in scripture of an "abundant life." The dream can easily become a nightmare! Christian hope is different; while it includes that God will provide, it is rooted in our complete trust in God. It defines who we are and grounds us in obedience to God's laws, thereby defining how we live. Humans are acquisitional creatures. We like to collect things. We seem to think that if we can surround ourselves with enough stuff, and it holds enough prestige for us, then somehow, we'll really be someone! There are endless demands and desires, far beyond our means, so we work harder or go further into debt, until, one day, we say, "That's enough!" We're exhausted and have no time for our things, let alone friends and family. Somehow, enough is always just out of reach; its just a little bit more. The scriptures say that God wants us to have abundant life, but this path does not lead to what is intended. The secular world appeals to that part of us that wants to be special and implies that we can obtain it by outward evidence.

The Christian hope proclaims that we are special because God is our Father, our Maker. We are set apart by knowing and loving the heavenly Father. It truly has nothing to do with us. The decision to give our lives over wholeheartedly to Jesus the Savior and decide from that day on to live by the will of God changes everything. It isn't always easy; turning away from God occurs almost constantly; you must know God so completely that you know that you can only find wholeness through forgiveness and a new life. We move toward deliverance as we pray, study, and give in his name.

Let Us Pray
October 2
Matthew 6:6–15

The Lord's prayer is one of the most treasured instructions we have from Jesus. It is rich and full, sincere and simple, complete and adequate. Unfortunately, we often misuse the Lord's prayer. We mumble it distractedly, we sing it overdramatically, we rattle it off mechanically. How has this come to be? One problem is that we know it too well. We repeat it so often that we come to use it thoughtlessly, without regard for the really awesome petitions we are repeating. We have committed it to memory—true. But all too frequently, we have not taken it to heart.

The Lord's prayer was not intended to be repeated as the only prayer ever given on our knees, but as an example. Jesus said: "This, then, is how you should pray" (Matthew 6:9). The message was to give our prayers the reverence, the simplicity, the directness, and the ethical balance of one like this. Each phrase carries its own message and could become a full prayer in and of itself. Let us truly be aware of the sacred holiness of God in heaven. Let us recognize that we serve a coming kingdom here and now. Let us come into a proper attitude toward earthly needs and worldly temptations. Let us truly have forgiveness now and to come. Let us deeply sense the power and glory of God forever. If we can do this, we may find the full understanding of the Lord's prayer to be a key to real spiritual power for us.

Our Father
October 3
Luke 11:1–13

Prayer is how our souls interact with God. Jesus teaches his disciples to approach God as, "our Father." Most of the time, we have repeated the words so quickly that we don't stop to think about them. It is hard to even wrap our minds around the fact that God is "our" Father! The use of the word *our* is significant, because it points out that we are not alone, even in prayer. One of the major difficulties of prayer is our selfishness. Jesus, then, gives us the right perspective as he prays, "Hallowed be Thy name." When we address our heavenly Father, we must be reminded to center our lives in him who is greater than ourselves.

The word *father* has special meaning. In the original language, the word was *"Abba,"* more closely translated as "Daddy." Simply saying the word daddy softens most of our hearts. Even if your earthly daddy was not ideal, it is comforting to know that the heavenly Father is truly perfect; he is the manifestation of love. If we humans are able to give to those we love, how much more will the heavenly Father do so. He makes more than ample provision for each of us. He is in heaven but also right here with us, in our midst.

Jesus guides us to speak to God first about his nature and goodness, before bringing our own needs, transgressions, and struggles. This is not to remind God of what he is like, but to remind ourselves of who God is. This helps us learn to apply his plans to our lives rather than to attempt to mold the Lord into our plans. Putting God first is our first lesson in spiritual efficiency. In recognizing his holiness we begin to achieve a right attitude toward all of life. True prayer begins with the recognition that God is near, that he accepts all of us as we are, and that life itself is holy because God is holy.

Thy Kingdom Come
October 4
Luke 17:5–21

When we say, "Thy kingdom come," we mean that God reigns sovereign in our lives. His reign is contingent upon ourselves, for the kingdom is truly within us. In reality, we often say these words while thinking that the kingdom will only come in paradise. As Christians, we are responsible for making the world around us better. How desperately we need to be reminded that it is God who reigns. Our days are immersed in the empires of this world. We face demands from the government, social obligations, work, and even our own homes and family. These empires claim authority over life and limb, when, really, they are simply creations of humans, not of God. Our primary allegiance belongs to God.

Through the centuries, humans have tried to wiggle around this "Thy kingdom come" bit. The reality is that we all have reservations. Sinful humans cannot obey the law of love. Even with the help of God, we are unable to do what we know we ought to do—to love our God with all our hearts, minds, souls, and strength … and our neighbor as ourselves. The kingdom of God has entered into history in Jesus Christ, but in its fullness, the kingdom is yet to come. Jesus revealed truth, love and power, but the final consummation will occur when he returns.

We are not left idle; there is much to do. We must look beyond ourselves and toward those less fortunate. We can seek improved education and distribution of world goods. Most importantly, we learn to love our neighbor, regardless of race, creed, and color.

Thy Will Be Done
October 5
Matthew 26:30–46

How many of us truly believe that prayer is an effective force in our world? If we were to go out into the world and poll popular opinion, we would find that prayer falls into the category of, "Praise the Lord and pass the ammunition!" In other words, prayer is OK when your back is up against the wall, but you will still rely on what you can physically do. The Lord's prayer states: "Thy will be done on earth, as it is in heaven" (Matthew 5:10). It is one thing to say that, but how do we know what the will of God is?

The will of God is that we should put into action our knowledge of him in Jesus Christ hand in hand, walking in fellowship with each soul. We must develop and promote a sensitivity to the needs of our world and our neighbor. We need to hurt together and rejoice together. In reality, the will of God requires a decision. It involves the individual conversion and dedication of each one who would be an adopted Son of God.

Jesus's prayer in the garden of Gesthemane was that the cup be taken away from him. "Yet not as I will, but as you will (Matthew 26:39). He knew, as we know, that the flesh is weak, but with God, all things are possible. In our own minds and hearts, we cannot do the will of God, but with the Holy Spirit guiding us and giving us the power, we can know and do his will. It is easy to think it is impossible. You might not even want to do what God has set before you. With courage, our own willingness, and the power of the Holy Spirit, we can each take the single next step ahead. That is what God asks of us.

Give Us This Day
October 6
Matthew 6:17–33

God is aware of our needs. He knows we have needs. Most of us have much more than we need, and can chastise ourselves all day about our material abundance in the face of want elsewhere. But we still need bread. Bread is central to live. It is the word signifying the necessity of sustenance to flesh and blood. God knows we need bread, and we must trust him to provide not only for ourselves, but for whomever is hungry.

It is another lesson to consider that Jesus prayed for bread; he did not pray for cake! He was teaching us that material luxuries can rapidly lead us away from God. It is difficult to draw the line designating where bread leaves off and luxury begins. Overconcentration on things can end in our being enslaved to them. The use of the word *us* helps us see that where we have overabundance, we need to reach out to see where we can share with those who do not.

This day. Today. Another reminder to avoid getting ahead of ourselves. We want what we want, and we want it *now*. God can become a slot machine, into whom we plug a supply of prayers and from whom we expect a return of properly merchandised hopes. When we focus on anything beyond today, we are acting as if our future was in our own hands, not the hands of God. We are not promised tomorrow and yet spend so much time preparing for it! This is the root of anxiety, as the scripture lesson points out: "Do not worry about your life, what you will eat or drink; or about your body, what you will wear. Is not life more important than food and the body more important than clothes?" (Matthew 6:25). Consider focusing on today, and the joy and troubles before you, and you will have come a long way toward seeing God's will on earth.

And Forgive ... Even ... Us

October 7
Luke 23:26–34

True prayer is at one and the same time a most humiliating and a most sublime thing we do. It is starkly humiliating, because in prayer, we stand with naked souls, unmasked thoughts, true selves before God. Prayer is soothingly sublime because it renews twisted and broken fellowship between ourselves and our God. Prayer is not something we do naturally as many suppose. Though we seem compelled to pray particularly in times of stress, it is not something we do well or easily.

We need forgiveness, for none of us are faultless or without offense. The relationship of fellowship with God was broken in the Garden of Eden with Adam and Eve. The sins of each day are almost countless: negative thoughts, hasty words, lack of self-control, opportunities lost, lack of forgiveness, laziness, and procrastination, and on and on and on. So God made his provisions. We put up a dam; God built a fish ladder. Jesus saves us from our disobedience to a renewed fellowship. Jesus brings our petition to God with the endorsement of our belief and trust in him.

We are forgiven as we forgive. Unless we forgive, we have no understanding of forgiveness. It is not hard to say, "I forgive everyone who has ever wronged me" without thinking of any specific wrongs. Add in the specific instances of being wronged, and how that affected our lives, and we have a different story. Disobedience, dangerous choices, loss of trust between each other, these things hurt. Yet we need to forgive and be forgiven. We ourselves change as we forgive. It renews a softness of heart toward those who have wronged us. Good relationships require soft hearts.

But Deliver Us
October 8
Psalm 40

Can or does God ever lead men into temptation? Certainly, God does not tempt us; we are tempted by the enticement and allurement of our own desires. The statement "And lead us not into temptation" is a very accurate translation of the Greek phrase. It is important to look at the whole sentence: "Lead us, not into temptation but deliver us from evil" (Matthew 5:13). God will lead us. He has, however, given us the freedom to decide, and he cannot lead us until we give ourselves into his leadership. We must surrender. This is only the beginning, for we also have to attempt to live by his leading. This means listening to his voice when our own voice tries to crowd him out. This means using our own will to turn away, with his guidance. There will be temptation, but God takes us beyond ourselves to a higher good: the fellowship of the great commandment: Love God with all your heart, soul, mind and strength; and love your neighbor as yourself.

God's leading also delivers us from evil. He allows us to triumph over our sinful desires with the Holy Spirit within us. We can hold up the highest ideals, though we are unable to keep them ourselves. With God's guidance, we can apply them to our lives and return to them when we fail. God allows us to be a part of our own deliverance! We first resist temptation through the support of our fellow believers and humble prayers; then, having failed to resist the evil, we can find the forgiveness of God that renews and lifts one to walk once again.

For Thou Art Eternal
October 9
Matthew 6:5–15

The closing of the Lord's prayer as it is now said is: "For thine is the kingdom, and the power, and the glory forever. Amen." This ending is added as a footnote in many versions of the Bible, and in Luke, it is not stated at all. Many Bible scholars conclude that the ending was not originally said by Jesus. However, it rounds out the prayer so satisfactorily, and has been found in manuscripts as close to the original as fifty years, so most of us would not want to omit it. This phrase is really a confession of faith—God does reign, this is a fact. His reign is invisible but undeniable. Anyone who has seriously considered this earthly existence has come to an awareness of the instability of earthly things and the need to grasp things that are eternal. This is God's kingdom.

God's power is equally challenging to completely define. He is able to create everything out of nothing. He can cause and calm the storms; he filled the ocean and gave it limitations; we are but a speck in the universe he created. He is also involved in the intimacy of a rosebud, a baby's smile, and a warm sunny day. God can redeem a soul. He can deliver us from pride and arrogance and greed. He can open our eyes. He is the epitome of love—love that does not demand return but requires a personal choice to accept. This is God's power.

Glory. God's glory is in every living thing. It is in everything around us. It is in a quietly helping hand. It is doing the right thing regardless of where we are or under what circumstances or who happens to be around. Glory is recognizing that the only source of life is God himself and humbly living that every day. To live lives in humble obedience to God's ways, and giving him praise: this is God's glory.

Amen. So be it.

A Vision of Who We Are
October 10
Mark 10:46–52

At a certain age, most of us are forced to wear glasses. Be it bifocals or trifocals, or just for reading, they are a bit of a challenge, but at least with them, we can see! What a privilege it is to see. When the glasses allow the letters to become clear, it opens up a whole new perspective. The story of Jesus healing the blind man describes one of the most powerful moments in the ministry of Jesus. A man is singled out, and asked, "What do you want me to do for you?" Can you imagine hearing that question? Then, being told, "Your faith has made you whole" (Mark 10:51–52).

It is beautiful, yet so many still turn away. The unique claim of Jesus was that in the fullness of time, God sent his Son to bring the message that God's will is to unify all life in the Creator in order that all life may live joyously and abundantly. Jesus is God's hug for the world. We are either restored by it or repelled by that hug. Jesus is the work of God incarnated. He is not just anyone; he is the most potent friend we can possibly have for these days and for eternity. In healing the blind man, Jesus fulfilled prophecy from hundreds of years prior to his coming and caused there to be vision where there had never been vision before. When we accept Jesus as our friend and Lord, we realize the fullness of our own beings. We are God's people, and we have the purpose to spread that life-giving knowledge to all persons. Jesus is a guide to the blind, and a light to those who are in darkness. He calls us to be the same.

Christs Reveals

October 11
Hebrews 1:1–4

Prior to Jesus, God spoke to humans through the prophets and through the lives of Abraham, Isaac, and Jacob. Moses was a key prophet as well. In Jesus, however, the testimony is that God himself, in the person of his only Son, is present among us. This is God we can touch. This is God of whom we can ask questions. This is our primary family, flesh of his flesh; brothers and sisters together. This is great news, because nothing is more important than a loving family.

Children are so refreshing. As adults, we grow more staid and less effusive. But the children of the family love so transparently. How wonderful it is to hear a child say something like, "I love you with my whole heart!" and be overjoyed to be with their family. We are the children of God, and God is love. The more love we have and the more love we pass on means we will be blessed, and we will be a blessing. Thanks be to God.

Come What May
October 12
Job 13:13–16, 42:10–17

All most of us know about the book of Job in the Old Testament is that Job was a patient man. Despite all the adversities that beset him—and they were great—still he didn't give up and deny God. In fact, Job was an impatient man. He impatiently listens to his advice-giving friends and storms at God, wanting to plead his righteousness. He disagreed with the venerable belief that suffering was a punishment for sin. He, himself, was an evidence that experience proved the belief wrong, he felt. One of the most quoted verses in Job is: "Though he slay me, yet will I trust in him" (Job 13:15). This catches the major message of Job: That salvation comes in ultimate trust in God and that ultimate trust brings face-to-face confrontation and peace.

Job knew he was righteous to the extent that his humanity permitted. He also accepted the fact that all things come from God, both the good and the bad. Honest evaluation of our own actions, and appropriate confession and repentance, allows rightness with God. Come what may, trust and grace are the eternal guarantees. Job comes to realize that the only hope for him is to ultimately trust his creator to be gracious and merciful. He caught a vision of God and suddenly recognized that his righteousness was not the laborious work of his hands but the gift of God. He saw that the greatest possession was not wealth or even health but fellowship with God. What happens to us in this world, then, is basically incidental. Our fellowship with God and humankind is essential.

This eternal truth offers help in times of uncertainty and anxiety. We must always do what we can, according to the information we have. After that, we must trust God if we believe he is Father and is concerned for his creatures. God doesn't overthrow the sins of humans, but he forgives them and opens a pathway to reconciliation. We can affirm in gladness and confidence that in trouble, a sure and steadfast reliance upon the Lord will bring perspective. We can witness that in developing a way of life that places God at the center and shares of ourselves in significant ways, there is a blessing from God. Come what may, he is with us.

Devoutly Kneeling
October 13
Luke 18:9–17

It is news when a person devoutly kneels and takes the solemn promise and vow of fidelity to God. The vows are important: Do you confess Jesus Christ as your Saviour and Lord and pledge allegiance to his kingdom? Do you receive and profess the Christian faith? Will you be loyal to the church with your prayers, presence, gifts, and service? Becoming a Christian—professing Jesus—does not require that you devote yourself to the church. However, without the church, growth as a Christian is virtually impossible. The church is not its denomination, building, pastor, or programs. The church is the body of Christ—the people.

With that, prayer is critical. Prayer changes perspectives. Prayer cultivates the inner life. Prayer helps discipline the body to serve the soul. When we pray, we stand before God as we are—there is no façade, no "public smile"—we can simply rise with our hand upon a central source of power and focus. There are so many distractions. We are too busy to be good spouses, good companions to our children, good friends, good employees, to take time to experience the quiet presence of God. Quiet time does not have to be a specific time, or even a specific period of time. It can be a breath, a pause, a moment to really be alone with our inner selves.

Surrender of our whole selves to God allows all of our outer commitments to be integrated into a single true self, whose whole aim is to humbly walk in the presence and guidance and will of God. Only so, may our lives be unshakeable, because we are clear down on bedrock, rooted and grounded in the love of God. In this way, we can live a prayerful existence in which all of life can be given the face of holiness, in which prayer and heavenward awareness are undergirding elements of each moment. This is a revolutionary way of living. It is living by devoutly kneeling in which religion isn't something to be added to our other duties, but where the life with God is the center of life, and all else is remodeled and integrated by it. The deepest need of humans is not food and clothing and shelter, as important as they are; it is God.

Dual Citizenship
October 14
Matthew 22:15–22

We like to think that debates are a modern way of politics, but in reality, what is new is our access to them. Now we have the feeling of participating even from our own homes! Really, debates fuel much of our own inner battles regarding our future and our nation. In the days of the Old Testament, a running battle was going on. During the time of the tribes and wandering in the wilderness, God was King. God provided manna and meat and water. God provided order and direction. Once the Israelites settled, they begged for a human king, like everyone else! Of course, those kings were fraught with human frailties and ultimately landed them in exile and anguish. Finally, the people and the prophets began to speak of a one who would yet rise up and save them … a savior, a messiah. As we know, eventually, one came, but many doubted. How could this one be the promised deliverer? Where were his armies? What was his plan? What were his trappings of power? What evidence was he showing of conquering?

The current powers that be were bent on discrediting him and asked many questions that were designed to trap him. Any answer was wrong and no answer at all was also wrong. The question was, "Is it right to pay the imperial tax to Caesar or not?" (Matthew 22:19). Jesus wisely asked for a coin and fouled their plans by answering with the famous phrase, "Give back to Caesar what is Caesar's and to God what is God's" (Matthew 22:21). Wow.

This brings out the fact that our faith gives us a dual citizenship. We are citizens of our nation, and we are citizens of our Lord's kingdom. The challenge lies in determining what is God's. One way is through our faith. A primary work of faith is to know, deeply and at the core of our being, that all things came from, are created through, and belong to our God. A second way is through our labor of love. Here, we are required to humbly accept that we are sinners in need of a savior. The third way is to be steadfast in hope. In this, it is critical to believe and act on the belief that we can make a difference. One of the biggest dangers in our dual citizenship is to think we simply don't count. With and through Christ, we can and do count. Dual citizenship is a big task. But then, our God promised us significance, not ease, usefulness, not compliance, and partnership, not puppetry.

Except a Man Die ...
October 15
John 12:20–26

"Except a grain of wheat falls in to the earth and dies, it remains alone; but if it dies, it bears much fruit" (John 12:24).

Some say that the difference between an atheist and a Christian is the open grave. For one it is the end, for the other it is part two. Faith tells us the person who saves their life loses it. It tells us that giving is living. It tells us that service is our best measure of greatness. It is recorded that a king of Israel died without being acknowledged. What a lonely, eerie epitaph. It causes one to look at life and ask, "How can I live so that it makes a difference that I'm alive?"

If a person is to be born again, there is some dying to do. Let's consider a few areas of dying. Is anyone holding a grudge? Kill it. Is anyone nursing a sorrow? Git rid of it. How about the words: "I want it" or "I want to" as the best reason for a purchase or an action? Yes, there's some dying to do, and it's hard to die. But it is the only way to live!

In addition to dying to self, we also need to spend life to retain it. We need to give, share, love, respond. John Barclay put it this way: "No doubt we will exist longer if we take things easily, if we avoid all strain, if we sit at the fire and husband life, if we look after ourselves as a hypochondriac looks after his health. No doubt we will exist longer—but we will never LIVE at all. Only by spending life do we retain it."

Finally, by service comes greatness. Jesus said, "If anyone serves me, he must follow me; and where I am, there shall my servant be also; if anyone serves me, the Father will honor him" (John 12:26). The devil must hate people that dedicate their lives to the mission field. Many of this world would say they are suckers to waste their lives that way. I don't think so. "He who loves his life loses it, and he who hates his life in this world will keep it for eternal life" (John 12:25). Jesus assures us of it, and he should know.

Gospel Partnership
October 16
Philippians 1:3–11

Loneliness is a terrible feeling. Sometimes you can be so lonely that it seems like your life means nothing to anyone. Despite the agony, loneliness can also be a great teacher. This is because it can drive us to learn that we are never really alone. By the grace of God, we are never without the fellowship of the Holy Spirit and others in the family of the faith. When Paul wrote the letter to the Philippians, he was a prisoner. Undoubtedly, he experienced extreme loneliness, even despair that his suffering was without purpose. Yet out of this time came the invaluable epistles to the churches he had planted along his journeys. Rather than complaining about his situation, he encouraged the young churches through prayer and example. He reminded them that they were in partnership with the one who really matters, our Lord.

This partnership comes in worship and prayer. Paul knew that he was not really alone. His prayer was linked with other prayers, with common joyous experiences together. Worship in the fellowship of Christ brings strength, refreshment, and encouragement. Together we confess and find forgiveness. The fellowship of the Christian faith is absolutely unique. Love, tolerance, warmth, and freedom are nurtured by the Holy Spirit that does not exist anywhere else on earth.

These experiences bring about another partnership, one of witness. In addition to building one another up, part of the purpose of the body of Christ is to come together in witnessing about our faith and inviting others to join in the fellowship. For this witness to be effective, it must be shared in love and discernment, steeped in sincerity, and above all, be given to the glory of God. These factors allow others to focus on God, not on the humans sharing their experience. In this way, we can come alongside those who are lonely with a true and lasting solution. Serving together to God's glory is the only answer that will satisfy into eternity.

He Is the Man!
October 17
Matthew 3:1–17

The wilderness of Judea is a lot like the badlands of North Dakota. Barren, treeless hills rumble down into parched valleys. Water is the key to life, and greenness betrays its presence. John the Baptist was a man whose character fitted the countryside of Judea. Spartan, single-purposed, ascetic, "a voice crying in the wilderness" (Isaiah 40:3). He brought those who responded to the Jordan River. There, water baptism was a vivid demonstration of new life in old soil. His actions caught the attention of the priests and Levites, who asked, "Are you the Christ?" "No," he screamed, "I'm here to prepare the way for the Christ." It is easy to be distracted by those who make a big show of things, but are not the Real Thing. John unrelentingly pointed to Jesus Christ as the Messiah, the Lamb of God, knowing he was the Man.

He is. Jesus is the central figure of the acts of God in history. He's the one to watch, to follow, to give your heart to. He is the Master. John was the perfect example of what we should be in the process of bringing others to know Jesus. He pointed to the truth and then got out of the way. As humans, we worry about our own selves; we want to be thought well of, liked. It is easy to get in the way. Our duty is to point to the Christ, not to be him. It is possible to become enamored with the human personality and walk right by the Lord.

Let us learn from John the Baptist and share boldly about Christ, then step out of the way for him to do the rest.

Holy Boldness
October 18
Hebrews 4:14–5:6

Everyone has experienced the sense of feeling unloved, unworthy, unwanted. These feelings are not present all the time, but at some time or another, we have all had them. As Christians, we are called to bring God's grace to those who do not know it. The writer of Hebrews put it this way: "that we may receive mercy and find grace to help in time of need" (Hebrews 4:16). What great words! At any given moment, we can be on either side—in need of mercy, or able to extend help. God knows what we need. That is why he gave us Jesus. Jesus has been where we are! He can identify with our needs, because he has experienced the pain that the world puts in our paths.

Jesus is the perfect guide for our faith pathway, because he not only understands where we are, he has been where we are going. He knows the truth of what God wants for us. He reveals God as loving father, loving spirit. Jesus knows firsthand that we can approach the throne of God with holy boldness and receive mercy and find grace to help in time of need. Do you feel hurt, unlovely, unloved, unwanted, unworthy? God loves you. The Lord wants you freed. The Lord wants to lead you home. Reach out and grab life. Reach out and grab eternity. Live with holy boldness.

Let Us Examine Our Souls
October 19
Luke 12:13–31

God is at work. It is uncertain at what point God-at-work will next come to fruit, but it is happening. Each day, the good news of Jesus of Nazareth is a new experience. Wisdom does not always go with success. In this world, we must be careful of allowing those things that advance us to get in the way of our acceptance of the voice of God. We need to examine our marriage with the material. Life is temporary; the soul is eternal. That which we work for in this world has no place in eternity. God wanted us to have delight in the things of this world—his creation. The danger is becoming entangled in these things to the detriment of our faith in the one who made them.

It is not important what you place your trust in, but in whom you place your trust. In America, there is such an overabundance that we worry more over surplus and taxes than about poverty and hunger. We have unlimited means to solve our problems, and still the solution escapes us. Our national and personal problems require spiritual answers, not more resources.

The good news is: Trust God. We are in danger of centering our attention on our possessions and ignoring what is happening to our souls. In the attempt to be wholly self-sufficient, we forget that the real necessities by which we live are not humanly produced. They are from God. If we cut ourselves off from that source, we are doomed. Let us examine our souls, our relationship with God. He will provide the things of this life.

Momentous Moments
October 20
Mark 10:35–45

A momentous moment is an experience that draws us to transforming insights. It is when we let God into our lives with the kind of trust that allows us to be led by him. There is a sense that God is so completely present, that from then on, we know we will move toward God. Despite the doubts, the backsliding, the sins of omission and commission, Godward is the path. This does not mean that we have actually arrived, simply that we know where we are headed. Once we have a sense of direction, it becomes the source of our joy. God is our inspiration, and his love never runs dry. There is ministry in the life of every baptized Christian. No matter what the specific job title, our work is dedicated to the Lord. The frustration of the everyday-ness of work is transformed. When we see what we are doing not as a task or duty but as a ministry, every job is a calling from God, a place in which to serve others in his love. This realization leads to a shift of attitude. There is a change from wanting to be served to wanting to serve, from focusing on trivial things to reaching toward loving cooperation with others to build community and loving families. Attitude puts Jesus Christ on the throne of our lives, trusting in God, rejoicing in the people of God, and rising above everyday situations to look for loving solutions.

To gain such insights, we need only to be open to God's momentous moments. Then, his power and energy will flood our souls, making every part of life sacred.

Moving from Conformed
to Transformed
October 21
1 John 2:1–6

Nothing is more central to how we approach life than our mind-set. We can either be thermometers, which just register what goes on around us, reflecting it, or we can be thermostats, aware of what is going on and changing it, making it reflect the will of the Father. The issue of conforming or transforming is not a new one, but it is a constant one. It is so easy to fall into the world pattern. We would like to be transforming people, but we get caught up in this world. We need the power to be faith thermostats. We need to tap into the power that lies deep within us. Only God can change us inwardly by a complete transformation of our minds. The process takes place as we study about him, immerse ourselves in the culture of the church, and offer ourselves in service to others.

With this mind-set, we can look at the world around us with the eyes of someone who cares and is willing to put others first. The secular society around us needs a moral center. That is one of the reasons Christians are here. Our mission is to spread scriptural holiness across this land. Our means is to take our bearings from the God who would transform us completely. Transformation is a lifelong process and takes time and energy, but the results are out of this world!

Nutshell Truth
October 22
Matthew 22:34–46

The greatest commandment of them all is: "To love the Lord your God with all your heart and with all your soul and with all your mind" (Matthew 22:37). The second is to love your neighbor as yourself. This is a nutshell truth. Sometimes, our familiarity with this passage makes it hard for us to understand what a magnificent truth it is. It is difficult to separate this vividly simple set of commandments from the confusing complexity we experience every day.

Our own bodies function based on the most basic principles of microbiology. Our DNA knows exactly what to do to keep us alive. If the information contained therein was written out in ordinary language, it would occupy a hundred thick volumes. The Great Commandment is to us and our present and future what the nucleic acids DNA and RNA are to our bodies. The heart is our cellular nucleus of human emotion. The soul has the quality of awe. There is no anatomical equivalent to emotion and soul, yet each of us has experienced elation, disappointment, and connection with others that defies understanding. The mind is the most secular of the realities of life known as qualities. It can gather and mingle and mold and remember and reason. We can differentiate between dreams, fantasy, illusion, and reality. We can even tell whether that is in the past, the present, or the future.

The connection of heart, soul, and mind is crucial to our understanding of God. Together they bring powerful wholeness. Our Creator, our God, the Lord of life meant that those powerful capacities should be linked together and committed to him. It is how we are designed.

The Kingdom Is Like a Festival

October 23
Matthew 22:2

Life rarely feels like a festival. Even in the midst of our festivals, we hold back. We wonder and worry about tomorrow. There are hardships, inconsistencies, betrayal, and sadnesses with which to cope. There are people all around us who are distressed, just praying for a word of hope. Everyone has their own troubles. Yet Jesus compared the kingdom of heaven to a marriage feast—to a festival! If we look at life in view of what God intends and what God has already done, it is certainly worth celebrating. God wants his people to know joy and to live in joy, rejoicing.

Joy is actually a perspective—a positive perspective. All around us are everyday realities that discourage. The beauty of the gospels is that in the face of the failures we experience time after time, there is still hope. God can overcome our tragedies. Nothing can happen that is so bad that the light of Christ cannot lighten the gloom. The festival is celebrating the knowledge that God is in control, and we can put our trust in him. We still have to respond to God's invitation to the festival; no one is going to force us to join in the celebration. Entering the kingdom of heaven requires planning and preparation. When we prepare ourselves for the festival that God offers through prayers, praise, worship, and study; God will be faithful and bring us joy and fulfillment. We can choose to center on our blessing, looking for someone to thank, and looking forward to the festival.

Things that Are God's

October 24
Matthew 22:15–22

I think we would all agree that money is an important part of our everyday life. It is essential, useful, but can also be distracting and negative. The phrase "render unto Caesar that which is Caesar's" (Mark 12:17, RSV) has actually made its way into current language. Every time we pay taxes, we remember this phrase! But what about the second part of that verse? "And to God what is God's." Have you ever considered that we who claim Christ and have made sacred commitments to God are the coin of God's realm? Each one of us bears the image of God!

When judgment day comes, God may ask Jesus to show him the results of his work. He will point to *us*. What will that look like? Will you be shiny and bright or mangled and defaced? The coins of the realm that are bright and shiny are those who are responsive to God's Word. They rejoice in the body of Christ and find joy in prayer and service in the kingdom of God. As a coin of God's realm, you are valuable; you have the image of Christ stamped into your heart! With that, there is empowerment to be an instrument of God, to be useful to the kingdom. The coins of America all have "In God We Trust," and "E pluribus Unum." That phrase is Latin for "many joined in one." We are pulled together in God's realm, bearing God's image.

To Lose Is to Win
October 25
Matthew 16:25

The desire to win is universal. As much as we believe the saying "It's not whether you win or lose, but how you play the game," the drive to win is so great that winning is the goal. In the right circumstances, that drive is good. It is what enables us to strive and achieve. The desire to win is what puts climbers on the top of Mount Everest and leads people to sail around the world singlehandedly in small sailboats. This is why it is so startling to hear Jesus say, "Whoever would save his life will lose it" (Matthew 16:25). That's incredible, implausible. It has been said that this is one of the profoundly true, basic paradoxes of life.

The most familiar analogy is to think of a seed—a grain of wheat. If it does not fall into the earth and die, it remains alone. If it dies, it bears fruit by growing into a full plant. Even something as simple as a campfire is a good illustration. The wood has to burn up to create the warmth and beauty of the fire. What a privilege life is, then. When we harness the desire to win with the truth that to give is to live, God's love gives us a great power. It is true that anything held too close becomes a problem. If we worry too much about our health, we become a hypochondriac; a person cannot have a friend without becoming a friend; even money is of no use unless it is invested. If we try too hard to hold on to life, we are dead while breathing. If we spend life Godward, then we are really alive even if the body is weak.

The world's formula for greatness is wealth, power, and position. God's formula is that to serve is to become great. Through history this has been shown to be true—Lincoln, Ghandi, Mother Theresa. Most of all Jesus, the greatest servant of all, has brought the most change to the world.

Transformation

October 26
Romans 12:2

People want something different than blind conformity to the world's standards. There is a debate about whether people can change. The Christian faith maintains an insistence that transformation is not only possible but essential. Meanwhile, the world persistently doubts that people can change. We don't want to be naïve or unrealistic about this ability, especially where employed personnel are involved. Yet Jesus Christ of Nazareth, the Son of God, had the audacity to proclaim that we could be transformed. Perhaps the key is what we set our eyes upon, what vision lies ahead, and what we want to have happen.

One thing is clear; if there is to be transformation, surrender of the old ways is crucial. Psalm 51:7 says, "The sacrifice acceptable to God is a broken spirit; a broken and contrite heart."

It isn't that God wants us to be broken; we need to be changed to a new direction. We need to surrender our own willfulness, selfishness, and vengefulness. We need to give up the desire to shape our own destiny, to be in control. We must get out of the center, and put Christ in control.

It is so easy to conform to the world. The world tells us if there is trouble, we need to get even, to "make it right." The crux of transformation is to be patient in trouble and constant in prayer. These are healing and redemptive words. With God as our guide, we can begin to move steadfastly in the direction of transformation.

What Is Worship?

October 27
Isaiah 6:1–8

Worship leads to a renewed self-commitment to God. It is a double process—first of placing ourselves under the creativity of God, and second, of releasing ourselves from those enthrallments that prevent God from working his will in us. Humans have, in every age, worshiped. In primitive stages, worship was closely associated with magic and was largely humankind's attempt to control the environment, which dictated its destiny. In more sophisticated times, worship has been the human attempt to know himself or herself. Isaiah was an adviser to the king before he became a prophet. However, his encounter with God changed everything. It made God *real*. God became a reality and a presence.

One of the biggest problems today is that economic good times blind persons to the continuing need for worship—to maintain, to recommit, to achieve balance. Worship includes several components. Primarily: adoration, confession, renewal, and dedication. The transcendence of God is tied in with the mortality of humans in the experience of worship. Adoration and forgiveness through confession transform us to rightness with God that leads to personal meaning and identity. Rightness with God brings renewal, and service is an outpouring of energy and activity that follows the experience of true connection with God. Dedication to service is cause for true celebration. This leads us back to the beginning! Worship is the means to a life of meaning and true joy. Humanity can only experience wholeness in the presence of our Creator, God, and in service to him.

What Will It Be?
October 28
John 12:20–26

Human beings have learned that experience, training, expertise, and service are the things that pay off. Seeing something through one's own vision and working at it day after day and watching it grow—that's the payoff for humans. Giving one's life away for and through another is beautiful, maybe even more beautiful than dying. Why did Jesus have to die? Christ's dying was to reveal our human willfulness. It is shocking to realize what humans are capable of. Our degradations can be complete. We are all made of the same stuff. It is easy to think ourselves above such atrocities as genocide and murder. However, we know ourselves well enough to know that we too kill the spirit, even of those we love. More often than we like to admit, our unkind thoughts toward those we don't know are like a nightmare.

It would have been nice if Jesus could have lived to a ripe old age and died a natural death. But our pride would never have been revealed and our haughtiness would have destroyed us. Dying as he did is a prototype for us to reveal that we could even kill God if we got it into our heads to do so. How many times have we snuffed him out in our hearts as it is? Yes, we are capable of killing God—unless we catch a new vision of wholeness, partnership, and interdependence. If that beautiful grain of wheat that is Jesus falls into the earth of your heart and germinates and catches life there, his horrible death will bear the fruit he foretold.

What happens with the germination of a grain of wheat is that the grain expands and assimilates the life nutrients around it into a new life. Our dying of our old self with its "gimmie" nature and a rebirthing of a new nature assimilates a Christ lifestyle. In the words of the verse: "Unless a grain of wheat falls into the earth and dies, it remains alone" (John 12:23, RSV). Except our pride dies, except our fear dies, except we reach out, *we* remain alone.

Which Is It ... Insured or Really Ready?

October 29
Matthew 25:1–13

Remember back to the time when you first fell in love with Jesus. Your heart was on fire, you knew the difference between right and wrong, and your ideals were unblemished. What happened when you went back to your "regular" life? You got busy with the day-to-day struggles, and slowly by slowly, the world crept back in. You didn't mean to stop going to church or reading the Bible, but there was just so much to do that something had to give. We know that Jesus Christ is returning and that the hour will not be known. We are to be ready for that day, every day. Many of us lean back on the forgiveness of God and think that all will be forgiven. This is like having insurance. You know that you need God, but he takes a back seat to everyday living.

The Christian faith is always optimistic about a new start. There is a way back to God through confession, repentance, and forgiveness. But to know that God is love and will forgive does not mean there will not be consequences. Sometimes, the moment of need comes, and you truly miss out on something that cannot be replaced. Further, you cannot obtain that experience through anyone else; it can't be borrowed. Such things are character, wisdom, personality, love, and faith. If you are really ready—fresh and vibrant in your faith, you will never miss the opportunity to experience the best God has for you. He wants you to have life abundantly, not half-heartedly. Be ready; the best is yet to come.

Whose We Are
October 30
1 Corinthians 11:23–29

One of the hardest conversions is a person who has been immunized by a little mild Christianity. One who has been introduced to the ideals but never committing to the Master. Culturized by Christmas and Easter but never really knowing the power. Classified by nominal membership but never really knowing Whose we are. Lukewarm Christians have been around since the days of the early church. In Revelation, Jesus addresses them as neither cold nor hot. Holy Communion reminds us Whose we are and what we are about. One thing is required in a life that is directed toward God—truly giving your heart to him, truly asking him to be your rule and guide, truly receiving him. This knowledge leads immediately to action. We must know and live the faith, maintain the household of faith, and tell the story.

Living the faith means to get your priorities right. To serve the Lord and those who depend on you with hard work and trustworthy behavior. Taking Communion together is a part of maintaining the household of faith. Bread is the symbol for food that keeps us alive; juice is the symbol of Christ's broken body on the cross. He died so we may know the one true God, who is life for us now, and eternally. After the first Communion, Christ commissioned the disciples to take personal responsibility to tell the story of what occurred there. This is real life. We must remember always, Whose we are and what we are about.

Widened Hearts
October 31
2 Corinthians 5:20–6:13

Paul dearly loved his Corinthians, but he had trouble with them. Their backgrounds from the corruption in their city led to resistance to the disciplines of the faith. He charged them with divisiveness, disloyalty, lack of love, drunkenness at Communion, lack of generosity, disruptiveness, and disorderliness. The first letter to the Corinthians addressed many of these things. The second letter was a bit more gentle; Paul has widened his heart to them and asks them to do the same. As the seat of our emotions, a widened heart is what makes the faith possible. Without open hearts, we could not believe. A widened heart means a heart open to receive and respond to words like character, value, truth, honesty, worth, kindness, thoughtfulness, self-control, purpose, dignity.

As such, the widened heart enriches the faith. Having the values of seeing self before others allows us to express our faith in action, such as helping those less fortunate and reaching out to the lonely. Finally, a widened heart possesses everything. The problem with most of our earthly possessions is that they do not bring the joy we expected. In Christ, we can possess life and death, the present and the future, because we are Christ's and Christ is God's. Even hardships and sorrows in life can be transformed into blessing when we possess God's love and find his fellowship in everything. Let us widen our hearts to the Spirit of Christ whose peace and joy are even this moment our own.

Band-Aid Religion
November 1
Matthew 7:13–27

Pretty much every one of us has used a Band-Aid at one time or another. They are a handy gadget, a triumph of technology, protecting a wound temporarily from dirt and damage. Many people think of religion as a type of Band-Aid. It is a quick fix in time of hurt. Prayer can be expedient when the going is rough. There is so much evidence that this is so—things like hospital baptisms, death-bed Communion, late-night counseling calls. However, a Band-Aid doesn't heal anything. It only protects a wound for a time. Healing only comes in the health of the body. Therefore, be encouraged to prepare and condition the soul! Be aware that the disciplines of Christian life bear their fruit: good will, love, joy, peace, patience, gentleness, honesty, integrity, devotion—and many others.

Further, we may need to be reminded that Band-Aids cannot help deep wounds. A healthy body is the only protection. We need to build our soul health on a firm foundation. There needs to be regular communication with God and Jesus in prayer. One benefits greatly from regular study of the Bible. It is vital to work out your faith by helping others as well. Our soul health depends on good habits much like our bodies' health. Eating well, exercising, and avoiding bad habits goes a long way toward keeping our physical health in shape. It matters what we think and how we live. No organ of our bodies is as vital to the whole self as is the soul. It must be made healthy and whole daily, or great will be the fall of it. We may need religious Band-Aids; they'll help if the soul is healthy.

Come unto Me
November 2
Matthew 11:1–30

This passage of scripture has been called the "great invitation." It typifies the many times Christ called people to him throughout his life. He called the disciples from their lives, he called Zacchaeus, he called the children, and he called the sick and burdened to "come unto me." He calls us not only to share our burdens but, more importantly, to reveal his Father to us.

It is interesting that the call does not demand action, but it does require it. We must choose to say yes to him, or our silence rejects him. There are so many things that call to us for attention these days—the world, our families, our work, and even the church itself can be a distraction from the true source of life—Christ.

In addition to the simple call, this passage goes on to say, "all who are weary and burdened, and I will give you rest" (Matthew 11:28). Christ calls all; no one is excluded. There are no special criteria for coming to Christ, no restrictions as to who may come. We must simply accept his invitation, his compassion, and rest.

What exactly is meant by rest? Here, Jesus is offering not literal rest but the rest that comes with a right relationship to God. The carefree life is not the life free from care, but the life that is freely given to God. The soul of a person must give itself up, for it is incomplete alone. The decision to place our lives in his hands and to give our hearts fully to him is personal. With that commitment comes the rest he promises.

Eh?
November 3
Psalm 19:14

Communication is at the root of many, perhaps most, relationship troubles. We complain that we are not heard, yet how many times have you caught yourself straying in thought while someone else is speaking? Communication is at the root of many deeply Christian acts as well: repentance, forgiveness, sensitivity. It is not simply the act of speaking, but the transmission of information from one to another. Jesus spoke often of those who "listened but did not hear."

We must learn to communicate effectively. Everything we do says something, not just words, but actions, tone of voice, and even silence. It is not easy to keep the lines of communication open. We start taking one another for granted, gradually tend to go our own way, and suddenly wake up strangers or angry. One valid technique is to never let the sun go down on a disagreement. You may have some late nights, but then each day is a clean slate, with a bright new beginning.

Separation is the essence of the problem with communication. When we are separated from one another, life becomes very empty and frustrating. This is so with humans, and even more so with God. Isolation is one of the supreme forms of punishment. With separation from love, the spirit withers.

Openness is the beginning of the solution. This requires a willingness to be understanding, to be sensitive. It could also be used in the sense of being open to new possibilities. Such as, open to receive another person; open to the Spirit of God; open to our own need for correction or improvement. This allows a connection on the emotional level—where we are most human. When we allow ourselves to be acceptable in the sight of God, then we begin to grow in his grace.

Enter into Joy
November 4
Matthew 25:14–30

It's a tough world out there! Broken promises, canceled guarantees, tough financially, competitively, relationally, and on and on. There are plenty of illustrations, but each of us knows this truth because we have experienced it personally. The question is, how do we deal with it? The parable of the talents is about money. Each servant was given a sum in accordance with his level of trust. The first two doubled the money and were praised. The third, however, buried it and was proud that none of it was lost. He was thrown out on the street. It seems pretty rough. If the master is God, where is the forgiveness? That's the point. It is too easy to make God into our own image. We'd like a God we could control. But if we are going to enter into the joy of heaven, we have to take God the almighty seriously.

Jesus invested everything into us. We need to get creative with the gift of joy and eternal life to give him a return on his investment. Faith isn't about keeping what you have to yourself; it is about sharing it with everyone around you. That takes some risk, that takes an investment of time. It takes letting go of your own fear of discomfort and putting it on the line for God. The amazing thing about God is that when you truly let go and trust him, he will bless you back tenfold.

Hope: No Pushover
November 5
Isaiah 2:1–5

What does the word *hope* stir inside you? On one hand, there is that hope that some desire will be fulfilled. On the other, hope can be seen as visionary, unrealistic, fantasy. None of us want to be naively hopeful. But it is amazing how tenacious hope can be. There is truth in the phrases "hope against hope," and "hope springs eternal."

Biblical hope stems from memory, posterity, and new life. We hope for the future because we remember the past. Each year progresses from Advent to Christmas and from Lent to Easter. This helps remind us of our roots as God's people. We know that God chooses to work through unusual, even hopeless circumstances like promising a nation to an elderly, barren couple; and presenting the King of kings as a tiny infant.

Posterity speaks to that which stretches beyond our own generation. We know that how we live today determines, in large measure, how our children will be able to live tomorrow. We each want to have left something worthwhile for those who follow. We hold fast to the hope that what we have left will abide.

New life certainly brings hope. One look at a newborn will melt any heart! Biblically, new life means so much more than that. It is the symbol that a person always has another chance to change. The final completion of God's promise is New Life in a big way. There will be a new heaven and a new earth. Those who believe and trust in Christ will all be together to enjoy the ultimate result of hope.

Hope, a Gift of God
November 6
Psalm 80:1–7

Hope is the one thread that never breaks. Hope is the feeling that what is desired is also possible. In the case of people, hope is about the person in whom expectations are centered. Hope is not dependent on us, but on the actions of *God*. Consider the image of the potter and the clay. A glob of clay is plopped on a wheel and starts spinning. Through the spinning, something purposeful, wonderful begins to happen. The clay becomes a useful but weak form, awaiting the fire of the kiln. Only after shaping, firing, and glazing does the clay become usable. Without the potter, the clay remains just clay.

Every individual Christian is consecrated of (set apart for) God. Each is dedicated and marked, belonging to God—different from the regular run of people. Each Christian is a part of something much bigger than a single person—a part of a great company of other Christians that spread across the entire globe. More importantly, our usefulness is not dependent on our own power, but on the power of God. Without this undergirding, hope can easily be rubbed out by the harsh realities of everyday life. Christian hope is not based on power, position, money, or even achievement; it is a gift of God awaiting us.

I Am Infallible ... for the Most Part
November 7
Matthew 9:1–12

The experience of the Lord in one's heart, mind, soul, and body—and the good news that pervades such an experience—can and does change things. Unfortunately, it does not make a person infallible. One of my favorite posters reads "I AM INFALLABLE," but the A is crossed out and an I is scribbled in. And below, in blotchy ink, are the words "for the most part." The reason I like it so much is that it is so true to life. We do like to take the reins in our own hands and make like we are immortal. We do like to act like we are some kind of little tin gods. So, it is good to be humbled a little, to be made to know that God is God, and we are not!

The reality is that despite a true, life-changing acceptance of Jesus Christ, we do not always live up to the ideal of being a Christian. There is an inconsistency between our expectations and what we actually do. We must acknowledge that our human condition is such that our best is a striving, a working-at-it, an endeavoring toward.

So how do we resolve the difference between the ideal and the actual? By being *real*. It is critical to be honest, filled with a desire to have integrity, striving for the highest ideals but knowing that our only hope is in the grace and mercy of God. Christians aren't superior to anyone else. But we have a different perspective. We know that we are fallible instruments, but God can change us, he can use us, and he is still willing to take us on as partners.

Imitators of God
November 8
Ephesians 5:1–20

Have you ever noticed that we live in an age of imitation? All around us are plastic flowers, veneer wood, pleather. Imitation can be both encouraged or berated. It can be considered as a mockery or faithful reflection, forgery or striking reproduction, echo or mirror. One of the most important issues relates to what is being imitated. In the case of God, a Christian strives to reproduce God's attitudes of love and kindness and forgiveness and mercy in his or her own life.

A second important distinction is the difference between being an imitator versus an imitation. An imitation is cheap, inferior, counterfeit. The goal of a Christian is to be genuine, to follow the Master, using his pattern by which to cut the cloth.

One of the reasons this was so critical in Paul's time was that in that time, immorality, slavery, and even the abandonment of infants and children were common practices. They were justified, rationalized, and accepted. What Paul is saying is that these practices were so evil that they shouldn't even be talked about. Contrast this with what we are called to do as Christians. We are called to stay in the light—focusing on all that is good and right and true. To succeed, it required such a radical change from the prevailing society that it was vital for the Christians to stand together, as imitators of God. Is it really any different today?

In God's Good Time
November 9
Psalm 25:1–10

None of us are really very good at waiting. The phrase "in God's good time" is a good phrase; it gives us peace; it gives us a chance to stand back a little bit and allow God to guide the course of events. It is not, however, an excuse for our not doing anything; we are to be partners with him in the process. One of the things that this phrase indicates is that God is involved with life. He wants good to result among us. After all, look what he has done! He has come to us; he is Immanuel, God with us. He is in our Lord of life—Jesus—and he is in the Holy Spirit—our teacher and guide. Furthermore, it is his promise that he will come again and take us unto himself.

Another meaning of this phrase is that God calls us to rejoice in the moments that we have. It is so easy to get derailed by fussing about how much there is to do. But the moment is all we have. This moment is when we can reach out in our hearts and prayers to those closest to us. We can use the moments God has given us to bring about what is becoming. We are the persons God has to change the world, to transform our environment, to create what will be history. It is now God's good time; now is the fullness of his time.

In His Name
November 10
John 1:35–41

Our name is very important to us. It represents our identity, our history, our roots. In fact, many parents send their children out the door with a reminder, "Remember who you are!" Given that we want to represent our own names well, it is not too much of a jump to say that we want to represent the name of Jesus well. He is our Savior and Lord. How we live, as Christians, can tarnish or polish that name. We can lift it up or drag it down. Of course, it is true that even if we all failed him, Jesus is the name above all other names.

The name Jesus means, "God saves." When we add Jesus, who is the Christ, it becomes a matter of belief and faith. There is no hard proof of this, only conviction. There is good reason to believe, of course, but the real proof comes in what believing in him makes of us! Our own development is not based solely on what he does for us; rather, what we are willing to do in his name. There are no quick solutions or easy answers. Faith requires an element of sacrifice of our time and effort. We may expect material gifts, and he gives imperishable ones. We expect power; he gives servanthood. We expect control and are given service to others.

These gifts bring change to our very beings. We become of service to others rather than being served; we comfort others rather than being comforted; we mature our faith in reaching out to those in need. It is a great thing to follow in the name of our Christ. If you will be open to this, you can expect unexpected joy, humble strength, and qualities that do not fade away but are eternal.

Judged
November 11
Matthew 25:31–46

Judged. The words depicting the final judgment are a bit sobering. There is no turning back, no opportunity to change your mind. Jesus states: "Whatever you have done to the least of these, you have done unto me" (Matthew 25:40). In the final analysis, the basis of judgment will be: How did we treat those less fortunate than we? Christ in disguise. It is not a trick; it is a reminder to see and treat others as we would see and treat Christ. There is a "least of these" in each of us. Each one of us can become closed in by our feelings of inadequacy. Each of us can be disabled by a sense that we have little to give. Each of us can be crippled by the fear that we are not good enough, or smart enough, or in a position to be of use. It is this part of us that blocks the gospel of good news, prevents us from living freely and holds us off from trusting God for the needs of each day. It is this insecurity that promotes us to be judgmental. It is this fear within that makes us want to blame others. We find blame because our fear needs shoring up.

The opposite of love is not hate ... it is fear. Fear is what finds fault. Perfect love casts out fear. It is what lives all the way into eternity, and the darkness cannot put it out. None among us is so secure, so optimistic, so positive, that there is no "least of these" within. That portion of us needs the nurture of prayer, the comfort of knowing Christ, the encouragement of God's worshiping people. Our assignment in the parables is to find ourselves there and to let God's truth find us. So that we may be made whole, so that we may be nurturers, so we may enter the inheritance our Father prepared for us from the foundation of the earth.

Moments of Truth
November 12
Matthew 25:1–13

The story of the bridesmaids and the groom is kind of a tough one to hear sometimes. There are ten bridesmaids, and five run out of oil. The others do not share, and those without the oil are shut out of the celebration. That doesn't seem quite fair. Of course, we are talking about eternal life. God is compassionate and loving, so surely he won't actually shut anyone out of heaven. Surely, God will prevail with all people, right? Yet when it comes down to it, are we really ready? Or are we napping and unprepared?

The maidens who declined to share their oil were not really being mean; the oil was a symbol of the quality of their relationship with the groom. This kind of thing can't be shared! The character of our relationship with Christ is much more than a one-time decision. It involves living the life of a follower of Christ. It requires building the relationship, by responding with gratitude in thousands of little ways over a lifetime.

This is not something that can be borrowed or handed down. Each individual must make a decision for himself or herself. Must take on the responsibility of being prepared for himself or herself. It is sometimes said that God has no grandchildren. If my parents make a decision to follow Jesus and become a child of God, they can't pass that on to me. I have to make my own decision to become a child of God. The time is now. It is never too early to begin the relationship. The bridegroom is coming. Are you ready?

Person Power
November 13
Joshua 24:15

One of the amazing and stimulating characteristics of Jesus was his ability to look deeply into the personality of individuals and see them—not only for what they were—but for what they could become. As a person came to know Jesus, that quality would grow and develop, transforming them into the person Jesus expected. Many biblical stories document the miraculous changes that can take place. Look at Abraham, Moses, Peter. All of them were normal, flawed people who came to live up to what God had planned for them.

God is at work in us right now, bringing us toward his ideal, giving us "person power." It is astonishing what can happen when you really grab on to that ideal! We often sell ourselves short. We stop from sharing or contributing because we think, "I'm just a …" (a housewife, a salesman, a clerk, a nobody). In God's world, there are no "nobodies." Each of us is made in his image to glorify him and please him. What a difference it makes to simply believe that phrase: You are created to please God. When we become the person he sees, incredible things can happen.

In order for this to occur, we have to say with Joshua, "As for me … I will serve the LORD" (Joshua 24:15). This means to recognize that the world is a distracting place and to set aside some of those things. We are then able to join God on the journey he has designed for us in a divine God-human partnership. With God, each of us has the capacity to reconcile, to heal, to bring peace in Christ's name, and to make a difference in this world. Now that's *person power!*

PTL

November 14
Psalm 150

PTL. Three letters with a very powerful meaning: Praise the Lord. In the '70s and '80s, there were innumerable little buttons people would wear. There were smiley faces, peace signs, flower power, and many more. Initials were always a little puzzling; you had to ask what they stood for. This was with some fear, not knowing what charity or political slogan they might stand for. Praise the Lord was an answer that gave some relief! There are barriers to brazenly shout out *praise the Lord*! We are all sinners; we agonize over poverty, starvation, cruelty, and pain. We must remember that to praise the Lord is not about congratulating ourselves on how lucky we are, or somehow superior to others. It means much more than that.

Praising the Lord acknowledges the source of our being. God is praised because salvation, glory, and power belong to him. Gratitude, reverence, and trust are the elements of real praise. Those who praise the Lord are those who know their dependence on God. Praise should be offered in all circumstances. Gratitude is an attitude of the heart and mind. Once we get our attitude right, gratitude comes naturally, spontaneously, and with joy and gladness. The psalmist concludes with, "Let everything that breathes praise the Lord!" (Psalm 150:6). It calls us to the majesty and power of God. It reminds us that God is God, and we are not. The wonder of God is not that he is high and holy, but that he stoops to save the human soul.

Religion with a Bounce
November 15
Micah 6:1–8

What does the Lord require of us? When we begin to examine our souls to see if there is any development there, we search for meaning and purpose. This passage answers the question in one of the most eloquent ways expressed in the Bible. "What does the Lord require of you? To act justly, and to love mercy, and to walk humbly with your God" (Micah 6:8). What a simple admonition. Yet how easy it is to pervert justice and how difficult it is to maintain it and administer it. Jesus reminded us that how we judged others would be used to judge ourselves. It really boils down to trying to put ourselves into the other person's shoes. In this way, acting justly leads to understanding mercy. Judgment without mercy is often vengeance. Together with mercy, or kindness, the purpose of justice is to restore. It is interesting to note that in this statement of Micah, two of the requirements deal with humans and only one with God. It is futile to talk about God unless we are in good relationship with our fellow humans. Acting justly and loving mercy require us to give of ourselves.

In the act of giving to others, we find humility. We can learn to trust God rather than ourselves—making God our primary focal point. It is so easy to put earthly things before God, which becomes idolatry. We idolize what we truly give ourselves to. We obtain what we set ourselves after, and that becomes our reward. Walking humbly with God and making him the priority in life leads to the eternal. When we walk with God, there comes a spring to our step, a bounce in our faith. As our Lord Christ is within us, joy comes to us.

Shoulder to Shoulder
November 16
Luke 22:24–32

One of the most impressive and thrilling sights to Christian people is to see another person stand and pledge their life to Christ in moving sincerity. No one makes the decision to accept Christ in the same way. Some come by it gradually, some suddenly. For some it is a studied thing, for others, an impulsive response. You may have a picture in your mind's eye of your own decision—a picture of decisions made around a campfire or in a church service ... or most anywhere on God's earth. When one joins the fellowship of Christ, you join the ranks of many others who have gone before you in the same experience. Christ set up the church to serve and support one another. In fact, wherever such service occurs *is* a church. Jesus himself came to us a king, yet a servant.

We stand shoulder to shoulder in learning—through scripture and history and in the joy of teaching the next generation. Shoulder to shoulder, we also share. We share joys and sorrows, dreams and failures. We take one another as we are and help each other to a quality of life that comes from a deep relationship to God. In true Christian fellowship, this also extends beyond our walls to help others in their times of need. Each opportunity for service is the call of God. For being a Christian is not a solitary activity; it is being an active member of the fellowship of Christ.

The Be Happy Attitudes

November 17
Matthew 5:1–10

Everyone wants to be happy. It is a universal goal. The trouble is that it is not really a goal; it is a by-product, a side benefit. The beatitudes spoken by Jesus are rather startling when we really take a look at them. Some modern translations use the word happy instead of blessed. Happy are the poor, happy are the sad, happy are the humble, and so on. That concept truly does not fit in today's world. We learn that happiness is about winning, being rich and well fed, getting our own way. So what is Jesus saying here? The world is upside down!

It is really the outlook—the perspective—that is critical here. These beatitudes are revolutionary. They call for a way of life that is opposite of the way the world thinks and works. A way of life that sees humility, love, trust, and fidelity as prime values. Persons who are won to that way of life are not in pursuit of happiness, but, amazingly, are incredibly filled with joy. Such persons do not claim that they are perfect, but they know that they are converted. Their fundamental desires have been turned in the direction of the will of God.

In the beatitudes, Jesus takes us by the hand and says, "Find happiness within your soul as you see to the happiness of another." "Congratulations to you when you empty your hearts of pride and turn your heart to the Lord." "Calm down. Discover the joy in the simple things of life." Our essential belonging is in the unity of the body of Christ, and in that belonging is profound joy.

The Bible's Golden Thread
November 18
Jeremiah 31:31–34

We live in a day of many conflicts. There are, of course, those on the national and international news, and those around religious beliefs. There is such rapid change around us that it is hard to say what is right—what will bring peace and righteousness. The golden thread that runs through the Bible and which points in the right direction is found in one word: covenant. Covenant means a contract, an agreement, a binding pledge. Certainly there are plenty of those in our world! Hardly any avenue of our lives is not touched by contracts. We agree to be at certain places at certain times; we exchange our time and talent for money at work; even behaving in a certain way is a type of contract. Each person is expected to live according to the moral code.

Between humans and God, the first covenant begins with creation. God made us. He did this because it is in his nature to love. He made us so that we could love him and he us. Love needs to give itself away to be true. It needs to receive in order to be whole. The familiar stories of the Old Testament are filled with covenants—to Abraham, Isaac, and Jacob; to Moses and the Israelites coming out of captivity; to David, that his "house" would be forever. God always kept his side; humans had a lot more trouble following theirs.

The greatest covenant occurred when the Word became Flesh and dwelt among us. Jesus died so that we imperfect humans could be reconciled to the perfect God through his precious blood. How do we keep our part of this covenant? We recognize our faults and mistakes and return to believing in God; then live life like we mean it. The Bible's golden thread is the story of salvation to joy and peace. It is the way to life, now and eternally.

The Holy Spirit

November 19
Acts 2:1–12; John 16:4–15

Try to think of a term that would show power, life, and strength but be invisible and real. The wind is like that; you can't see it, but it's there. In fact, the former name of the Holy Spirit was the Holy Ghost. The Hebrew word for ghost is the same as for breath. So, this name suggests the Holy Breath of God. The Holy Spirit is invisible but as real as wind or breath.

Of course, most often we think of the Holy Spirit as part of the Trinity. After Jesus left the earthly scene in bodily form, he sent the Holy Spirit to be the Advocate. This brought fulfillment in human experience—he helps us understand the words, the acts, and the symbolism of the Bible. The Holy Spirit makes the gift of God's love available for each one that will follow God's path. He aids us to accomplish our full potential in salvation. In salvation, we find wholeness, significance, purpose, and genuine, deep happiness.

> Come, Holy Spirit
> Love divine
> Rest thy hand upon
> This shoulder of mine
>
> Pierce this prideful heart
> With love
> That greater obedience
> I might give
>
> Fill my empty soul
> With Thy presence glow
> And make, in each next hour
> Thy love through me to flow.
> —Norman R. Lawson

A Good Old-Fashioned Thanksgiving

November 20
1 Thessalonians 5:18; Colossians 3:12–17

Thanksgiving. What memories. All of us pick some certain stage in life that becomes our composite picture of Thanksgiving, and it rings a nostalgic bell in our insides, making us at once happy and sad. Thanksgiving is an appropriate festival for America. It is our attempt to acknowledge that at the roots of our heritage, God the almighty is center stage. We have been fortunate. We have worked hard. And God has blessed us; we give our thanks in gratitude. There is a growing cloud over Thanksgiving. It is not about a lack of thankfulness but a concern over those who continue to starve. How do we give "thanks in all circumstances" (1 Thessalonians 5:18), when things are tough?

Paul's words from Colossians give some clues as to appropriate actions in tough times. First, put on compassion, kindness, patience. These attitudes lead to harmony and unity among those around us. Second, let the peace of Christ rule in your hearts. Let the word of Christ dwell richly. Fear is what causes us to withdraw and blame our loneliness on someone else, not taking the trouble to care about us. If we let peace rule in our hearts, we are able to reach out to others and quell loneliness and fear. Third, do everything in the name of the Lord Jesus. The key is acting on what we believe. *We* can all do something about the need in the world around us. Simple things, such as giving to the food banks, donating warm coats and blankets to the shelters, and inviting lonely people to join our circle go a long way toward lightening the needs around us.

This Thanksgiving, put on love with your family, let peace rule in your heart with friends, and reach out in faith to those less fortunate than you. It will be a good, old-fashioned Thanksgiving.

Leftovers
November 21
Romans 12:9–12

I love leftovers … the first time. After that, I eat them rather begrudgingly, so as not to waste good food. Christian living has a parallel with even leftovers. Just as we love the initial meal and enjoy the second, our faith grows colder as we get away from the inspiration that brought us to believe. At the height of the moment—whether it was at a campfire, seminar, revival, or even a particular reading—we are fired up and ready to go. Then, when we return to the frustration and disappointment of everyday living, we lose the excitement and resolve to change that we started with. The passage in Romans gives a few pointers as to how to keep things fresh.

Rejoice in your hope. Hope is an outlook on life. It is an outlook that is fully aware of life's opportunities, possibilities, and demands. In contrast to many things, however, it has a backing in the sense of God's divine purpose and our part in it. Hope reminds us that we are a part of God's kingdom and that a great destiny awaits us.

Be patient in tribulation. One of the fascinating aspects of faith is that God *always* wins. In the midst of the tough times, it helps to know that you are on the winning team! Without faith, this critical fact is missing. Every day takes on a better perspective when you know the ending! It is possible to be patient in times of trouble, because although the exact path is unclear, you know that the end result will be amazing.

Be constant in prayer. Neither hope nor faith have any power without prayer. Prayer is what connects us to God. Hope and faith do not come naturally; they come from a constant contact with the One who makes them possible. Regular, honest, and humble connection is what brings the joy of salvation. It takes time. Paul said it in his letter to the Romans: "Love must be sincere. Hate what is evil; cling to what is good. Be devoted to one another in love. Honor one another above yourselves. Never be lacking in zeal, but keep your spirtual fervor, serving the Lord. Be joyful in hope, patient in affliction, faithful in prayer" (Romans 12:9-12). "Do not be overcome by evil, but overcome evil with good" (Romans 12:21).

Thank God!
November 22
Philippians 1:3–11

Thanksgiving Day. It is a day unique to America—a day celebrated in this country out of a historical past and revered because of its obvious worth. We need to say thanks. We need to acknowledge that God is the source of all our lives. That in him we live and move and have our being. That the origin of our material benefits resides in the provisions he has made for our needs. Yet there is a deeper source of thanks that we do not often express—the thanks for God's guidance and protection. This is especially true when we didn't even know his gentle presence.

Consider the following poem from one of our congregation:

> One Day for Thanks
> One day for giving thanks; and yet the sun
> Sends abundant reassurance with each ray
> Through all the year; and seed selects no one
> Day's interval for growing want away
> From earth; there is no stipulated hour
> Alone of one brief season when eyes may see
> The intricate slow opening of a flower
> And the long rhythms of a wind-blown tree.
> —Anon

We set aside only one day a year for thanks. Let us show our gratitude with each miracle of creation we witness every day.

Thanking God with All My Heart

November 23
Psalm 9:1–2; Colossians 3:15–17

The Good Book is right in calling us to thanksgiving and praise. Thanksgiving is a result of being a partner with the living God who loves you with his whole heart. You matter to him. The Bible truly overflows with thanksgiving; there are over four hundred references to thanks, encouragement and praise! More than enough for one a day. The trouble is … us. We are so prone to complain, blame, rationalize, be indignant. We are "me-ists." This is nothing new; look back at the Israelites. They complained about everything as they were released from bondage in Egypt. There wasn't enough water, food, meat; freedom was worse than slavery, they said. They blamed others, lusted after things they couldn't have, resisted authority, were greedy for power, and refused to believe God could provide what he promised. Incredible. Yet … take a look around. How much better do we do? Thank God for the Bible. There are words for us there, such as Colossians 3:15: "Let the peace of Christ rule in your hearts, since as members of one body you were called to peace. And be thankful."

Let Christ *rule* in your heart. There is a terrific struggle going on inside us. Feelings and desires clash; trust and distrust battle; uncertainty fights cockiness—let Christ rule. How? Peace and thankfulness. Consider what you are grateful for—it all comes from God. Think on these words: Rule. Dwell. Praise. Thank. Let Christ rule. Let the word dwell. Let the praise flow. Give thanks in all things. Wow. The Bible applies to life every day.

Thanks a Lot!
November 24
Matthew 6:14–15

We place a terrible burden on one another by our critical spirits. We are so quick to judge, to criticize, to pick apart. We readily see what's wrong with the other guy. Yet we hold our own faults so close we can't see them ourselves. We intend to inspire improvement and better performance. What we get is bitterness, lower performance, and hostility. How can we overcome such a thing?

First, it is helpful to put yourself in another's shoes. This is not an easy trait to develop. It requires sensitivity. It requires imagination. The dynamic behind this understanding is that it promotes sharing, rather than stifling it.

Another consideration is to act instead of reacting. Unfortunately, when we react without thinking, it is often negative. If you have thought ahead about your response, it is much more likely to be a positive one. Finally, be appreciative. We often fail to be appreciative if we have centered too much on ourselves. Focusing on the amazing gifts God has put in front of us makes a big difference here. If we can see the hand of God in every living thing, and every other human, it is easier to keep the center in the right place.

God made us to live life fully and well. He made us to be happy and bright, to respond to his love. He gave us a way out of darkness, through forgiveness. Sometimes it takes a special care to come to that place. But God is in the everyday. He longs for our joy right here and right now. Each day, take time to look up to God and say, "Thanks a lot!"

The Peace Corps at Home
November 25
2 Corinthians 5:16–6:2

Peace is made by coming to trust one another and to work for each other's good. Peace is made through responsibility, the concerned person and nation, a willingness to lift each up for the common good. Peace is infinitely harder to wage than war. At home, we are the Peace Corps when we are responsible mothers and fathers, sensible and thoughtful children, useful and hard-working citizens, and concerned and willing Christians. Indeed, we are the church in action whenever we act in compassion, whenever we lessen hate and anger, whenever we act on behalf of all humankind for a better world.

The church must continue to support Christians at home, as well as reach out as an instrument of God to the world. It is not a chapel for the devout alone; it is an outpost for God's mission. We are at war. At war with callousness, at war with apathy, at war with emptiness, and sickness of the soul to death. A large part of worship is a reawakening to what God did and does in history! We are compelled to be in a constant state of change and renewal. We *are* the ambassadors of Christ twenty-four hours a day. The job of the Christian is to show that God is at work in the world to redeem men, to restore them to their true humanity, and to maintain them in this relationship. The church is not a building; it is the body, the family of Christ. *We*, each and every one of us (not just the ordained pastors), are the church. It is time to move out like soldiers on a scouting mission. God has laid his hand on us to be volunteers for the Peace Corps … at home.

There's Power in an Open Hearth
November 26
Revelation 3:14–4:1

Have you ever lied, cheated, or stolen? How about when you promise yourself and your family this moment or that moment or this afternoon or that evening, with every good intention. Then something comes up—a crisis, an emergency—and you suddenly become a liar who cheated time from your family with promises you would repay later, promises you often don't keep. Everyone borrows against some future time in order to meet some pressing present need. It is terribly easy to let it become a habit. Then it tears apart families and marriages.

We need to reorder our lives! But on what basis? We need to look back at the early days of a relationship, or a movement, like Christianity. When something is new, you are transformed. You can't keep it to yourself; you have to share what is happening in your life. The strategy of the early church was to open their homes to each other in order to share the news of what God was doing in their lives. Too often the image of the world about your home is that it is a place of escape. A place to get away, to withdraw. But if a home is empty of laughter, joy, and nurturing relationships, it is an empty and hollow place.

What to do? Choose a family, invite them to your home, and share love and laughter, tears and tough times with them. Sharing a meal is such an easy way to make a bond. Share how the Word is applying to your everyday life. Nurture each other, and you will find a new energy to share your faith.

There in Our Need
November 27
Isaiah 9:2–7

It is a curiosity of life that regardless of how smart we are, how secure we are, how much we have of this world's goods, we are always in need. We need energy to get through the long days, we need strength for staying well and healthy, we need to know how to get along. Further, there are spiritual needs—to feel the sorrows of life as well as the joys. Without Jesus Christ as our wonderful counselor, we can't make it through! The good news is that our God knows this. God cares so much that he comes after us. God literally comes alongside us and invades our space! He finds us wherever we are and takes us by the hand and joins us in our need. This is truly amazing! Clearly, he won't force himself on us; we can always refuse the outstretched hand. But to know that God is actively present in our times of need is really mind-blowing! When Jesus came to earth and dwelt among us, he understood firsthand what it is like to live on earth. He was tempted, he was hungry, he was angry, he was tortured, he was loved, and he was betrayed.

It is important to be energetic, to set goals, and to strive mightily with all our physical and mental strength. But when we decide we are going to "do it ourselves," we are either headed for self-pride or big failure. God actually set up this world as we know it such that we are always in need. Just as a child needs a parent, we need God. Isaiah put it well: he is our "Wonderful Counselor, Mighty God, Everlasting Father, Prince of Peace" (Isaiah 9:6). Now that's who I want on my side.

Transferred ... from Darkness to Light

November 28
Acts 26:18

Between jobs, the military, school changes, and so on, pretty much everyone has experienced a transfer of some kind. The key of being transferred is to go *from* one thing and *to* another. In the passage for today, Paul is quoting Jesus' words to him at the time of his conversion. To be delivered from the dominion of darkness and transferred to the kingdom of God was truly a miraculous thing.

From a faith perspective, we all change in this way when we accept Jesus as our Lord and Savior. We go from helpless sinner to glory in the power of Jesus! Faith is from and to something. It is from darkness to light. It is salvation from that which is bad, destructive, lesser, to that which is good, constructive, greater.

While it is nice to feel that we are in the light immediately, the truth is that there is something of the light and something of the dark in each one of us. How do we shift the balance from darkness to light within ourselves? First, we must set ourselves on a positive belief. A person's set of beliefs sets the course of their life. It could lead one to shame and dishonor or blessings and peace. The next step of the process is to determine what or who we believe in. That's why God came to us in the form of a man. Jesus demonstrated an accurate image of ourselves and what God had planned for us. Through the scriptures, we can get to know Jesus better. There is a huge difference between knowing someone and believing in him. This is Christ's vision for each one of us.

Two Worlds in Technicolor

November 29
Revelation 22:1–5

The fear of organized and dedicated persecution and death for proclaiming one's belief in Jesus Christ is what prompted the writing of the book of Revelation. Rome expected people to evidence their loyalty to the state by participating in the state religion. The Christians at that time saw that to accept this was to accept the right of the state to claim the absolute obedience of its citizens. This they could not do. The true Lord, both of the individual and of the nation, was Jesus Christ. The Christians to whom John was writing needed to be encouraged.

John told the people, and us, in vivid language, of how heavenly things related to earthly living for the Christian who was hunted. The first thing he told them is that God is *real*. As one reads this book, it is critical to ask, "How real is God to me?" Do I continue to enter the sanctuary with hush and awe? Can I truly and reverently sing, "Holy, Holy, Holy?" Is God alone King? To the writer of Revelation he is real. He rules in heaven and he rules in earth.

Another truth that emerges is that God is a God who *judges*. God can and does use the forces of this world to drive his children into repentance. Because he has chosen to leave us free to choose, he will not force us to repent or to love him. In our selfishness, we fall away and break relationship with the only source of our lives. The result of sin is self-destructive. God does not will destruction of his children but discipline, not retribution but repentance, not vengeance but that men should return to their true home.

Finally, God is *victorious*. Faithfulness triumphs. We are created to live in two worlds—this one and the next. If we forget it, then our lives become all of the horror of the worst of Revelation's consequences. As we remember it, the promises are fulfilled, and God will "wipe away every tear from our eyes" (Revelation 7:17). Come, Lord Jesus.

What Is Next?
November 30
John 11:1–27

We are here now, living pretty well, yet seem to be compelled to ask, somewhat fearfully, "What next?" It truly is one of the basic questions that has disturbed the human mind throughout history. We humans are completely dependent—individual but unable to survive without one another. Our lives are tenuous with the only separation between life and death a heartbeat, a breath. We strive to be all powerful in ourselves. We were born in the very image of God; we have a driving urge to worship him. All too often, we worship all else, and most surely ourselves. We try to become our own god whom we can control, and it is usually at the very point when we are seemingly the most powerful that we are the weakest. We sense our weakness and frailty, so we build up barriers. We try to be our own gods through entertainment, diversion, noise. We obtain financial, political, and personal power, then stand back and say, "Look what I have done!"

Yet we fail to see ourselves from God's eyes. We are nothing, have nothing he has not given us.

The story of humankind is broken relationships. The work of God is healing relationships. God *knew* from the beginning that humans would need healing—from the moment of Adam and Eve in the garden. How are the broken relationships healed? He chose to reach down by sending Jesus—love—to meet us. Jesus showed us true love to break down the barriers. How do we see this love on the cross? He bore the weight of our sins in death, then revealed the answer to what is next in his resurrection and eternal life.

A Christ-Centered Christmas
December 1
Luke 2:1–20

As we approach Christmas, we ought to center down on Christ. We spend so much time sending cards, buying gifts, worrying about who will bring what and sit where. What is more important about Christmas is that God gave a priceless gift to the world. We go through the Christmas season without truly giving thought as to what it is all about.

If this were your last Christmas, the last opportunity to feel the exuberant excitement of the reenacted Christ event—What would you want to be central? Quite a question, isn't it. One thing would be that it must be spiritually centered. You would want to remember how your heart feels, how the event impacts eternity. God chose to come as a baby, instead of as a typical king. This way, he enters into our hearts slowly, gently. A baby reminds us that the relationship with God and humankind is about joy, responsibility, growth, fruitfulness. A baby speaks without language and gives us a kind of sudden awareness that breaks through our normal reservations. Christ also brings assurance at Christmas. Assurance that the coming of Christ was not just a pleasant farce, but a massive Force. It is truly *God with us*—Immanuel.

If this was your last Christmas, you might want to truly give everything you've got. You'd do something unselfish, other centered, something with abandon. Giving is living; after all, the secret of life is to share. So, what is to prevent us from pursuing this course for *this* Christmas? The world is never going to get it. The world will remain caught up in commercialism. Having a Christ-centered Christmas is up to each one of us.

Ah, I See!
December 2
Luke 19:1–10

It is so critical today that people see the real Jesus. There is a big difference between being exposed to Jesus and seeing him for what he really is. This means seeing him with our minds and hearts and souls. Once a person has truly seen Jesus, their life automatically changes and becomes a life of faith and service.

One of the things that gets in the way of seeing the real Jesus is how we see other people. After all, we see the Bible scholar who cheats on his wife; the regular church attender who cheats his customers, and the woman who is sweet to your face but talks about you as soon as you turn away. Unfortunately, Christians are still human! Those who follow Jesus do not claim perfection; instead, they are striving for fellowship with God, trying to point others to the Way, the Truth, and the Life. This striving is an ongoing process—not complete as long as we live on this earth.

To see what Jesus does on this earth requires practice—like the professional driver who is trained to look far ahead to avoid danger, or the doctor who can make a diagnosis by watching someone walk into the room. We must learn to see beyond the human frailty, unrealistic expectations, and appearances to the act of God in ourselves—the very presence of Jesus in our lives. This requires us to see that, not only in ourselves, but to see the same potential in those around us. With this type of vision, we can gather together and work for the kingdom of God. Perhaps we can even catch a glimpse of what God sees as he looks upon us. He sees that we are a group of imperfect creatures struggling with sin and selfishness and desiring to walk through this life in a way he would want for us.

Christmas—Chaotic or Cherished?

December 3
Luke 2:1–20

Christmas is a wonderful time. It's a time of memories, happiness, and family. Yet Christmas can be absolutely chaotic. It can mean shopping, extra programs, extra visits, frustration. Thankfully, we can keep Christmas from being chaotic and shape it into something cheerful and cherishable.

Christmas is a joyous time. It is a celebration of Immanuel—God with us. What could be more worthy of celebration than God coming to earth in the flesh to be with us? God is no longer "way up there," he's here. With us. The purpose of Christmas is love, the divine love that gives depth to our interpersonal relations. Love is the staple food of the good life. It is that which helps us to put first things first, because our lives have a central and worthwhile purpose. Christmas characterizes the coming of Christ into the world as an answer to the hurt of humanity.

Christmas is essentially Christian. It cannot be otherwise. Our tendency to make it chaotic stems from the loss of this understanding. The world seems bent on making this happen. Every year, commercialism takes a broader place in our consciousness. We say, "Happy Holidays," or "Season's Greetings," instead of "Merry Christmas." We cross out Christ by calling Christmas Xmas. People search for Christmas carols that are not about Christ! This adds up to a confusion of ideas, a misplacing of values. Let's put Santa into perspective. Santa, and the idea of giving are a training ground for children and not the true Christmas message. Let's make Christ once again central. Pray earnestly that you may feel the true meaning of Christmas in your heart. Maximize the Christ in Christmas and minimize the worldly influence. Before your traditional gift unwrapping, say a prayer, say it out loud before the whole family—a prayer in humility and thanksgiving. We serve the purposes of our Lord in practicing the true meaning of Christmas.

Coming: Powerful Possibilities

December 4
Micah 5:2–4; Luke 1:39–56

Sometimes it is hard to know how to "do" Christmas. It reminds us of who we are and who we are not. Mostly, we try to control it or "do it right." What if we simply trusted our feelings about it? One of the surest ways to reach the true meaning of Christmas is to let the Christian truths pour into our spirits through music. It doesn't matter whether you are musical in the performance sense, music touches deep fibers in our makeup. More of our theology and our beliefs are contained in the music of Christmas, I think, than in the books of theology. The haunting strains touch the withdrawn spirit; the joyous lilt of Christmas carols bounces our lethargy into exuberance; the hope expressed in songs of simple faith tell us that coming with Christmas are powerful possibilities.

What is written in Luke 1:46–55 is also known as the Magnificat of Mary. Despite the burden of her situation, she knew she was blessed among women. God is mighty, transforming the mundane. Some tough times and grinding efforts have a way of becoming the times we remember with the greatest sense of worth. Many of us have trouble coping with life because we expect it to be easy! Wrong. People who cope with life successfully are those who understand discipline and denial, who recognize that life is a training school. When life is easy, we do not learn to cope. God's holiness can transform everyday things into holy moments. Love works. Trust Christmas. Fill yourself with Christmas. Know that powerful possibilities are coming as the Christ wins our hearts.

Expectations
December 5
Matthew 1:18–25

Have you ever stopped to think that no other religious holiday than Christmas involves gifts? In fact, no other American holiday involves gifts. Gifts at Christmastime grew up out of two examples: out of the example of the kings from the Orient and out of an awareness of the great gift of God to us. Our gift giving, then, is actually symbolic and illustrative. Unless we realize this truth, the exchange can be rather ridiculous. In another perspective, gift giving also heightens our expectations and piques our curiosity. There's something quite appropriate in our sense of expectation. Mary, too, was expecting.

Expectation can be divided into three parts: anticipation, preparation, and fulfillment. We all can relate to anticipation. Anticipating visits from friends and family, the beauty of the Christmas tree, and, of course, the gifts. Anticipation also connotes mystery. There is the mystery of rebirth and renewal. The gift of God coming into our lives is both mysterious and magnificent.

Preparation is the part of Christmas that is most likely to elicit a groan. In our human preparation, it is easy to get overwhelmed—shopping, buying, decorating, baking. Yet the traditions and memories are really what make the season so special. From a spiritual perspective, Mary's expectancy tells the truths of waiting, growing, and trust.

Fulfillment is the ultimate part of expectancy. Finally, the day comes. The outward event can be anticlimactic, especially if we forget to consider the real gifts of Christmas. God gave us Christ that we might have true fulfillment and complete joy.

Expectantly Waiting
December 6
Mark 13:24–37

What an amazing and unexpected turn of events that God chose to come in the form of an infant! Who would have thought it? As Christians contemplating the Advent, we are torn between hope and doubt. We want the coming again of Christ. We long for the intervening power and splendor that will cause every eye to see, every heart to know, every mind to understand, every soul to be inspired.

We know the difference a Christ-filled life has made for us. The gift of God is a wonderful gift! It is beyond imagining before receiving it. In Christ, we know a rich sustaining fellowship that cares, cherishes, shares, and lifts one another up. Yet so many are oblivious to the possibility of knowing the joy of being a part of the family of God. They get caught up in their own pursuits and do not see. In fact, some are afraid of the church.

Expectancy is a new and transforming ingredient. Expectancy turns waiting into watching. It is a perspective of hopeful outcome. That is why we Christians are a hopeful people. We expect that we can and do make a difference. Those of us who are of the root of Jesse are leaning toward hope in the midst of a world that leans toward doubt. Thanks be to our God and to our Christ.

Faith
December 7
Luke 1:38

It's tough to be patient. In an age of instant gratification, it is hard for us to capture a long-term perspective. Impatience is also a characteristic of the Christmas season. Children can hardly stand those last few days—some of them start counting down on December 26 for the next year! It is tough to know how many people even grasp the spiritual significance of Christmas. That's why Christmas is truly a matter of faith. Christmas is a gift of God, and it is hope and love and joy, and it is based on faith.

Faith can be used as a verb—an action word. Faith is something to live by. Faith is something on which we act. You would have the right to be skeptical if I said I was a person of faith, and then I gave no evidence for it in my life. Faithful living involves living by truth, honoring justice, embodying fairness, exhibiting goodness. We expect results from faith. Faith is also always growing; it is never static; it is not once and for all. It is like a pilgramage that is in a constant state of being created.

One of the beautiful things about Christmas is that it gives us an opportunity to exercise our faith into action. Those who don't know the true meaning of Christmas may think it is all make-believe. They need to see God with skin on. That's just what Jesus was, and that is who we can be for someone who needs to see him. Everyone needs someone in their corner; we all have Someone in our corner. Who needs you to be Jesus with skin on? Who needs you in their corner?

Getting Ready
December 8
Isaiah 12:2–6

We are the ones who must translate the form of Christmas so that the true meaning of Christmas comes again this year. No-one else can do it for us. We know the meaning of Christmas. We know it is the incarnation. We know we must get ready spiritually for the highest gift of Christmas. But there is so much to be done that it makes one want to escape. Yet the Christian faith calls us to high ideals, hopes, and expectations. We are special servants of God, so a challenge that calls forth our best is always just beyond our reach. Otherwise, what difference do we make? We are called to be the difference, God being our helper.

It sounds kind of heavy. But when Christ is in our midst, he is not a burden; he is our friend; he is our pleasure; he is our joy. If we center on the Lord, there is cause for rejoicing. If we center our minds on what is not yet done for Christmas, that will pervade our whole spirit. But if we let ourselves rejoice in each little thing that gets done, the joy of it begins to sink in. If we focus on the true gift of Christmas, the rest is easier. Let us get ready to take Jesus into our hearts, making Christmas come once again.

Gold!
December 9
Matthew 2:1–12

Gold was one of the gifts brought to Jesus at his birth. We have attached the symbolism that it was intended to be used for a crown. No-one knows how it was actually used … this information has been lost to history. Perhaps it allowed the little family to escape to Egypt, following the warning Joseph received in a dream. There are several qualities of gold—beyond its monetary value—that we can identify as gifts that we can offer of ourselves.

Gold is a unique metal. It is more malleable than any other metal. It can be hammered into thin sheets or strung out into fine strands without losing its structure. It can be shaped into instruments and ornaments with intricate detail. As we approach our Master, we, too, can be best used if malleable. He can mold us and shape us into his will. Our response must be to withstand this shaping without crumbling. With a call from God, we can present ourselves as willing to draw out the best in each other and seeking to refine our own living toward being a worthy offering to the Lord.

A second property to emulate is durability. Gold can be buried, frozen, and exposed to fire without harm. It is almost impossible to destroy. A thin band of gold can be worn on one's finger for a lifetime! Service to God may require submitting personal frustrations in order to work with needy persons. It may entail ignoring criticism by committing to the church regardless of outward popularity.

Finally, gold is beautiful. Its beauty is inherent. It retains its luster without polishing. It cannot be counterfeited. Such is the beauty of Christ. His perfection is beyond compare. He came not only as the messenger from God, but as the message, bringing light to a dark world. We cannot attain such flawlessness on our own, only in his power. We can present ourselves as gold to our father—malleable in his hands, durable in his service, and beautiful in his likeness.

Hallelujah!
December 10
Psalm 147:1–11

The word *Hallelujah* means "Praise the Lord!" We Christians have something that is terrific. Our God is a God of salvation and glory and power. Whom should we fear? Our faith is a faith that saves lives from destruction, that makes families whole, and that creates light in a time of darkness. It is a faith about which we ought, rightly, to shout, "Hallelujah!"

Salvation belongs to our God. What every person needs to be saved from is hostility to God and his will. We were made to live in a relationship to God of trust and obedience and love. Unfortunately, we often want to be our own little tin gods. Sin is the denial of the relationship we were made for. It leads us to become rebellious and disobedient. Salvation means that we return to the right relationship to God through Jesus Christ.

Glory belongs to our God. The trouble we have with glory is that we tend to think of glory in terms of visible appearance. Glory is the recognition of God's majesty, power, and worth. To understand this requires that we honor his name, that we treasure him, cherish him, and hold him dear. To do this brings a deep sense of reverence.

Power belongs to our God. The power of God comes from his creativity. He made the world and all that is in it. He determines the number of the stars. Presumably, he also has the power to destroy the whole world. That is the reason the word *fear* is used. The fear of God is the recognition that finally he has our destiny in his hands, and that he has the power to cast us into outer darkness. It also brings the understanding that justice will be done. Our universe is one we can count on—the moral law can no more be broken than the law of gravity; it can only be illustrated. This brings forth our trust.

So, Hallelujah! Salvation, glory, and power belong to God!

He Is Coming
December 11
Luke 1:26–38

It is so easy to lose the excitement of Christmas. The true meaning gets lost in the hustle and bustle of preparations that really do not prepare our hearts for the event ahead. The announcement "He is coming" elicits, "My goodness, is it December already?" When it should cause us to fall to our knees and say, "Praise be to God!" How can we recapture the lost enthusiasm?

First, we must truly grasp that Christ's coming is God's fulfillment of his promises to humans. The prophecies that the early church saw as telling of Jesus were not picked at random. Consider the great messianic passages: "For unto us a child is born, unto us a son is given" (Isaiah 9:6), and "A shoot will come up from the stump of Jesse; from his roots a Branch will bear fruit" (Isaiah 11:1), and "The eyes of the blind shall be opened, the ears of the deaf shall be unstopped" (Isaiah 35:5). There are so many prophecies fulfilled in the birth of Christ that it seems impossible to not recognize Jesus as the fulfillment of God's promises. This was God himself dealing with the hardness of our hearts. Seeking by all means at the disposal of divine love to reconcile ourselves unto himself. The coldness with which we tend to confront Christmas seems to be because we have ignored or forgotten its import. We've forgotten the drama of salvation and who we are in that drama.

Furthermore, we stand on the other side of the cross. We know the significance of the child in the manger. We have the Bible, eyewitness accounts of his life, and the church itself to use as evidence of the power of his coming. Knowing the true meaning of Christmas, we will come to it with joyful anticipation, born out of a new relationship with our heavenly Father. May his coming fill us with the awareness that he is coming for *us*.

Immanuel—God with Us
December 12
Matthew 1:18–2:12

Christmas is eternal because God is with us. Christ is with us. Somehow, every year, the message of God in Jesus breaks through our tough hides, tears down the barrier of our crowded schedules, and penetrates the preoccupation of our busyness. The idea that God is with us all of the time is a bit overwhelming! God not only listens to our prayers, he listens also to our arguments. God is not only with us in church but also at the office and the home and even at the store.

Hush. Feel his presence. Settle down. Quiet. Still.

Allow this moment to soften the rush of moments that propel us so much of our days. Allow this quiet to refresh. Listen. Even if the ache of tired bones from preparations for Christmas overrides all other thoughts, there can be inner peace. Look at the excitement of children's faces, at a hope born, at a renewed joining in with the true meaning of Christmas.

We sometimes think that we make Christmas. We think we have Christmas if we have our homes splendidly decorated, if we have bought everyone gifts, if we sing Christmas carols. All of these things are valuable, and they help to prepare us. But what did we do to make Christmas? Really, we did nothing. Only God provided Christmas. We didn't provide for the coming of eternity into time through the humbleness of a completely dependent baby. It was God's doing that gave us Christ. For God so loved us that he gave us his only begotten Son.

The crux of Christmas is Immanuel—God with us. We are his hands. We are the hands of Jesus wherever we are, in whatever way we are able to express that his love is in our hearts. Each of us have our own means of expression. Be the very hands of God this Christmas season.

Keep Your Eye on the Gift
December 13
James 5:7–10; Matthew 11:2–11

It is easy to say, "Keep Christ in Christmas," but as always, it is easier said than done. When John the Baptist wanted to know about Jesus, he was told, "see for yourself,"—the deaf heard, the blind saw, and the lame walked. God made Christmas in sending the most fantastic, life-changing gift in history. No other prophet or teacher has made the impact on the world the way Jesus Christ has done. Focusing on the significance of that gift changes everything. Without it, our Christmases are empty and disappointing. So are our lives!

The fluff and puff of the Christmas season blurs the focus on The Gift. Most of us can't even remember Christmas gifts long enough to say thank you. As you select and receive gifts this year, think of the giver, remember and appreciate that relationship. The gift is only a symbol of the affection and good wishes of the giver. The enactment of opening the presents under the tree is intensely spiritual when you stop to think about it. That special time occurs all over the world, shouting out the Great Truth—God's gift to us. No exchange or gift receipt needed; just keep passing it along.

Love
December 14
Romans 8:39

Love. What a word! So powerful. So misused. Sometimes we hook up love and performance, insisting that love is some kind of reward for someone else's efforts. Love is not a reward; it is a quality of relationships! Sometimes we think that romantic feelings and sexual relationships are love. But, as delightful as romance is, and as scintillating as sexual relations are, unless there is deep and long-lasting commitment, it is not really love. In the church, we say, "God is love." Then we are casual about caring or insensitive in the way we relate to others, and observers wonder what we mean when we say that God is love and that we love God. The Christmas season is a season we all love, because it brings out love in us, and because it is such a wonderful demonstration of God's love in giving us this precious infant Jesus. We know that the whole reason that God came to earth was simply that we could be returned to the family of God and be a loved part of that family if, through brokenness, we had run away from home.

Christmas is coming, and we need to prepare our hearts to receive what God has given. The true glory of the Lord was revealed in the coming of Christ. Christmas is an event where the Word of God and the act of God will stand forever. Think about what God brought about. While the Hebrews were slaves, he came to them through the prophet Isaiah, telling them they would be restored. "For to us a child is born, to us a son is given, and the government will be upon his shoulders. He will be called Wonderful Counselor, Mighty God, Everlasting Father, Prince of Peace" (Isaiah 9:6). Isaiah reminded them that all was not lost, because God is love. God's Word stands forever. God loves you! This love came to us. Humble. In the beauty of infancy … to win our hearts.

Magnificent!
December 15
Luke 1:39–56

The trouble with Christmas is that it has had too long a run. The truth is that a thing can become so commonplace and so familiar that it comes to be taken for granted—the spectacular taken out of it, the magnificence tarnished and faded. How many Christmases has it been for you? How unable are you to catch the astounding magnificence of what our faith offers in the claim that God became embodied in a little baby in order to come among us and so to win us? It is possible to actually take this, our salvation, for granted. To take the Christmas event casually is blasphemy!

The Christmas event is new for each of us because we are different than yesterday or last year. We understand some things better now than we did last year, because some things have happened since we last thought about Christmas. Life is ever new. The arrival of Christ is fulfillment of prophecy. God, in his great wisdom, gave us Jesus, who fulfilled the prophecies by changing the expectations of men into the fulfillment of God.

The birth of Christ is magnificent because it is beyond humankind. The unusual circumstances of his birth and conception is of *God*. It is of the *Spirit*. It is for our salvation so that we can bridge the chasms which separate us and come once again into a perfect relationship with our heavenly Father. The birth of Christ signals the entry of a new order. Each person whose heart is warmed by the love of God becomes a child of God and has a right to dignity and respect. This new order catches the freshness of the acts of God in daily wonderment. It places priorities of godliness in our hearts. This new order does not take our faith for granted but brings to it eagerness, expectancy, and praise. May we know the birth of Christ is for us, and it is ever fresh and new, and magnificent.

More than a Carpenter
December 16
Luke 2:8–14

Jesus was more than a carpenter. It is surprising how much mental exercise is involved in carpentry. Of course, some physical strength is also required. Consider how much calculation goes into building even such a simple thing as a doghouse or a deck. Whether you are a carpenter or a scientist, a ditch digger or a dentist, you are always more than that. God always has much more in store for us. What you do for a living is your vocation. It is our avocation that puts us in ministry. This is what makes us constructive partners with God. Being in ministry with God is what makes life worthwhile.

The Christian faith has been the foundation of victorious living for over twenty centuries. It is rooted in the promise that if we will be God's people, he will be Immanuel—God with us. The promises of Jesus will meet every need. When you start to panic or feel stressed or lonely, stop. Look to your spirit, reorient, take time to let the Lord touch you once again. When we allow Christ to take up residency in our hearts, it helps us focus on what is worth doing. The Holy Spirit will teach us what is worth hanging on to and what should be let go. The Lord is our peace and joy, truly, the good news.

On Order
December 17
James 5:8; Isaiah 35:1–10

Most of us have placed an order for something we really wanted and found that it was back-ordered. Hopefully, it eventually arrived, albeit late, but as promised. This is how the human race has been with God. On order, on hold, never fully delivered. God's plan for us was Christmas for the whole earth. It was to be a masterpiece of music. First there is the joyous burst of new life and beauty. Then encouragement to the weak and feeble. Finally, there is peace and wholeness for everyone! Safety. Plenty. God's order is beautiful, idyllic. But in reality, it is yet to be. We have not been delivered peace; we do not see wholeness. There is poverty of body and of spirit everywhere.

God's plan is on hold. The scripture gives us some response for the delay. First, it is still ahead, and only God knows when the fulfillment will be. Second, the promise can be seen in individuals—Abraham, Sarah, Isaac, Jacob, David, Isaiah, and finally Jesus. For that matter, look around you at the mentors of your own faith—fathers, mothers, pastors. None are perfect except our Lord, but there is evidence of the promise.

What God has on order is us! Each of us can live as best we can right now, and we can fill part of the order. We can make the community around us the image of what is to be. Establish your hearts. The coming of the Lord is at hand. How will you help make the order complete?

Recapturing Our Carefreeness—
the Everlasting Father
December 18
Isaiah 9:2–7

If human fathers follow the guidance of the everlasting heavenly Father, it is possible to defeat the enemy! The steps of good men are directed, ordered by the Lord. Father means to be the bringer of order out of chaos. Jesus was particularly fond of calling God "Father." When God enters our lives, he immediately begins to bring order out of our chaos. When we put Christ at the head of our lives, we get order. It is vital to follow the guidance of his Father.

One of the best things in the world is to come alongside your children and gently guide them using the everlasting Father's hand. This way, we get to watch them grow in wisdom and in stature and in steady nurturing maturity. Let your steps be directed by the Lord. Micah 6:8 says that we are to "do justice, to love mercy, and to walk humbly with our God." With this, we will turn the word *everlasting* into a wonderful gift for the family and our lives.

In our broken world, one of the things that is missing is solid, godly parenting. This means to be there for your children. To be their scout masters, coaches, tutors, and guides. Don't just watch from the sidelines or, worse yet miss out on these critical activities. One meaningful relationship between a child and an adult can save that child from despair. So, if you do not have children, volunteer to be a mentor to a child that needs a relationship. If we all vow to follow the words of Micah, we can truly bring order out of chaos and defeat the enemy.

That Little Black Book
December 19
John 20:26–31

That little black book could mean any of a number of things. It could be a list of names with their dirty deeds, phone numbers of pretty girls, or a vital date book. In this case, it is the Bible. It has a wealth of information that never goes out of date, is power packed, and can change a life for eternity. No other single piece of literature has ever begun to rival it. It is the world's best seller year after year.

It is historic. Here is where God chose to act with his people, among them, side by side. It reveals the hand of God moving in the lives of humans. It is amazing what archeology and scientific research has unearthed. There are innumerable datable sites of biblical history. Irrefutable evidence has corroborated various biblical narratives, such as the siege of Jericho. With all the scrutiny of meticulous archeologists, nothing has been found that lessens the preeminence of the Bible as a unique religious document and masterpiece of literature.

It speaks of eternity. Eternity is the golden thread that runs through the entire sixty-six books. It is about God and humankind, humankind and God. It is a book of faith. Finally, it is personal. Once we touch the pages of scripture, we can never rightly feel we are nobody. In God's economy, there is value in each individual, he knows us by name. There are no persons in general described in the Bible; it is a record of persons in particular. Persons with pride, lust, greed. In fact, there is nothing that humans have done that the Bible has not observed. But with it all, we are pointed beyond it and ourselves to an ultimate and unfailing One. In that little black book are the words of life and salvation.

The Everlasting Father
December 20
Isaiah 40:28

The title "Everlasting Father" does not refer to whether or not the Father will continue to exist or for how long. It centers on the fact that his care and concern will be everlasting, never-ending. The everlasting father is a father who acts. Not "has acted," but is "presently acting." The words of Isaiah bring hope to a despairing nation, then and now. God cares more about this world than we can imagine. We cannot activate ourselves to be good beyond our own humanness. But we can catch a vision of the Son of God. We are in a position to do something about the needs of this world in concert with him and not in the foolishness of our own devices. The Everlasting Father is one who acts to save his children from destruction because he loves them too much to just let them go.

One of the very difficult things for us to learn is the frailty and impermanence of humans. God, having created us in his image, has had trouble with us ever since, because we are everlastingly trying to be or make our own god. That's why the first commandment is, "You shall have no other gods before me" (Deuteronomy 5:7). Once we get it down pat who we are and who God is, much of the trouble in our lives is eliminated. After all, there is nothing quite so troublesome as trying to be someone or something we aren't. The Everlasting Father acts in our lives and calls us to know our true selves. If we open our hearts to him, we will discover the kind of peace that comes from receiving the gentle blessings of God, for he longs to walk with us hand in hand.

The Hunger to Belong
December 21
Isaiah 7:10–25

Solitary confinement is the worst punishment society can inflict on a person. The reason is that we humans are social animals. We crave to belong; we need to belong. Any belonging is better than no belonging; any society is better than no society; the only thing worse than isolation is anarchy. We have all experienced the icy stab of exclusion. That is why Christmas is such a winsome season! God saw our hurt and isolation. God saw the brokenness and pain, and God moved to embrace us. Isaiah tells of the coming of the Messiah hundreds of years before it occurred. The other name for the Messiah is Immanuel—God with us. God became a man so that we could find our way back to him.

It is easy to be generous and inclusive with those we love. It is not so easy to include the down and out, the misfits, those who are not like us. We somehow want to exclude these people. It takes a visitation to turn us. When Joseph first heard of Mary's condition, he wanted to separate himself from her. It took a visitation from an angel of the Lord for him to see that God was more powerful than anything in this world. Joseph learned to trust God for the outcome and opened his heart to the family of God. Because of his tenderness, we have Jesus to take us by the hand and guide us into a better way—the way of belonging and inclusion.

The Preparer

December 22
Luke 1:76–80

If you find yourself dreading the busyness of the Christmas season more than looking forward to it, the provision of Advent as a time of preparation has been wisely made. Each of us need to understand anew the real impact of the actual coming of the Son of God. He came into history, life, and the soul of humankind. Expectancy is essential if God's spirit is to be poured out and received. This preparation was initially the task of John the Baptist. His role was prophesied hundreds of years prior to his birth by the prophet Isaiah: "The voice of one crying in the wilderness: prepare the way of the Lord" (Isaiah 40:3) John fulfilled the prophecy down to his wardrobe and diet! He alerted the people to anticipate the arrival of the Messiah, calling them to repentance.

Most of the text available about John the Baptist highlights his message of preparedness. He knew that he was not the anticipated Messiah but was called to gather the people for the arrival of the Messiah. His role is not unfamiliar in today's world. The best recommendation a person can have is that of a mutual friend. This holds true for introducing Jesus to others as much as to any other situation. The most common way for persons to be won for Christ is by hearing his message through a person they trust. Somehow, being introduced through a friend opens the way to a better reception—so the message can be heard.

The other vital piece of John's message was that of repentance. This is not a word used widely anymore, but the basis of its meaning is to turn around. When a person first considers the idea of turning to Christ, it invariably involves turning away from a different way of life. It calls for self-examination and recognition of a need to change to be able to receive the forgiveness and renewal of God's love.

The season of Advent is a holy one. It reminds us of the need for anticipation, expectancy, and preparation. The outcome is beautiful: salvation and peace.

The Shining Star
December 23
Matthew 2:1–13

The story of the wise men following the star to Bethlehem, to the crib of Jesus, is told only by Matthew. The significance of the story is that humans are brought from afar, and from every race, to adore the word become flesh. That star has come to be a symbol of the light of Christ shining in the world to many men. The disciples followed it too, in a sense. In their day, as with the wise men, to follow Christ was counted as foolish. Today, we feel surer of ourselves. We have the Bible, the church, millions of believers to encourage us. Yet it is just as easy for us to get lost along the way now as it must have been then. For, while the early believers had no clear trail, they also had fewer roadblocks.

The star shines through history to a renewal of wonder. How we need to recatch a sense of wonder. Nothing seems to surprise us anymore. When Christmas doesn't make your heart swell up until it nearly bursts, and makes you all soft inside, then you know that something inside you is dead. Do we really understand what a stupendous thing we celebrate in the event of Christmas? Unless we come to terms with our spiritual selves, all that is material turns hollow in our hands. The star shines to remind us that God is truly with us.

The star shines through in all languages and nations of the world. In all the world, each country carries its own customs in celebrating Christmas. But in every one, there is the figure of the Christ-child. He came for everyone. Every soul is equal before God. The wonder of the star should invite us to expect great things. To stop and wonder that nature itself shone out to worship Christ, the Son of God. God gave us his gift of love. This gift says, "Come unto me." It says that God is with us. Heaven is to be in fellowship with God. The star still shines bright in the hearts of believing persons everywhere.

The Sounds of Christmas
December 24
Luke 2:1–20

More than most times, Christmas is a season of many sounds. No other holiday carries the gift-buying tradition as much as Christmas does, which brings along with it the frenzy of shopping, crowded parking lots and stores, music, and frayed nerves. In the words of the Grinch, "all the noise, Noise, Noise, NOISE!" Much of the noise has come about due to commercialism. Christmas has become an opportunity to make lots of money, and businesses don't mind exploiting the holiday with visions of Santa, gifts, and the fear of disappointment. One wonders, in fact, if sometimes kids have actually lost their faith in God when they discovered Santa was a fake; if Santa is a hoax, then maybe all things invisible are untrue.

Thankfully, the rich music of Christmas is good therapy for the noisyness. It's pretty tough to stay frazzled listening to hymns of Advent and Christmas carols. They catch us up with their tunes and instill the meaning of God's work in us. There are such beautiful scenes played out in "It Came upon a Midnight Clear," "Silent Night," and even "Away in a Manger."

The meaning of Christmas that is found in the sound of a baby's low cry is the jewel that makes Christmas a time to rejoice. God became flesh so that humans could understand spirit. The mystery of God in the flesh calls us to settle in and consider the wonder of this act. God, in Jesus, left heaven as a baby, to coax us back to him. There is no threat in a baby, but this baby changed the world.

Unknown
December 25
Isaiah 35:1–10; Matthew 11:2–11

Jesus came into the world completely unknown. He was born in obscurity unheralded by the world. It is not usual, now, to think of Jesus as unknown. Surely everyone knows about Jesus. But curiously, the one who seems to be so well known is still substantially unknown. Christmas is, for so many, a day or a few days of vacation. For that matter, do we know, deep in our spirits and souls, that Christmas is not just a sweet sentiment but the very incarnation of God? Our God of creation loved us enough to take on our form and live among us—vulnerable, fragile, destructible. The coming of Jesus into human history is the event that changed everything. It gives us hope that the human experience has a chance.

With Christ known in us, we come to understand that our eyes, ears, and hearts are open to joy. The world is God's, and we are stewards; the whole world is our brother and sister. Knowing that God is among us should bring wild joy and ecstasy; full confidence in this brings a deep inner assurance. With God among us and Christ within us, we come to know that our future is in God's hands. What will be is now being created. The future is being born in new vision and understanding. It is possible, looking at our own personal reserve of strength, to feel defeated, desperate. But when we grab hold of the truth that our future is in partnership with the God of Creation, who would risk coming to us unknown as a helpless infant, to awaken in us our love and open us through that awakening to a new vision of the future, then a truly fresh Christmas becomes a reality.

What Was Done with the Gifts?
December 26
Matthew 2:1–23

One of the elements of Christmas that has gotten out of control is the gifts. We spend weeks, months even, preparing for the big day. Everything is set up beautifully; the house is decorated, lights are up, turkey in the oven … then the chaos begins. In a few moments, it looks like a hurricane blew through! Of course, many of the gifts were carefully selected and will be treasured. What about the rest? Some will be exchanged. Some will be regifted. Some will sit in a closet. Why do we exchange gifts on Christmas anyway?

Obviously, it is the birthday of Christ—God's great gift to us. In symbolic reference to that capital G Gift, we give gifts to each other. Yet, as obvious as it is, how often does the central meaning get smothered in the ribbons and wrappings? Some people think we ought not give each other gifts at all at Christmas. I believe we learn by doing. Children naturally love getting gifts. Yet Christmas is a time to learn that it is also fun to give.

Then there is the true gift. God gave us eternal life through Jesus in the ultimate sacrifice of all ages. Our redemption story is told throughout the Bible. It is worth more than a fleeting moment of attention as to how to use that gift. So many people have a drive that places all their energies into achieving something in the future but which never lets them enjoy the present. God gave us the earth and said it was good. He wanted us to so live our days together that we would enjoy them. He wanted us to love one another in the here and now, not in some distant and unattainable future. It may take hours of consideration to come to the insight as to how to truly give and also receive. God wants us to give of our love here and now. What will we do with the gift?

Which Scrooge for Christmas?
December 27
Isaiah 52:7–15

Ebenezer Scrooge. The name made famous by *The Christmas Carol*, written by Charles Dickens. It brings to mind a stingy, tightfisted, shriveled up, nasty old man, yelling, "Bah Humbug!" Interestingly, the thrust and intent of the story is conversion. It is the story of the miserly Scrooge who became the generous Scrooge and a man who brought blessings to others. The story exaggerates, of course; the truth is that there are always two sides to life—the beautiful and the ugly, the kind and the torturous, the sweet and the bitter.

Such is the nature of God's love. It is not some idealistic fantasy, indulging in rose gardens and sweet perfume. It is realistic, meeting us where we are, caring for the loved. God agonized over our lostness, so he came with the surest token of love available to our human experience—a baby. What else could have so thoroughly disarmed us and raised feelings of tenderness and openness? A baby, so we could hear and understand the angels: Glory to God! To come as a baby was not weakness. It was subtle strength. It was to woo and win us. It was to beseech our hearts. After all, what does it matter to God? He has everything. All powerful, all knowing, holding the final judgment—Why should God care about us?

The answer is love. Love must be freely given in response to his loving care. Love is the dearest truth. When there is love between humans and God, and between one another, then it is good, and all other problems pale in comparison. When there is anger and enmity and strife, when there is separation and brokenness, then it is not good. And that is the given. So, God doesn't have everything. He doesn't have those who are separated from him by their choice of separation and loneliness rather than fellowship with him. And the nature of love is such that he cannot force any to love him. Love must be won, earned, sought. The strength of God is not in his power to destroy. It is in his power to set right, to give growth, to nurture. It has the strength of truth in it. It has the bond of love in it—unbreakable. All of us struggle with a tendency to set our hearts upon our own gain rather than the glory of God. Let us kindle our kindness and love, which causes us to rejoice in and with our God.

Hunger and Thirst for Righteousness
December 28
Isaiah 55:1–3, 6–13

Few of us know from personal experience the ravenous longing of the starved man or the agony of a parched throat. We do know enough to realize that hunger and thirst are the master appetites of human nature. Israel is essentially barren without water. The audience to which Jesus spoke would have been very familiar with the sensation of hunger and thirst. Jesus was aware that the need for spiritual food and drink was equally important to the human as physical needs. Consider the feeling when you are under water, and the only thing you can think of is the need for air. Translate that into a way to think of your need for rightness with God.

This life has many hungers, and our appetites rage with many thirsts. Many earthly fulfillments create greater longings, which can never be satisfied. We seek to fill ourselves with too much food, too much drink, too much material wealth. Yet these do not satisfy. Some seek satisfaction in power or wealth, which are also insatiable. We are all vexed with varying degrees of discontent. Jesus sees our hungering and points us to righteousness. He is the only source of the bread of life and the living water.

Harmony between God and humans means equity for humanity in the realm of the Christ spirit. Righteousness is justice held in love. God is perfectly righteous. Our only path back to him is through Christ—the Way, the Truth, and the Light. If we seek a relationship with Christ with the same fervor we seek to fill our earthly hungers, we will be satisfied.

The Meek
December 29
Psalm 37:1–11

Meekness is not a quality we currently prize. It is often equated with weakness, but only the strong can be meek; only the tough can be tender. Jesus was meek but never weak. As a Christian, being meek means humbling oneself. We have to fight to subdue the almighty "I" and to hold down the all- important "me." The self must be disciplined, humble minded, reverent. Meekness also requires the abandonment of self-centeredness, to become God-centered. Self-centeredness ultimately brings not only slow spiritual death, but human poverty of spirit as well. This all takes time and effort. In truth, it cannot be achieved without the gift of God's love.

Jesus said, "Blessed are the meek, for they will inherit the earth" (Matthew 5:5). It is the meek who will inherit divine grace, forgiveness, redemption, sanctification, salvation, and eternal life through their humility. It is the meek who are able to see the great things in life. Contrast the proud and vain with the meek and humble in the following scenario. We are driving along the coast of the Puget Sound at sunset. We see the reddening skies casting their glow over the clouds and the changing hues of the rippling water, overlooking the islands with their deep green foliage. The proud, arrogant, hurried man see this scene and says, "Huh, better hurry, getting dark!" For the other man, the scene evokes the affirmation, "How can anyone who has seen this beauty believe there is no God?" Which of these men has inherited the earth?

The Merciful

December 30
Psalm 103:1–17

"Blessed are the merciful, for they will be shown mercy" (Matthew 5:7). The words of Jesus in the beatitudes echo many of the attributes of God seen in the Old Testament. As Christians, we long to be nearer to Jesus, and the beatitudes are guideposts, pointing a direction toward how to be more like him. The word *mercy* summons images of acts of kindness, and we place ourselves in the position of the one giving aid. Yet mercy involves more than that. It begins in feelings of compassion and sympathy, but mercy must also have in it a tenor of justice. Mercy shows compassion over and above what a person deserves. Mercy without justice would result in chaos.

Another facet of mercy is forgiveness. Mercy is not just displayed in acts of charity. Mercy is given in spite of just deserts. When one has been wronged, it requires mercy to forgo retaliation. One must pray for God's pardon for the person's offense. The ultimate act of mercy would be to revive harmony with the wrongdoer. Without the power of God's love, it is beyond the human nature to show true mercy.

The birth of Jesus represents a dramatic illustration of God's mercy. God brought a new face into this world that was destined to tell us things about God's nature and relationship to us. The whole story of salvation for all men is spelled out in the word *mercy*. Faith in Christ brings us back into harmony with God.

Mercy blesses the giver as much as the receiver. Without mercy, a person's heart can become hard with hatred and resentment. Mercy purges these emotions like gentle rain softens the hard, dry earth. Let us be merciful, that we might obtain mercy.

Our God Reigns
December 31
Isaiah 52:7–15

What a spectacular age we live in! We sit calmly and watch a television announcer tell us that we reach for the moon, go under the North Pole in submarines, and control destructive power enough to devastate this planet. Our minds are so accustomed to physical inventions, great and small, that we are barely even impressed. Our casual approach to these amazing events is similar to our approach to the spectacular significance that *our* God reigns. There is no significance in lunar orbits unless life has ultimate meaning.

As the spirit of Christmas wends its way into our consciousness, we become awake to the awareness that the greatest spectacular of life is that our God reigns. Regardless of our forgetfulness of him, he nevertheless is sovereign. He shall bring his purpose to pass. He reigns over the countless human accomplishments just as he inspired the writings of Isaiah. His ways aren't noisy spectacles, because the spectacular quickly pales and fades as its newness wears off, and we want something more.

God reigns in the ordinary events of common life. What could be more commonplace and ordinary than the birth of a baby? Yet no life ever lived on this planet has been so influential in the affairs of humans as that of Jesus. That holy infant life revealed to us God's own nature—his will, his purpose for humankind. For his purpose to come to pass, God must reign supreme in each heart. Hearts closed to him cannot acknowledge his reign.

Consider the Christmas carol, "Silent Night," by Joseph Mohr:

> How silently, how silently
> the wondrous gift is given!
> So God imparts to human hearts
> the blessings of his heaven
> No ear may hear his coming
> but in this world of sin,
> Where meek souls will receive him still
> the dear Christ enters in.

Let each of us know with certainty that our God reigns.

CPSIA information can be obtained
at www.ICGtesting.com
Printed in the USA
LVHW101331160722
723611LV00028B/1